Get the eBook FREE!

(PDF, ePub, Kindle, and liveBook all included)

We believe that once you buy a book from us, you should be able to read it in any format we have available. To get electronic versions of this book at no additional cost to you, purchase and then register this book at the Manning website.

Go to https://www.manning.com/freebook and follow the instructions to complete your pBook registration.

That's it!
Thanks from Manning!

T0100170

Julia as a Second Language

Julia as a Second Language

GENERAL PURPOSE PROGRAMMING
WITH A TASTE OF DATA SCIENCE

ERIK ENGHEIM

MANNING

SHELTER ISLAND

For online information and ordering of this and other Manning books, please visit
www.manning.com. The publisher offers discounts on this book when ordered in quantity.
For more information, please contact

  Special Sales Department
  Manning Publications Co.
  20 Baldwin Road
  PO Box 761
  Shelter Island, NY 11964
  Email: orders@manning.com

 Manning Publications Co.
  20 Baldwin Road
  PO Box 761
  Shelter Island, NY 11964

Development editor:	Marina Michaels
Technical development editor:	Milan Ćurčić
Review editor:	Adriana Sabo
Production editor:	Kathleen Rossland
Copy editor:	Christian Berk
Proofreader:	Jason Everett
Technical proofreader:	Maurizio Tomasi
Typesetter:	Dennis Dalinnik
Cover designer:	Marija Tudor

ISBN: 9781617299711
Printed in the United States of America

To my grandparents,
who paid for my first computer: an Amiga 1000.

brief contents

contents

preface

I began programming as a teenager, learning from fun books containing comic strips with wizards and turtles. I read magazines that showed me how to make my own simple games or cause silly effects to appear on the screen. I had fun.

But when I went to university, my books began discussing bank accounts, balances, sales departments, employees, and employers. I wondered if my life as a programmer would mean putting on a gray suit and writing code handling payroll systems. Oh, the horror!

At least half of my class hated programming with a passion. I could not blame them. Why did programming books have to be so boring, functional, and sensible?

Where was the sense of adventure and fun? Fun is underrated. Who cares if a book is silly and has stupid jokes if it makes you learn and enjoy learning?

That is one of the reasons I wrote this book. I wanted the reader to enjoy learning programming—not through cracking jokes but by working through programming examples that are interesting and fun to do.

I promise you, there will be no examples modeling a sales department. Instead, we will do things like simulate rocket launches, pretend to be Caesar sending a secret message to his army commanders using old Roman encryption techniques, and many others.

The second important reason why I wanted to write this book is because people keep asking me, "Julia? Isn't that a language only for science and scientists?" Julia has had major success in this area, which is why the Julia community today is full of brainy people working on hard problems, such as developing new drugs and modeling the spread of infectious diseases, climate change, or the economy.

But no, you don't need to be a genius or a scientist to use Julia. Julia is a wonderful *general purpose* programming language for everyone! I am not a scientist, and I have enjoyed using it for over 9 years now. With Julia, you will find that you can solve problems more quickly and elegantly than you have done in the past. And as a cherry on top, computationally intensive code will run blisteringly fast.

acknowledgments

This book has lived through several incarnations. At one point, it was a self-published book. Later, chance brought me in touch with Manning Publications, and we agreed to work on publishing my book. Back then, I did not realize how much work I was getting myself into. In my mind, I would do minor revisions to the existing book, but from all the feedback I got, I realized I had to make many revisions.

At times I felt like giving up. However, despite the difficulties, I believe the extensive system Manning has set up to aid us authors has helped me make a significantly better book. For that, I must thank Nicole Butterfield, who got me to sign on with Manning. I have had two Manning editors: Lesley Trites, in the early phase of the book, and Marina Michaels, who with her considerable experience and steady hand has helped get me over the finish line. I would like to extend a thanks to Milan Ćurčić, my technical development editor, who helped me a lot with his feedback in determining when material was understandable (or not) to my target audience. My copyeditor Christian Berk was invaluable for me as a non-native English speaker in correcting any odd constructs or grammar I may have written.

Furthermore, I'd like to thank the reviewers who took the time to read my manuscript at various stages during its development and who provided invaluable feedback: Alan Lenton, Amanda Debler, Andy Robinson, Chris Bailey, Daniel Kenney, Darrin Bishop, Eli Mayost, Emanuele Piccinelli, Ganesh Swaminathan, Geert Van Laethem, Geoff Barto, Ivo Balbaert, Jeremy Chen, John Zoetebier, Jonathan Owens, Jort Rodenburg, Katia Patkin, Kevin Cheung, Krzysztof Jędrzejewski, Louis Luangkesorn, Mark Thomas, Maura Wilder, Mike Baran, Nikos Kanakaris, Ninoslav Čerkez, Orlando

Alejo Méndez Morales, Patrick Regan, Paul Silisteanu, Paul Verbeke, Samvid Mistry, Simone Sguazza, Steve Grey-Wilson, Timothy Wolodzko, and Thomas Heiman.

Special thanks go to Maurizio Tomasi, technical proofreader, for his careful review of the code one last time, shortly before the book went into production. Finally, thank you to the creators of Julia. You have created the programming language for the future, which I believe will transform the computer industry. That may sound like hyperbole, but I truly believe Julia is a major milestone in the evolution of programming languages.

about this book

Julia as a Second Language is an introduction to the Julia programming language for software developers. It not only covers the syntax and semantics of the language but also tries to teach the reader how to think and work like a Julia developer through extensive focus on interactive coding in a read–evaluate–print–loop (REPL) based environment.

Who should read this book?

Julia as a Second Language is written for developers curious about the Julia programming language but who do not necessarily have a scientific or mathematical background. The book is also a good starting point for anyone who wants to explore data science or scientific computing, as Julia is a language very well designed for such work. However, that does not exclude other uses. Any developer who would like to program in a modern, high performance language that makes them more productive would benefit from this book.

How this book is organized

The book is organized into five parts, consisting of 18 chapters.

Part 1 covers the basics of the language.

- Chapter 1 explains what kind of language Julia is, why it got created, and the advantages of using the Julia programming language.
- Chapter 2 discusses working with numbers in Julia. It shows how you can use the Julia REPL environment as a very sophisticated calculator.

- Chapter 3 explains control flow statements, such as if statements, while loops, and for loops, by implementing a trigonometry function and calculating the Fibonacci numbers.
- Chapter 4 explains how to work with collections of numbers using the array type. Readers will work through an example involving pizza sales data.
- Chapter 5 is about working with text. This chapter walks you through making nicely formatted displays of pizza sales data with colors as well as reading and writing pizza data to files.
- Chapter 6 discusses how a program to convert Roman numerals to decimal numbers can be implemented using the dictionary collection type.

Part 2 covers the Julia type system in greater detail.

- Chapter 7 explains type hierarchies in Julia and how you can define your own composite types. This is one of the most important chapters because it also explains multiple dispatch, which is one of the most important and unique features in Julia.
- Chapter 8 introduces a rocket simulation code example we will use through several chapters. This chapter is focused on defining types for different rocket parts.
- Chapter 9 gets into depth on numerical conversion and promotion in Julia by building up a code example dealing with different units for degrees. This chapter helps cement an understanding of the multiple dispatch system in Julia.
- Chapter 10 explains how you can represent objects that are nonexistent, missing, or undefined in Julia.

Part 3 revisits collection types, such as arrays, dictionaries, and strings covered in part 1, but this time digs into more details.

- Chapter 11 goes into much more detail about strings, including topics such as Unicode and UTF-8 usage in Julia as well as their effects on your use of strings.
- Chapter 12 explains traits common to all Julia collections, such as iterating over elements and building your own collections.
- Chapter 13 walks through several code examples to show how sets and set operations are used to organize and search for data in many types of applications.
- Chapter 14 shows how you can work with and combine arrays of different dimensions, such as vectors and matrices.

Part 4 focuses on methods for organizing your code at different levels, including modularizing at the function level all the way up to packages, files, and directories.

- Chapter 15 digs deeper into using functions in Julia, with emphasis on how functional programming differs from object-oriented programming.
- Chapter 16 is about organizing your code into modules, using third-party packages, and creating your own packages for sharing code with others.

Part 5 digs into details that were hard to explain without the previous chapters as a foundation.

- Chapter 17 builds on chapter 5. You will get into the details of the Julia I/O system by reading and writing rocket engines to files, sockets, and pipes in CSV format.
- Chapter 18 explains how a parametric data type can be defined and why parametric types are beneficial for performance, memory usage, and correctness.

About the code

This book contains many examples of source code, both in numbered listings and in line with normal text. In both cases, source code is formatted in a `fixed-width font like this`. Code annotations accompany many of the listings, highlighting important concepts.

In many cases, the original source code has been reformatted; we've added line breaks and reworked indentation to accommodate the available page space in the book. In rare cases, even this was not enough, and listings include line-continuation markers (➥). Additionally, comments in the sourcecode have often been removed from the listings when the code is described in the text. Code annotations accompany many of the listings, highlighting important concepts.

Much of the code you write is in the Julia REPL (read-evaluate-print-loop) environment or in a Unix shell. In these cases, you see a prompt such as `julia>`, `shell>`, `help?>` or `$`. These should not be included when you type. However, Julia is normally able to filter out the prompt if you paste code examples into your terminal window.

Code meant to be written into a file will usually not be shown with a prompt. However, you can typically paste this code into the Julia REPL if you like.

You can get executable snippets of code from the liveBook (online) version of this book at https://livebook.manning.com/book/julia-as-a-second-language. The complete code for the examples in the book is available for download from the Manning website at https://www.manning.com/books/julia-as-a-second-language, and from GitHub at https://github.com/ordovician/code-samples-julia-second-language.

Julia version 1.7 or higher is recommended to run the example code in this book.

liveBook discussion forum

Purchase of *Julia as a Second Language* includes free access to liveBook, Manning's online reading platform. Using liveBook's exclusive discussion features, you can attach comments to the book globally or to specific sections or paragraphs. It's a snap to make notes for yourself, ask and answer technical questions, and receive help from the author and other users. To access the forum, go to https://livebook.manning.com/book/julia-as-a-second-language/discussion. You can also learn more about Manning's forums and the rules of conduct at https://livebook.manning.com/discussion.

Manning's commitment to our readers is to provide a venue where a meaningful dialogue between individual readers and between readers and the author can take place. It is not a commitment to any specific amount of participation on the part of the author, whose contribution to the forum remains voluntary (and unpaid). We suggest you try asking the author some challenging questions lest his interest stray! The forum and the archives of previous discussions will be accessible from the publisher's website as long as the book is in print.

Other online resources

Need additional help? The Julia language has an active Slack workspace/community with over 10,000 members, many of whom you can communicate with in real time. Find information about registration at https://julialang.org/slack.

- Julia Discourse (https://discourse.julialang.org) is the go-to place for Julia-related questions.
- The Julia community page at https://julialang.org/community has info about YouTube channels, upcoming Julia events, GitHub, and Twitter.
- Official documentation of the Julia language and standard library can be found at https://docs.julialang.org/en/v1/.

about the author

**ERIK ENGHEIM** is a writer, conference speaker, video course author, and software developer. He has spent much of his career developing 3D modeling software for reservoir modeling and simulation in the Norwegian gas and oil industry. Erik also spent several years as an iOS and Android developer. Erik has programmed in Julia and written and made videos about Julia since 2013.

about the cover illustration

The figure on the cover of *Julia as a Second Language* is "Paysanne Anglaise," or "English peasant woman," taken from a collection by Jacques Grasset de Saint-Sauveur, published in 1788. Each illustration is finely drawn and colored by hand.

In those days, it was easy to identify where people lived and what their trade or station in life was just by their dress. Manning celebrates the inventiveness and initiative of the computer business with book covers based on the rich diversity of regional culture centuries ago, brought back to life by pictures from collections such as this one.

Part 1

Basics

These chapters cover all of Julia at a basic level. Later chapters will expand on topics covered in this part. You will learn about working with numbers, arrays, if statements, for loops, text strings, basic I/O, and storing and retrieving data from dictionaries. Subsequent parts of the text then discuss these topics in greater depth.

Why Julia? 1

This chapter covers

- The type of problems Julia solves
- The benefits of a fast, dynamically typed language
- How Julia increases programmer productivity

You can choose from hundreds of programming languages—many of them much more popular than Julia. So why pick Julia?

How would you like to write code faster than you have done before? How about building systems with a fraction of the number of lines of code you normally require? Surely, such productivity will come at the cost of deplorable performance and high memory consumption. Nope. In fact, Julia is the language of choice for next-generation climate models, which have extreme performance and memory requirements.

I know such accolades may come across like a bad sales pitch from a used car salesman, but there is no denying that Julia, in many ways, is a revolutionary programming language. You may ask, "If Julia is so great, then why isn't everybody using it? Why are so many people still using the C programming language?" Familiarity, packages, libraries, and community matter. Mission-critical software built up in large organizations isn't just transitioned away from on a whim.

Many of you reading this book may not care about having the more efficient and productive programming language. Instead, what you care about is what you can build with it. The simple answer is: anything. Julia is a general-purpose programming language.

That may not be a satisfactory answer. You could build anything with JavaScript too, in principle. Yet you know JavaScript dominates frontend web development. You could write anything with Lua as well, but it is mostly used as a scripting language for computer games. Your primary interest in reading this book may be the kind of job Julia can land you.

Presently, the Julia community is strongest within scientific computing, data science, and machine learning. But learning Julia is also a bet on the future. A language with such strong capabilities will not remain within a small niche. If you read on, it will become clearer what Julia is and why it has such potential. I will also cover areas where Julia is not ideal.

1.1   What is Julia?

Julia is a general-purpose, multi-platform programming language that is

- Suited for numerical analysis and computational science
- Dynamically typed
- High performance and just-in-time compiled
- Using automatic memory management (garbage collection)
- Composable

That's a lot, and some of these things sound like contradictions. So how can Julia be a general-purpose language and also tailored toward numerical programming? It's general-purpose because, like Python, Julia can be used for almost anything. It's numerical because, like MATLAB, it is well suited for numerical programming. But it isn't limited to numerical programming; it's good for other uses as well. By *composable* I mean that Julia makes it easy to express many object-oriented and functional programming patterns facilitating code reuse.

1.1.1   *Pros and cons of statically and dynamically typed languages*

Let's focus on one aspect of Julia: the fact that it's dynamically typed. Usually, programming languages are divided into two broad categories:

- Dynamically typed
- Statically typed

> *In static languages, expressions have types; in dynamic languages, values have types.*
>
> —Stefan Karpinski
> Julia Creator

Examples of statically typed languages are C/C++, C#, Java, Swift, Go, Rust, Pascal, and Fortran. In a statically typed language, type checks are performed on all your code before your program is allowed to run.

Examples of dynamically typed languages are Python, Perl, Ruby, JavaScript, MAT-LAB, and LISP. Dynamically typed languages perform type checks while the program is running. Unfortunately, dynamically typed languages tend to be very slow.

In dynamic languages values such as numbers, characters, and strings have attached tags that say what type they are. These tags allow programs written in a dynamically typed language to check type correctness at runtime.

Julia is unusual in that it is both a dynamically typed language and high performance. To many, this is a contradiction. This unique trait of Julia is made possible because the language was explicitly designed for just-in-time (JIT) compilation and uses a feature called *multiple-dispatch* for all function calls. Languages such as C/C++ and Fortran use ahead-of-time (AOT) compilation. A compiler translates the whole program into machine code before it can run. Other languages, such as Python, Ruby, and Basic, use an interpreter. With interpreted languages, a program reads each line of source code and interprets it at runtime to carry out the instructions given. Now that you have an idea of what kind of language Julia is, I can begin discussing the appeal of Julia.

> **Language design and JIT compilation**
>
> In principle, a programming language is decoupled from the method used to run it. Yet you will find that I talk about Julia as a JIT-compiled language and Fortran as an AOT compiled language. Strictly speaking, this is imprecise. For instance, Julia can run through an interpreter as well. However, most languages have been designed for a particular form of execution. Julia was designed for JIT compilation.

1.2 Julia combines elegance, productivity, and performance

While performance is one of the key selling points of Julia, what caught my attention back in 2013 when I first discovered it was how well thought out, powerful, and easy to use it was. I had a program I had rewritten in several languages to compare how expressive, easy to use, and productive each language was. With Julia, I managed to make the most elegant, compact, and easily readable variant of this code ever. Since then, I have tried many programming languages but have never gotten close to what I achieved with Julia. Here are some one-liners that exemplify the expressiveness of Julia.

Listing 1.1 Julia one-liners

```
filter(!isempty, readlines(filename)) # strip out empty lines
filter(endswith(".png"), readdir())   # get PNG files
findall(==(4), [4, 8, 4, 2, 5, 1])    # find every index of the number 4
```

Having been programming since the 1990s, I have had periods where I have felt I had enough of programming; Julia helped me regain my joy for programming. Part of the reason is that once you master Julia, you will feel that you have a language in your tool-box that works as a member of your team rather than against you. I think many of us have had the experience of working on a problem we have a good idea of how to solve, but the language we are using is getting in our way. The limitations of the language force us to add one hack after another. With Julia, I can build software the way I want without the language putting up obstacles.

Another aspect that adds to your productivity and sense of fun is that Julia comes bundled with a rich standard library. You hit the ground running. You can get a lot done without hunting all over the web for some library to do what you want. Julia has you covered, whether you want to do linear algebra, statistics, HTTP, or string manipulation or you want to work with different date formats. And if the capability you want isn't in the standard library, Julia has a tightly integrated package manager that makes adding third-party libraries a walk in the park. Programming with Julia almost makes you feel guilty or spoiled because you can build rich and elegant abstractions without taking a performance hit.

Another essential advantage of Julia is that it is easy to learn. This ease of learning can help Julia gain a larger community over time. To understand why Julia is easy to learn, consider the famous *Hello world* program written in Julia:

```
print("Hello world")
```

When run, this code writes the text *Hello world* to the screen. While trivial, many languages require a lot of complex scaffolding to do something that simple. The following is a Java program which does the same thing:

```
public class Main {
    public static void main(String[] args) {
        System.out.print("hello world");
    }
}
```

That exposes the beginner to a lot more concepts all at once, which can be overwhelming. Julia is easier to learn because you can focus on learning one concept at a time. You can learn to write a function without ever seeing a type definition. With a lot of functionality available out of the box, you don't even need to know how to import external libraries to write helpful code.

1.3   *Why Julia was created*

To truly understand what Julia brings to the table, you need to understand better *why* Julia was created in the first place. The creators of the Julia programming language wanted to solve what they have called the *two-language problem*.

This problem refers to the fact that a lot of software is written using two different programming languages, each with different characteristics. In the scientific domain, machine learning and data analysis dynamic languages are often preferred. However, these languages usually don't give good enough performance. Thus solutions often have to be rewritten in higher-performance, statically typed languages. But why does this preference exist? Why not write everything in a traditional high-performance, statically typed language?

1.3.1   Scientists need the interactive programming that dynamically typed languages offer

Scientists began writing software, including large weather simulations, in Fortran[1] and neural networks[2] in C or C++.[3] These languages offer the kind of performance you need to tackle these large-scale problems. However, these languages come at a price. They tend to be rigid, verbose, and lacking in expressiveness—all of which reduce programmer productivity.

The fundamental problem, however, is that these languages are not suited for *interactive programming*. What do I mean by that? Interactive programming is the ability to write code and get immediate feedback.

Interactive programming matters a lot in data science and machine learning. In a typical data analysis process, data is explored by a developer loading large amounts of data into an interactive programming environment. Then the developer performs various analyses of this data. These analyses could include finding averages and maximum values or plotting a histogram. The results of the first analysis tell the programmer what the next steps should be.

Figure 1.1 shows this process in a dynamically typed language. You start by running the code, which loads the data, which you can then observe. However, you don't have to go through this whole process after you change the code. You can change the code and observe changes immediately. You don't need to load massive amounts of data over again.

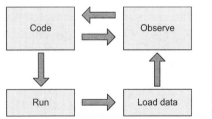

Figure 1.1   In dynamically typed languages you can ping-pong between coding and observing. Large data sets do not need to be reloaded into memory.

Let's contrast this experience with the use of a statically typed language, such as Fortran, C/C++, or Java.[4] The developer would write some code to load the data and

---

[1] Fortran is an old language for scientific computing.
[2] Neural networks are a kind of algorithm inspired by the workings of the human brain.
[3] C and C++ are related and widely used statically typed languages for systems programming.
[4] Java is used for a lot of web server software and Android phones.

explore it, without knowing anything about what the data looks like. They would then have to wait for the program to do the following:

1 Compile
2 Launch, then load a large amount of data

At this point the developer sees a plot of the data and statistics, which gives them the information they need to choose the next analysis. But choosing the next analysis would require repeating the whole cycle over again. The large blob of data has to be reloaded on every iteration. This makes each iteration exceedingly slow, which slows down the whole analysis process. This is a static, noninteractive way of programming (figure 1.2).

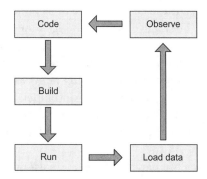

Figure 1.2 **Statically typed languages require the whole loop to be repeated.**

1.3.2   *Developers in other fields also need the interactivity a dynamically typed language offers*

This problem isn't unique to scientists; game developers have long faced the same problem. Game engines are usually written in a language such as C or C++, which can compile to fast machine code. This part of the software often does well-understood and well-defined things, such as drawing objects on the screen and checking if they collide with each other.

Like a data analyst, a game developer has a lot of code, which will need numerous iterations to work satisfactorily. Specifically, developing good game play requires a lot of experimentation and iteration. One has to tweak and alter code for how characters in the game behave. The layout of a map or level has to be experimented with repeatedly to get it right. For this reason, almost all game engines use a second language that allows on-the-fly change of code. Frequently, this is a language such as Lua,[5] JavaScript, and Python.[6]

With these languages, the code for game characters and maps can be changed without requiring a recompile and reloading of maps, levels, and characters. Thus

---

[5] Lua was originally made as a configuration language, but today it is primarily used to write games.
[6] Python is one of the most popular languages for data science and machine learning today.

one can experiment with game play, pause, make code changes, and continue straight away with the new changes.

Machine learning professionals face similar challenges. They build predictive models, such as neural networks, which they feed large amounts of data to train. This is often as much of a science as an art. Getting it right requires experimentation. If you need to reload training data every time you modify your model, you will slow down the development process. For this reason, dynamically typed languages, such as Python, R, and MATLAB, became very popular in the scientific community.

However, because these languages aren't very fast, they get paired with languages such as Fortran and C/C++ to get good performance. A neural network made with TensorFlow[7] or PyTorch[8] is made up of components written in C/C++. Python is used to arrange and connect these components. Thus at runtime you can rearrange these components using Python, without reloading the whole program.

Climate and macroeconomic models may get developed in a dynamic language first and tested on a small dataset while being developed. Once the model is finished, many organizations hire C/C++ or Fortran developers to rewrite the solution in a high-performance language. Thus there is an extra step, complicating the development processes and adding costs.

1.4   Julia's higher performance solves the two-language problem

Julia was created to solve the problem of needing to use two languages. It makes it possible to combine the flexibility of a dynamically typed language with the performance of a statically typed language. That's why the following saying has gained some popularity:

> *Julia walks like Python, runs like C.*
>
> —Popular saying in Julia community

Using Julia, developers within many fields can write code with the same productivity as with languages such as Python, Ruby, R, and MATLAB. Because of this, Julia has had a profound impact on the industry. In the July 2019 edition of *Nature*, several interviews were conducted with various scientists about their use of Julia.

For instance, the University of Melbourne has seen an 800x improvement by porting computational models from R to Julia. Jane Herriman, Materials Science Caltech, reports seeing tenfold-faster runs since rewriting her Python code in Julia.

> *You can do things in an hour that would otherwise take weeks or months.*
>
> —Michael Stumpf

At the International Conference for Supercomputing in 2019 (SC19), Alan Edelman, one of the Julia creators, recounts how a group at the Massachusetts Institute of

---

[7] TensorFlow is a popular machine learning library and platform for Python.
[8] PyTorch is a popular machine learning framework for Python.

Technology (MIT) rewrote part of their Fortran climate model into Julia. They determined ahead of time that they would tolerate a 3x slowdown of their code. That was an acceptable tradeoff for gaining access to a high-level language with higher productivity, in their view. Instead, they got a 3x speed boost by switching to Julia.

These are just a few of the many stories that abound today about how Julia is revolutionizing scientific computing and high-performance computing in general. By avoiding the two-language problem, scientists can work much faster than before.

1.5   *Julia is for everyone*

These stories might give the false impression that Julia is a language for brainiacs in white lab coats. But nothing could be further from the truth. It turns out that a lot of the traits that make Julia a great language for scientists also make it an excellent language for everybody else. Julia offers

- Strong facilities for modularizing and reusing code.
- A strict type system that helps catch bugs in your code when it runs.
- A sophisticated system for reducing repetitive boilerplate code (metaprogramming[9]).
- A rich and flexible type system that allows you to model a wide variety of problems.
- A well-equipped standard library and various third-party libraries to handle various tasks.
- Great string processing facilities. This ability is usually a key selling point for any Swiss-Army-knife-style programming language. It is what initially made languages such as Perl, Python, and Ruby popular.
- Easy interfacing with a variety of other programming languages and tools.

While Julia's big selling point is that it fixes the two-language problem, that does not mean the need to interface with existing Fortran, C, or C++ code is alleviated. The point of fixing the two-language problem is to avoid having to write Fortran or C code each time you hit a performance problem. You can stick with Julia the whole way.

However, if somebody has already solved a problem you have in another language, it may not make sense for you to rewrite that solution from scratch in Julia. Python, R, C, C++, and Fortran have large packages that have been built over many years, and the Julia community can't replace those overnight. To be productive, Julia developers need to be able to take advantage of existing software solutions.

In the long term, there is an obvious advantage to transitioning legacy software to Julia. Maintaining old Fortran libraries will often require a lot more developer effort than maintaining a Julia library.

The greatest benefit is probably in the combinatorial power Julia gives. There are certain types of problems that require the construction of large monolithic libraries.

---

[9] Metaprogramming is code that writes code. It is an advanced concept not covered in this book.

Julia, in contrast, is exceptionally well suited for making small libraries that can easily be combined to match the functionality offered by large monolithic libraries in other languages. Let me give one example.

Machine learning, a hot topic, powers self-driving cars, face recognition, voice recognition, and many other innovative technologies. The most famous packages for machine learning are PyTorch and TensorFlow. These packages are enormous monoliths maintained by large teams. There is no code sharing between them. Julia has a multitude of machine learning libraries, such as Knet, Flux (see https://fluxml.ai), and Mocha (see http://mng.bz/epxG). These libraries are tiny in comparison. Why? Because the capabilities of PyTorch and TensorFlow can be matched by combining multiple small libraries in Julia. Explaining more about why this works is a complex topic that requires a much deeper knowledge of Julia and how neural network libraries work.

Having many small libraries is an advantage for general applications. Anyone building any kind of software will benefit from the ability to reuse existing pieces of software in a multitude of new ways, instead of having to reinvent the wheel. With legacy programming languages, one often needs to repeatedly implement the same functionality. TensorFlow and PyTorch, for instance, have a lot of duplicate functionality. Julia avoids duplication by putting a lot more functionality in libraries shared between many machine learning libraries. As you work through the chapters in this book, it will become increasingly clear how Julia can pull this off and why this capability is hard to achieve in many other languages.

1.6   What can I build with Julia?

In principle, you can use Julia to build anything. However, every language has an ecosystem of packages and a community that may push you toward some types of development over others. Julia is no different.

1.6.1   Julia in the sciences

Julia has a strong presence in the sciences. It is used, for example, in

- Computational biology
- Statistics
- Machine learning
- Image processing
- Computational calculus
- Physics

But Julia covers many more areas. For instance, it's used in energy trading. The American Federal Reserve uses it to build complex macroeconomic models. Nobel Laureate Thomas J. Sargent founded QuantEcon, a platform that advances pedagogy in quantitative economics using both Julia and Python. He is a strong proponent of Julia, since the big problems in macroeconomics will be difficult to solve with other programming languages. In interviews with Lukas Biewald, Peter Norvig, a famous artificial intelligence (AI) researcher working at Google, has expressed how he thinks the machine learning world would benefit greatly from switching to Julia.

I would be happier if Julia were the main language for AI.

—Peter Norvig
Author of *Artificial Intelligence, A Modern Approach*

Life sciences is another obvious area for Julia. By 2025, 2-40 exabytes of human genome data will be collected every year. Most mainstream software cannot handle data at that scale. You will need a high-performance language, such as Julia, that can work with a variety of formats on a variety of hardware at the highest possible performance.

At the time of writing this chapter, COVID-19 is still a major challenge in the world. The Julia package Pathogen is used to model infectious disease and has been used by COVID-19 researchers.

1.6.2   *Nonscience uses of Julia*

What about its nonscience uses? Julia also has a multitude of packages for other interests:

- Genie—A full-stack MVC web framework
- Blink—For creating Electron GUI apps in Julia
- GTK—For making Julia GUI applications using the popular Linux GUI toolkit GTK
- QML—For creating cross-platform GUIs using the QML markup language used in the Qt GUI toolkit
- GameZero—For beginner game developing
- Luxor—For drawing vector images
- Miletus—For writing financial contracts
- TerminalMenus—For allowing interactive menus in the terminal
- Gumbo—For parsing HTML pages
- Cascadia—A CSS selector library for web scraping, extracting useful information from web pages
- QRCode—For creating images of QR codes popular with ads to show machine-readable URLs

As you can see, Julia has packages for general-purpose programming.

1.7   *Where Julia is less ideal*

In principle, Julia can be used for almost anything, but being a young language means the selection of libraries is not equally comprehensive in every area. For example, the selection of packages for web development is limited. Building something like a mobile application would not work well with Julia. It is also not great for small, short-running scripts—the kind you often write in Bash, Python, or Ruby. These limitations are due to Julia being JIT compiled.

That means Julia programs start more slowly than, for example, Python or Bash programs but begin to run much faster once the JIT compiler has converted critical parts of the code to machine code. There is an ongoing effort in the Julia community to reduce this problem, and there are myriad ways it can be tackled. Solutions include better caching of previous JIT compilations to being more selective about when something is JIT compiled.

Julia is also not ideal for real-time systems. In a real-time system, the software must respond to things that happen in the real world. You can contrast this with, for instance, a weather simulator. With a weather simulator, it doesn't matter what happens in the world outside the computer running the simulation.

However, if your program has to process data arriving from a measuring instrument every millisecond, then you can't have sudden hiccups or delays. Otherwise, you risk losing important measurements. Julia is a garbage-collected language. That means data no longer used in your program gets automatically recycled for other purposes. The process of determining what memory to recycle tends to introduce small random delays and hiccups in program execution.

This problem cannot be overstated. Robotics that require real-time behavior are being done in Julia. Researchers at MIT have simulated real-time control of the Boston Dynamics Atlas humanoid robot balancing on flat ground, which was done to prove that Julia can be used for online control of robots by tweaking how it allocates and releases memory.

Julia is not well suited for embedded systems with limited memory. The reason is that Julia achieves high performance by creating highly specialized versions of the same code. Hence memory usage for the code itself would be higher in Julia than for, say, C, C++, or Python.

Finally, just like Python, Ruby, and other dynamic languages, Julia is not suited for typical systems programming, such as making database systems or operating system kernels. These tasks tend to require detailed control of resource usage, which Julia does not offer. Julia is a high-level language aimed at ease of use, which means many details about resource usage get abstracted away.

1.8   What you will learn in this book

If you already program in another language, this book is for you. Every programming language has a unique set of features, tools, and communities. In this book, I focus on Julia's unique characteristics as a language and on the tools and programming community built up around Julia, including the following integral aspects:

1   Interactive programming using a read–evaluate–print loop (REPL)[10]
2   Science- and mathematics-oriented code examples
3   Julia's unique *multiple-dispatch* feature and type system

---

[10] REPL refers to an interactive command line for a programming language.

4 Functional programming and how it compares with object-oriented programming

5 Package-oriented development over app-oriented development

Julia's REPL-based development means you can launch the Julia command-line tool and start typing Julia expressions, which get evaluated when you press Enter:

```
julia> reverse("abc")
"cba"

julia> 3+5
8
```

I follow this approach through most of the book; it may be unfamiliar to readers who come from languages such as C/C++, Java, and C#, but in the Julia community, this development style is often favored. The REPL environment is used for experimentation, testing, and debugging.

Because Julia is used heavily in data science, machine learning, mathematics, and science, I use many science- and math-oriented examples in this book, such as calculating sine values or simulating a rocket launch, rather than building a website or an inventory system. I keep the mathematics in this text at a high-school level.

In this book, you will find in-depth coverage of Julia's multiple-dispatch system and type system. These systems matter because they are a crucial reason Julia achieves such high performance. Because many Julia beginners are confused about these systems, I go into somewhat greater detail on these topics.

Because the software industry is still dominated by object-oriented programming languages, it can be disorienting to jump into the more functional programming style of Julia. Thus I have devoted space to show how the same problems can be solved in a functional and object-oriented style. Many of the preferred functional programming practices are used throughout the book.

When working through this book, you will not see a lot of applications made—that is, the kind where you click an icon, and it launches. Nor will you see command-line tools made in Julia that can be run from the console. This choice will be new to, for example, Ruby and Python developers, who are very accustomed to building software as command-line tools.

The Julia community is, instead, very package oriented. They encourage you to build packages over standalone applications, as these can more easily be shared with others and reused. This preference is reflected in the Julia toolchain and package manager. Julia doesn't prevent you from building applications, but this book will get you into the package-first mindset. Build a package first, and then turn that into an application.

The package-oriented mindset is visible in how Julia's tools tend to be delivered. The package manager and debugger are handled by loading particular packages into the Julia interactive environment and issuing commands there instead of in the shell. This way of working might be familiar to MATLAB and R users. One tends to focus on packages rather than applications in these two languages.

A typical statistician, scientist, or data analyst using Julia may load up favored packages into their Julia environment and execute Julia commands rather than clicking on some application made using Julia. The Julia REPL will typically be an integral part of most Julia workflows.

Summary

- Static typing makes it easier to construct high-performance programming languages and catch type mistakes before the program is run.
- Dynamic typing makes it possible to make highly interactive programming languages. For programming that requires rapid iteration, this is an advantage.
- Development of scientific code often requires the ability to experiment on large datasets easily. This requires interactive programming offered by dynamically typed languages.
- Scientific code often needs high performance, which dynamically typed languages normally cannot offer.
- Julia is able to solve the two-language problem by offering a high-performance, dynamically typed language. This ability drives the adoption of Julia in performance-demanding fields, such as climate modeling, astronomy, and macro-economic simulations.
- Julia is not limited to science but is also an excellent general-purpose programming language.

Julia as a calculator

This chapter covers

- Working with integers, floating-point numbers, and fractions
- Using variables to store long numbers
- Creating reusable calculations by defining functions
- The most basic types in Julia

Even if you never end up using Julia as your primary language, you may still value it as a replacement for your desk calculator. Julia can even double as an advanced high-school graphing calculator (figure 2.1). As a bonus, it's completely free to use.

Remember you have to walk before you can run, and exploring numbers is a great way to get introduced to the core concepts of Julia. Since Julia is not just a general-purpose programming language but specifically tailored towards numerical computing, manipulating numbers plays a unique role in Julia.

In this chapter, you will look at the aspects of Julia that let you do the same kinds of things in Julia that you would do with a calculator. Of course, you may object that you don't intend to use Julia as a calculator, but this is simply a way to give you the foundation to understand the more complex topics.

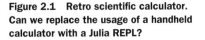

**Figure 2.1 Retro scientific calculator.
Can we replace the usage of a handheld
calculator with a Julia REPL?**

2.1 *The Julia command line*

If you have Julia properly installed and configured (see appendix A), you can type
Julia at your terminal prompt to start the Julia REPL. This interactive command-line
program reads your input much like a calculator and prints out the result as soon as
you hit enter. The REPL is a place for testing your code, looking up documentation,
and installing third-party software.

In this chapter, you will focus on evaluating mathematical expressions in the REPL.
The next code example demonstrates how to launch the Julia command line from the
terminal (console) application. After it has launched, type in 2 + 3 and hit enter. Julia
evaluates this expression and prints 5:

```
$ julia
               _
   _       _ _(_)_     |  Documentation: https://docs.julialang.org
  (_)     | (_) (_)    |
   _ _   _| |_  __ _   |  Type "?" for help, "]?" for Pkg help.
  | | | | | | |/ _` |  |
  | | |_| | | | (_| |  |  Version 1.6.0 (2021-03-24)
 _/ |\__'_|_|_|\__'_|  |  Official https://julialang.org/ release
|__/                   |

julia> 2 + 3
5
```

You can do far more complex operations than adding two single-digit numbers. In the
next example, you perform some very common mathematical operations, including
getting the logarithm, sine, and square root. rand is a mathematical function that evaluates to a random number between 0 and 1:

```
julia> 4 * 5
20
```
Complex expressions can be nested with parentheses.

```
julia> (1.5 + 3.5)*4
20.0
```

```
julia> 2^3
8
```
Exponents; taking two to the power of three

```
julia> log(2.71828^4)
3.999997309389128
```
The natural logarithm of 2.71, also known as Euler's number e

```
julia> sin(3.1415926/2)
0.9999999999999997
```
Get sine of π/2 radians.

```
julia> sqrt(9)
3.0
```
The square root of 9

```
julia> rand()
 0.14765146459147327
```
Generate a random number from 0 to 1.

2.2   Using constants and variables

Remembering all the digits in numbers such as 3.1415926... (π) or 2.71828... (Euler's number *e*) is tedious. In fact, it is impossible, since both numbers are what we call *irrational numbers*, which means they have an *infinite* number of digits. Therefore, it is much better to give each number a name—or, to be more accurate, an *identifier*.

> **IMPORTANT** *Variables* and *constants* define areas in memory in which values (data) are stored. Think of memory as a long list of numbered mailboxes, each holding a value. To avoid remembering the number of the mailbox containing a value, affix a named identifier. You can change the value of a variable after it has been created but not the value of a constant.

Identifiers can be used to give names to constants, variables, types, and functions in Julia. pi (π), golden (φ), and Euler's number e are identifiers used to refer to numerical *constants*. Both constants and variables simplify remembering long, complicated numbers:

```
julia> using Base.MathConstants
```
You can make common mathematical constants available to Julia. pi is always available, but the others are not.

```
julia> pi
π = 3.1415926535897...
```

```
julia> e
e = 2.7182818284590...
```
Euler's number is commonly used with logarithms.

```
julia> golden
φ = 1.6180339887498...
```
The golden ratio is often used in the arts for aesthetic reasons and appears in nature, such as the spiral arrangement of leaves.

```
julia> catalan
 catalan = 0.9159655941772...
```
Catalan's constant

With these constants, it becomes more convenient to write mathematical expressions. You also get more accurate results because it isn't possible to write *e* or *π* with enough digits. These are irrational numbers with an infinite number of digits. Mathematicians don't actually know if Catalan's number is irrational, but it is modeled as an irrational number in Julia:

```
julia> log(e^4)
4.0

julia> sin(pi/2)
1.0
```

You are, however, not limited to using built-in constants. You can define your own in Julia with the const keyword and use them in calculations instead of number literals:[1]

```
julia> const foo = 3481
3481

julia> const bar = 200
200

julia> foo + bar
3681

julia> const qux = 8
8

julia> qux + 2
10
```

You might be wondering about the funny-sounding names foo, bar, and qux. These are nonsense words commonly used in code examples to inform the reader that they can pick *whatever* word they like in this case. These are different from words like if, while, const and function, which are reserved words; you are not allowed to use them as variable names.

When writing Julia identifiers, you can mix and match cases. foObAr and FOObar are equally valid. But Julia is case sensitive, so they will be treated as *different* identifiers.

> **TIP** Julia's identifiers are case sensitive. foo, Foo, and FOO will not be treated as the same identifiers by Julia. That is standard practice in most modern programming languages today.

You can add numbers as long as they are not at the start of the word. Thus f00bar is valid, but 1oobar is not. You should be used to similar rules from other programming languages.

---

[1] A number literal is made up of digits from 0 to 9 instead of being expressed as a named variable.

Julia is unusual in its frequent use of Greek letters, such as π, θ, α, and Δ. The reason for this is that mathematics is usually written using Greek letters. When a mathematical equation is implemented in code, it becomes easier to read the code if it looks similar to the equation.

To accommodate this, the Julia creators built in special features in the Julia REPL and Julia editor plugins to make writing Greek letters and other Unicode characters easy. For example, in the REPL environment, you write a backslash, then you write the name of the character you want, and then you press tab:

```
julia> \pi
```

After I hit the tab key, this turns into

```
julia> π
```

The following is an overview of some popular Greek letters and Unicode characters you may like to use in your code, with some comments on what they usually mean.

Character	Tab Completion	Usage
π	\pi	Circle equation
θ	\theta	Angle
Δ	\Delta	Difference or change in something
e	\euler	Euler's number (important in logarithms)
√	\sqrt	Square root of a number
φ	\varphi	The golden ratio

What makes variables different from constants? Creating variables is very similar, except you don't use the const keyword:

```
julia> y = 7
7

julia> z = 3
3

julia> y + z + 2
12
```

So what exactly is the difference? This REPL interaction demonstrates the difference between variables and constants:

```
julia> const x = 9
9

julia> y = 7
7
```

```
julia> x = 12
WARNING: redefinition of constant x. This may fail, cause incorrect answers,
or produce other errors.
12

julia> y = 8
8
```

In this example, you made x a constant and y a variable. Notice how Julia warns you that you are trying to change the value of a constant. While this may indeed work, Julia makes no guarantees it will, which is why Julia gives you a warning. Never make your code rely on undefined behavior.

> **USEFUL HOTKEYS** Use Ctrl-D to exit Julia. Ctrl-C will break execution of some code that has gotten stuck. Clearing the terminal screen varies between operating systems. On Mac, use Command-K to clear the terminal, and use Ctrl-L on Linux.

Restart Julia to make all identifiers available again.

2.2.1 Assigning and binding values to variables

The = operator is used to assign a value to a variable in Julia. Comparing two expressions for equality is done with a double equal sign ==. However, to be accurate, what Julia does is not an assignment but *binding*. To better understand how binding works, I will present a code example in which the variable x is first bound to the value 2. Next it is rebound to the value x + 3:

```
julia> x = 2        ⊲─┤  Set the initial
2                      │  value of x to 0.

julia> x = x + 3    ⊲─┤  Increment x
  5                    │  with two.
```

If this code example had been a language such as C/C++, Fortran, or Pascal, then the system would have put aside a slot of memory to hold the x variable. Each time you assign a new value to variable x, the number stored in this memory location would be changed.

With binding, it works differently. You have to think about each calculation as producing a number that gets put in a different memory location. Binding involves moving the x label itself to a new memory location. The variable moves to the result rather than the result moving to the variable. Figure 2.2 shows the step-by-step explanation and should help clarify how this works.

1 The value 2 is stored in memory cell number 2. You attach the label x to this value, which is equivalent to the initial assignment statement x = 2.
2 Julia begins to evaluate x + 3 in the expression x = x + 3. It stores the result of this calculation at memory cell number 4.

3 To complete the evaluation of the x = x + 3 statement, Julia moves the x label to memory cell 4.

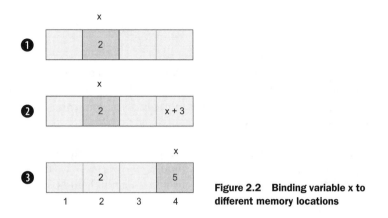

Figure 2.2   **Binding variable x to different memory locations**

But why do Julia and other dynamically typed languages perform binding rather than assignment? With a language such as C/C++ you can write statements such as the following.

Listing 2.1   Assignment in C/C++

```
int x = 4;
x = 5;

char ch = 'A';
ch = 'B';
```

This works because the compiler will make sure you never attempt to put a value that cannot fit inside the memory slot set aside for the variable x and variable ch. In a dynamically typed language, any value can be assigned to x, and thus, it cannot have a predefined size in a predefined location in memory.

2.2.2   *Using the ans variable*

There is a special variable in Julia that only exists when you use Julia interactively, called ans (answer). The Julia REPL assigns the value of the last expression you evaluate to it. Expressions in normal programs are not assigned to it.

Many people will be familiar with a similar variable if they have used advanced calculators. ans is a variable that always holds the result of the last calculation. This behavior is practical, as it allows you to easily use the result from the last calculation in the next calculation:

```
julia> 3 + 2
5
```

```
julia> ans*4
20

julia> ans
20

julia> ans - 8
12
```

2.2.3   What is a literal coefficient?

If you read mathematics, you may have noticed that something like $3 \times x + 2 \times y$ would be written as $3x + 2y$. Julia lets you write a multiplication in the same manner. We refer to these as *literal coefficients*, which is shorthand for multiplication between a number literal and a constant or variable:

```
julia> x = 3
3

julia> 2x
6

julia> 2*(3+2)
10

julia> 2(3+2)
10
```

Literal coefficients only work for actual number literals. π, e, and φ, for instance, are not number literals. You can write 2π but not $\pi2$ because the latter would imply an identifier.

There is a subtle difference between using literal coefficients and performing multiplication. See if you can make sense of the following example:

```
julia> x = 5
5

julia> 1/2x
0.1

julia> 1/2*x
2.5
```

What is going on here? `1/2x` is interpreted as `1/(2*x)`. Literal coefficients have higher precedence than division.

2.3   Different number types and their bit length in Julia

Julia has a variety of different number types such as signed integers, unsigned integers, and floating-point numbers with different bit lengths. If these concepts are unfamiliar to you, I advise you read about different number types in appendix B.

Let's focus on what is particular to Julia. In Julia, signed integers are named `Int8`, `Int16`, `Int32`, `Int64`, and `Int128`. The number suffix indicates the bit length of the number. Unsigned integer type names are formed by prefixing with a `U`, which gives you `UInt8`, `UInt16`, `UInt32`, `UInt64`, and `UInt128`.

While running code, it is often practical to know the minimum and maximum value of a particular integer type. You can use the `typemin` and `typemax` functions to discover minimum and maximum values. For instance, `typemin(Int8)` returns -128 because an 8-bit integer cannot represent smaller values than -128. `typemax(Int8)` will return 127:

```
julia> typemax(Int8)
127

julia> typemin(Int8)
-128
```

The default bit length of a Julia number literal is a signed 64-bit integer. You can easily verify that using the `typeof` function, which returns the type of the input argument:

```
julia> typeof(1)
Int64
```

How do you form numbers of other bit lengths then? If you want to create a signed 8-bit number, you write `Int8(x)`, where x is the number you would like to turn into an 8-bit number. This works for any number type. Naturally, if you try to input a number too large for the bit length, you will get an error message:

```
julia> y = Int8(42)
42

julia> typeof(y)
Int8

julia> typeof(Int16(4))
Int16

julia> UInt8(256)
ERROR: InexactError: trunc(UInt8, 256)
```

You should know that, unlike other popular dynamically typed languages such as Python, Ruby, and R, Julia doesn't automatically pick a number type large enough to hold the result of an arithmetic operation. In Julia, if you add two `Int8` values, the result will always be an `Int8` value.

Other dynamic languages would have upgraded to an `Int16` if the result was too large to represent as an 8-bit integer. In Julia, you will instead get an overflow. Read appendix B if the concept of integer overflow is unfamiliar to you.

Sometimes even `Int128` isn't large enough to hold a value. In these cases you use `BigInt`, which can hold an integer of arbitrary size. This flexibility is paid for in higher memory consumption and lower performance, so only use `BigInt` when you have to.

2.3.1 Writing numbers using different number formats

How you write a number and how that number is actually stored in memory are two different things. The numbers `0b1101`, `0x0d`, and `13` are stored as exactly the same binary number in computer memory. Julia defaults to showing all signed numbers in decimal format and unsigned numbers, such as `UInt8`, in hexadecimal format:

```
julia> Int(0b1101)
13

julia> Int(0x0d)
13

julia> UInt8(13)
0x0d
```

Hexadecimal numbers are popular in low-level, bit-oriented programming. This is because four bits can be represented by exactly one hexadecimal digit. Octal numbers are also popular because exactly three bits can be used to represent one octal digit.

> **Hexadecimal and octal numbers**
>
> Decimal numbers are created by combining digits from 0 to 9. Octal numbers are created by combining digits from 0 to 7. Thus the number 8 would be written as 10 in the octal number system.
>
> With hexadecimal numbers, there is a problem because the digits in the hexadecimal number system have to cover values 1 to 15; however, there are only symbols for digits 0 to 9. The solution has been using letters for digits beyond 9; thus the value 10 is represented as A, 11 is represented as B, and so on. F stands for 15. The largest value an 8-bit unsigned integer can hold is 0xff, which translates to 255 in decimal.

To write an octal number, use the `0o` prefix—you don't need to understand this very well. The point is making you aware of the fact that there are different ways of representing the same number. This is to avoid confusion when playing with *unsigned* integers in this chapter, as Julia defaults to displaying them in hexadecimal form:

```
julia> 0o5 == 0b101
true

julia> 0o6 == 0b110
true

julia> 0o7 == 0b111
true

julia> 0o10 == 0b1000
true
```

```
julia> Int(0o10)
8

julia> Int(0o23)
19

julia> 2 * 8 + 3
19
```

2.4   *Floating-point numbers*

Like integers there are floating-point numbers of different bit length. In Julia the default size is 64 bit, which means each floating-point number consumes 8 bytes of memory. By using more bits you can not only represent larger numbers but also represent numbers with higher precision. However, precision is not always important. For scientific calculations precision is important, but when calculating (e.g., for computer graphics), precision matters less. One pixel out of millions that is slightly wrong in position or color does not matter much. The most common floating-point types, Float64 and Float32, can be written as number literals:

```
julia> 42.98            ◄───┐   A 64-bit floating-point
42.98                       │   literal. You can verify
                            │   that with typeof.
julia> typeof(ans)
Float64

julia> 34.23f0          ◄───┐   A 32-bit floating-
34.23f0                     │   point number
julia> typeof(ans)
Float32
```

Notice the use of the f0 suffix to make the number of a 32-bit floating-point number. Why isn't there just an f like in Java and C/C++? This is due to the literal coefficients feature. If you look at the following REPL session you may be able to figure out what is going on:

```
julia> 0.5f
ERROR: UndefVarError: f not defined

julia> f = 2
2

julia> 0.5f
1.0

julia> 2f
4
```

If you try to write a 32-bit floating-point number like in Java or C/C++, Julia thinks you are trying to multiply a number with the variable f. In the first case this fails because you have not yet defined the f variable. In the second case it works because f has been defined.

How about other floating-point values, such as 16-bit values? In these cases you need to perform an explicit conversion:

```
julia> x = Float16(3.5)          ◁——┐   Convert a 64-bit
Float16(3.5)                         │   floating-point value
                                     │   to a 16-bit one.
julia> typeof(x)
Float16

julia> z = Float16(4) + 5f0
9.0f0
                                     ┌   Mixing numbers of different bit
julia> typeof(z)          ◁——————————┤   length causes Julia to pick the
Float32                              └   largest type to store the result in.
```

2.4.1 *Performing operations on integers and floating-point numbers*

While you can do many of the same operations on floating-point and integer numbers, the operations don't always have the same kind of results. And there are operations that only work on certain number types.

For instance the \ division operator gives floating-point numbers as result. That is not always what you want. When working with integers you often want the quotient and remainder instead. This is achieved with the `div` and `rem` functions:

```
julia> 4/2            ◁——┐
2.0                      │
                         │   Regular division
julia> 5/2            ◁——┤   operator gives
2.5                      │   floating-point
                         │   result
julia> 5.0/2.0        ◁——┘
2.5

julia> div(5,2)       ◁——┐   Integer division, which
2                        └   gives an integer result

julia> rem(5,2)       ◁——┐
1                        │   You also get a remainder,
                         │   which you obtain with %
julia> 5%2            ◁——┘   the operator.
1
```

2.5 *Defining functions*

You've already been exposed to some functions, such as *sin*, *cos*, and $\sqrt{}$. These are functions you can find on a regular calculator; they take a number as input and return a number as output. But what is the fundamental idea behind functions? And secondly, are functions in mathematics and in Julia the same kind of thing? The details differ, but conceptually, they are the same kind of thing. Functions have zero or more inputs called *arguments*. They can be considered to be returning a value or evaluating to a value. Consider the volume of a sphere:

$$V = \frac{4\pi r^3}{3}$$

How good are you at remembering exactly how this calculation is performed? I often have to look it up. You could perform this calculation in Julia by writing the following code:

```
julia> r = 4.5            ◄──────── The radius of the sphere
4.5

julia> V = 4*pi*r^3/3     ◄──┐  Storing the volume of
381.7035074111598             the sphere in variable V
```

Variables and constants make it easy to remember long, complicated numbers. In many ways you can think of functions as an extension of this idea. They allow you to remember complicated calculations. Instead of remembering what numbers to multiply and divide, you only need to remember the name of a function:

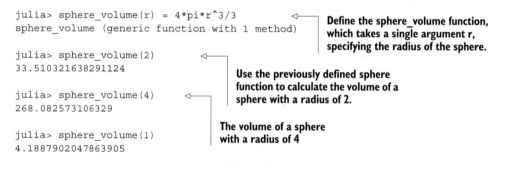

```
julia> sphere_volume(r) = 4*pi*r^3/3        ◄──┐  Define the sphere_volume function,
sphere_volume (generic function with 1 method)    which takes a single argument r,
                                                  specifying the radius of the sphere.

julia> sphere_volume(2)     ◄──┐
33.510321638291124             │  Use the previously defined sphere
                               │  function to calculate the volume of a
julia> sphere_volume(4)     ◄──┘  sphere with a radius of 2.
268.082573106329

                               Define the volume of a sphere
julia> sphere_volume(1)        with a radius of 4
4.1887902047863905
```

Notice that when you define a function, unlike a variable, you specify one or more arguments. Arguments are variables in your calculation that you want to change each time you perform a calculation. For example, when calculating the volume of a sphere you want the value of π to be the same each time; hence π is not an argument to the function. The radius, however, is an argument because you are interested in calculating the volume of spheres of different radii:

```
foo(x, y, z) = 2x + 4y - z
```

In the preceding code snippet you see a simple function definition. It's a function with the name foo, taking three different arguments named x, y and z. You could have just a few or many arguments. The rules for how you name them are the same as for any Julia identifier.

2.5.1 Storing function definitions in a file

Writing the definition of every function you want to use in the Julia REPL every time you restart Julia would be impractical. Instead you can store function definitions inside separate source code files.

> **CODE COMMENTS WITH #** You can write comments in your code to remind yourself what various parts of your code does. Comments start with a hash or pound sign: #. Anything after the hash symbol is ignored by the Julia compiler.

This file can then later be loaded into the Julia REPL when the functions contained within are needed. Let me demonstrate with an example. You will create a file called volumes.jl. Inside you store functions to calculate the volume of a sphere, cylinder, and cone.

Listing 2.2 volumes.jl source code file

```
# Volume calculations
sphere_volume(r)      = 4π*r^3/3
cylinder_volume(r, h) = π*r^2*h
cone_value(r, h)      = π*r^2*h/3
```

You can get the code in this file into Julia in three different ways. Perhaps the least sophisticated way is simply copying and pasting the text into the Julia command line. Alternatively, you could load the file when you start Julia:

```
$ julia -i volumes.jl
               _
   _       _ _(_)_     |  Documentation: https://docs.julialang.org
  (_)     | (_) (_)    |
   _ _   _| |_  __ _   |  Type "?" for help, "]?" for Pkg help.
  | | | | | | |/ _` |  |
  | | |_| | | | (_| |  |  Version 1.6.0 (2021-03-24)
 _/ |\__'_|_|_|\__'_|  |  Official https://julialang.org/ release
|__/                   |

julia> cone_value(2, 4)
16.755160819145562
```

However the more flexible solution is using the `include` function. This removes the need to restart your Julia REPL session:

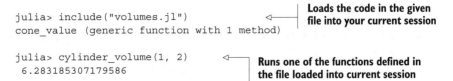

```
julia> include("volumes.jl")
cone_value (generic function with 1 method)
```
← Loads the code in the given file into your current session

```
julia> cylinder_volume(1, 2)
 6.283185307179586
```
← Runs one of the functions defined in the file loaded into current session

You can make changes to the code in this file and reload it using `include` to capture changes in the function implementations.

2.5.2 *Working with functions in the REPL*

Once complex calculations have been stored inside functions, you can easily reuse those calculations. But how do you deal with a large number of functions? The Julia REPL offers many ways to help.

If you start typing the first letters in a function and press Tab, Julia will attempt to complete the function name. If you start typing sphere, then hit the Tab key, Julia will complete this as sphere_volume. Sometimes there are many possible completions. In these cases you can press Tab twice to get a full list of possible completions:

```
                                    Press Tab twice here to get the full list of
                                    functions starting with the word find.
julia> find      ◁─┘
findall    findlast   findmax!   findmin!    findprev
findfirst  findmax    findmin    findnext
```

On the web page of the Julia programming language you can also find a manual, which gives you a complete list of all the functions built in to the Julia standard library. You can access the manual on the following webpage: docs.julialang.org/en/v1.

2.5.3 *Functions everywhere*

Functions are central to Julia. In fact, even common mathematical operators are defined as functions in Julia. Let me give you some examples:

```
julia> 5 + 3      ◁──┐
8                     │         It looks like you are using
                      │         an operator, but it is
julia> +(5, 3)        │         actually a function call
8                     │         written on infix form.
                      │
julia> 8 - 2      ◁──┘
6

julia> -(8, 2)                  The benefit of using + as a function
6                               is that you can use more than two
                                arguments (e.g., you can use it to
julia> +(2, 3, 5)   ◁─────      add up multiple values).
10
```

These are operators called like regular
functions. This is called prefix form.

To describe the placement of identifiers, use the following terms: prefix, infix, and suffix. Thus +(3, 4) would be considered a *prefix* form, while 3 + 4 would be the equivalent *infix* form.

How do you know if you can use a function on infix form? It's simple: the function name needs to be a symbol. For instance you cannot use a function named foo on infix form. Let's make some to demonstrate:

```
julia> x(a, b) = a^2 + b^2
x (generic function with 1 method)

julia> x(4, 10)
116

julia> 4 × 10
116

julia> 2 × 3
13
```

Here we made a function named × (write \times), and because it takes two arguments and is a symbol, we can use it on infix form. The simplest way to get a symbol is writing a LaTeX-like abbreviation and pressing tab (e.g., \Delta for Δ). Symbol completion will work in the Julia REPL and many Julia code editors. The LaTeX-like abbreviations supported by Julia can be found in the official Julia documentation at https://docs.julialang.org/en/v1/manual/unicode-input/.

2.5.4 *Functions to work with numbers*

You have already seen a number of functions you can use to operate on numbers, but Julia has a large collection of them. I would like to show some of the most useful ones, in particular for working with integers and floating-point numbers. Previously, I showed some operations on integers and floating-point numbers. However now you know that operations are really just functions. All of these variants are equivalent:

```
julia> 9 % 6
3

julia> %(9, 6)
3

julia> rem(9, 6)
3
```

The principle in Julia is that you should never *have to* use special Unicode symbols. Operations such as integer division can also be performed with simple functions:

```
julia> 9÷4
2

julia> ÷(9, 4)
2

julia> div(9, 4)
2
```

In fact, if you hit the ? key and write an integer division, you will get the built-in help system showing you that div has two names:

```
help?> div(9, 4)
  div(x, y)
  ÷(x, y)
```

The quotient from Euclidean division. Computes x/y, truncated to an integer.

It is very useful to know how to round numbers in different ways. Julia has the functions floor, ceil, and round for this purpose:

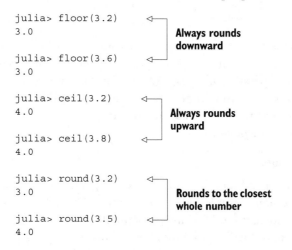

```
julia> floor(3.2)
3.0
```
Always rounds downward

```
julia> floor(3.6)
3.0
```

```
julia> ceil(3.2)
4.0
```
Always rounds upward

```
julia> ceil(3.8)
4.0
```

```
julia> round(3.2)
3.0
```
Rounds to the closest whole number

```
julia> round(3.5)
4.0
```

But if you are rounding to integers, then you probably want integer types:

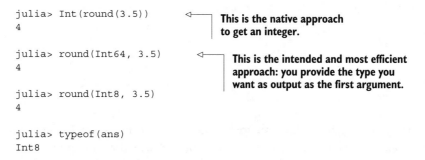

```
julia> Int(round(3.5))
4
```
This is the native approach to get an integer.

```
julia> round(Int64, 3.5)
4
```
This is the intended and most efficient approach: you provide the type you want as output as the first argument.

```
julia> round(Int8, 3.5)
4
```

```
julia> typeof(ans)
Int8
```

2.6   *How to use numbers in practice*

A lot of the details covered here are not things you need to think about when doing normal coding. I don't want you to pack your brain with too many unnecessary details. The key point here is providing you with an understanding of how numbers work in Julia. This is not unique to Julia, but it may be unfamiliar to developers coming from other dynamic languages, such as Python, R, or Ruby.

To make things easy for yourself, here are some simple rules to follow:

1 Just use the default integer and floating-point sizes. Only consider smaller or larger numbers when performance or the nature of your problem demands it.

2 Prefer signed integers to unsigned. It is very easy to make a mistake using unsigned numbers. To make it easy for yourself, stick with signed numbers most of the time.

Summary

- Julia supports different kinds of numbers, but the two most important types are integer numbers and floating-point numbers.
- Unlike numbers used by mathematicians, numbers used in programming have particular bit lengths. This determines how large and small of values you can store. For instance a signed 8-bit integer cannot store numbers smaller than -128 or larger than 127.
- Variables give names to numbers. Functions give names to calculations dependent on zero or more arguments.
- Assigning a value to a variable means sticking an identifier on that value. Reassigning another value to the same variable means moving the sticker to the new value. This is called binding.
- Two numbers that look identical in memory can look different on your screen because they are of different type.
- You can input numbers using a variety of different formats: binary, decimal, and hexadecimal. Unless you do systems programming, decimal will usually be the preferred format.

Control flow

Control flow is what separates a computer from a mere calculator. Calculators are for computing single expressions. Computers, on the other hand, have the ability to repeat the same calculations with different inputs numerous times without human intervention. Computers can choose to perform one calculation over another based on whether or not a condition holds true.

In this chapter you will explore code examples oriented around producing mathematical tables. You will learn about tables for trigonometric functions, as such tables are well known and of historical importance. Later you will explore conditional execution to help track the growth of rabbits using a method developed by Italian mathematician Fibonacci 800 years ago.

3.1 Navigation and trigonometry

In the age of sail the use of mathematical tables became more widespread, and a need to develop ways to automate the calculation of these tables developed (navigation is based on the calculation of angles and the sides of triangles; figure 3.1). This meant calculating trigonometric functions such as sine, cosine, and tangent.

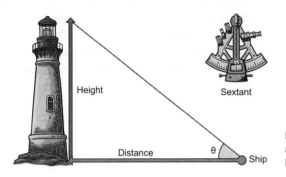

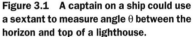

Figure 3.1   A captain on a ship could use a sextant to measure angle θ between the horizon and top of a lighthouse.

Nautical maps contain heights of different lighthouses. Thus if you want to know your position at sea while close to shore, you could measure the angle between the horizon and the top of a lighthouse of known height. This would give you the distance to that lighthouse. However all of these calculations require calculating trigonometric functions such as sine and cosine, and sea captains of the 1700s did not have pocket calculators (table 3.1).

Table 3.1   A simple trigonometric table

angle	0°	30°	45°	60°	90°
sin	0.000	0.500	0.707	0.866	1.000

Instead they used mathematical tables. Large, printed tables detailing the value of sine, cosine, and tangent for different angles were common tools for navigators of the time. Let me just refresh you on your high-school math if you have not used trigonometric functions in a while. Looking at the triangle in figure 3.2, sine, cosine, and tangent are defined as follows:

$$\sin(\theta) = \frac{b}{h} \qquad \cos(\theta) = \frac{a}{h} \qquad \tan(\theta) = \frac{b}{a}$$

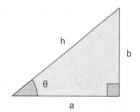

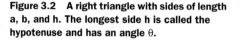

Figure 3.2   **A right triangle with sides of length a, b, and h. The longest side h is called the hypotenuse and has an angle θ.**

So for example, the sine of an angle is equal to the length of the opposing side divided by the longest side (the hypothenuse) in a right triangle (one angle is 90°). Today you use a calculator to calculate these trigonometric functions. But what if you lived before 1972[1]? How would you do these calculations by hand? There is, in fact, no canonical way of calculating sine and cosine. Instead there are various methods of *approximation.* A popular method of calculating sine is called the *Taylor series:*

$$\sin(x) = \frac{x}{1!} - \frac{x^3}{3!} + \frac{x^5}{5!} - \cdots$$

You can write this in a more compact and generalized form as

$$\sin(x) = \sum_{i=0}^{n} (-1)^i \frac{x^{2i+1}}{(2i+1)!}$$

But mathematical tables are not limited to trigonometric functions. Tables are useful for many other functions to reduce the amount of hand calculations required.

This spurred Charles Babbage to begin the construction of a massive mechanical calculating machine called the Difference Engine in 1819 (figure 3.3). It could calculate multiple values for tables by repeating the same calculation many times over. In modern programming terms it was creating the tables using loops. Loops are based on evaluating (running) the same code multiple times as long as a given condition holds true. In all programming languages Boolean expressions are used to define conditions. You will follow in Babbage's footsteps by creating such loops in Julia.

Your goal is implementing trigonometric functions in Julia using the Taylor series. Before that is possible you need to develop your understanding of Boolean expressions, which make it possible to understand while loops, for loops, and if statements. You will develop this understanding through a number of smaller code examples, printing out numbers, adding numbers, and converting from degrees to radians.

---

[1] In 1972 Hewlett-Packard released HP-35, the first calculator with sine and cosine functions.

Figure 3.3 A part of Charles Babbage's Difference Engine, which was a precursor to the Analytical Engine—the first mechanical general-purpose computer

3.2 *Boolean expressions*

One of the first things you learn about in elementary school is Boolean expressions. Ironically, most students never practice using them for anything. Nobody tells you they are one of the most important parts of any programming language. You have already looked at numerical expressions, such as *3 + 5*; these evaluate to a number. Boolean expressions, in contrast, evaluate to true or false. They are easier to grasp with some practical examples:

```
julia> 3 > 5          ◁——— Is 3 larger than 5?
false

julia> 8 > 3          ◁——— Is 8 larger than 3?
true

julia> 8 == 5 + 3     ◁─┐
true                     │  Check if values are equal.
                         │  This is not an assignment
julia> 3 == 5         ◁─┘  operator.
false

julia> 3 ≤ 3          ◁─┐
true                     │  Less than
                         │  or equal
julia> 3 <= 3         ◁─┘
true
```

In the example you use a Unicode version of the *less than or equal* operator. Several Boolean operators have Unicode variants. The following table shows you how to write some of them in the Julia REPL:

Character	Tab Completion	Description
≤	\leq	less than or equal <=
≥	\geq	greater than or equal >=
≠	\ne	not equal !=
≈	\approx	isapprox(x, y)

Boolean expressions return Boolean values, of which there are only two: `true` and `false`. Remember how I said everything is numbers inside a computer? Boolean values are no different:

```
julia> typeof(7 > 3)        ⊲───┐  Boolean expressions
Bool                             │  give values of type
                                 │  Bool.
julia> typeof(false)
Bool

julia> reinterpret(UInt8, false)   ⊲──┤ The false value
0x00                                   │ is stored as a 0.

julia> reinterpret(UInt8, true)    ⊲──┤ true is stored
0x01                                   │ as a 1.
```

Unlike many other programming languages, Julia actually allows you to perform arithmetic on Boolean values. In arithmetic, Boolean values are treated as 0 or 1:

```
julia> true + true
2

julia> 3true + true
4

julia> true + false + true
2

julia> false + false
0
```

For clarity it is best to avoid using Boolean values as numbers. However there are cases when this is very useful. Julia developers frequently use it to count how many things are true. In chapter 4 you will see an example of this.

3.2.1   *Compound statements*

Boolean expressions can be combined with the || and && operators. These perform what are called logical *OR* and logical *AND* operations. Thus given a variable x, I could ask, for example, if it is smaller than 4 *or* larger than 10:

```
julia> x = 3
3

julia> x < 4 || x > 10
true

julia> x = 5
5

julia> x < 4 || x > 10
false
```

Alternatively, you could ask if x is larger than 4 *and* smaller than 10:

```
julia> x > 4 && x < 10
true

julia> x = 12
12

julia> x > 4 && x < 10
false
```

Next you will use Boolean expressions to define conditions for repeating the same code multiple times.

3.3 *Looping*

The simplest looping construct in any programming language is the while loop. It allows you to repeat the same code over and over again as long as a Boolean condition is true, as shown in the following listing.

> **Listing 3.1 A simple `while` loop**

```
i = 0
while i < 5
    i = i + 1
end
```

All the code between the keywords `while` and `end` gets repeated over and over again as long as the condition `i < 5` is true. You could copy and paste this code into your Julia REPL, but you would not see any output. Why? Because `while end` is an expression that evaluates to `nothing`. That may sound a bit abstract, so let me give an example: 3 + 4 is an expression that evaluates to 7. You could store the value of an expression in variables like this:

```
julia> x = 3 + 4
7

julia> y = while false end          ⟵  Pointless while loop
                                        that terminates
                                        immediately

julia> typeof(y)          ⟵  The Julia REPL does not
Nothing                      print nothing values.
```

The while loop example illustrates a couple of different things. The loop itself evaluates to a value, just like *3 + 4*. You store this value in variable y. However you cannot see the value in the REPL because it is of type Nothing.

   Also notice that it is perfectly possible to place a while loop on a single line. Whitespace is not significant in Julia like it is in Python; in Python you must remember to indent statements belonging to a loop. But whitespace does play a role in Julia. Consider these three assignments:

```
x = 4
y = 8
z = 3
```

If you want them on a single line you need to separate them with a semicolon:

```
x = 4; y = 8; z = 3
```

You might wonder why I stored the value of the while expression in a variable. I did that purely for teaching purposes, to make you aware of the fact that nearly everything in Julia is an expression that evaluates to a value. Even an assignment evaluates to a value (see listing 3.2). While this may sound like a theoretical curiosity of no interest to you, it does have many practical consequences. It makes the REPL show what value you gave a variable in an assignment statement. You will also see the benefit of treating everything as an expression later in the chapter when if statements are discussed.

Listing 3.2   The assignment evaluates to a value

```
julia> z = 3 + 2
5
```

> **NOTE**   Calling an assignment a statement is technically wrong because everything in Julia is an expression. However I will use the word *statement* about many expressions in this book. The reason is that it makes it easier to distinguish between assignments and control flow, such as if statements and while-loops, and more mathematical expressions.

The REPL will always show the value of the outer expression and not the inner expression. For instance if you evaluate 1 + (3+2), you will never see 5 printed because that is the value of subexpression 3+2. Likewise you will not see i = i + 1 inside a loop. To *see* the value of i for every iteration, you need to explicitly tell Julia to print the value to the console. This is done with the print and println functions:

```
julia> i = 0
0

julia> while i < 5
           i = i + 1
           print(i)
       end
```

```
12345
julia> i = 0
0

julia> while i < 5
           i = i + 1
           println(i)
       end
1
2
3
4
5
```

From these examples you can probably tell the difference. `println` is short for *print line*. It prints a variable on a separate line. You can use `print` and `println` to explicitly print values outside of loops, but that is rarely needed:

```
julia> print(3 + 4)
7
julia> print(i)
5
```

3.3.1 Flowchart

Text doesn't visualize the control flow of a program very well. You have to know the semantics. Because of this, flowchart diagrams, which depict the flow of programs using boxes and arrows, used to be very popular (figure 3.4).

Start and stop of program   Action to perform   Input and output   Decision making

Figure 3.4   Standard flowchart boxes

In the past, students would be taught to design their programs as flowcharts and then write the code. The popularity of object-oriented programming caused flowcharts to fall out of use, as they cannot model object relations. However, flowchart diagrams are still very useful in teaching control flow in a program. If you are not familiar with loops, flowcharts can help you develop an intuition for how they work (figure 3.5).

The square boxes represent actions performed, while the diamond-shaped boxes represent decisions where the flow of control branches into different directions. If the condition is i < 5 ? is true, then the flow will follow the arrow marked with yes. Otherwise control flow would follow the no arrow.

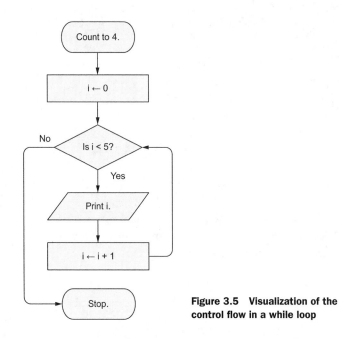

Figure 3.5   Visualization of the
control flow in a while loop

3.3.2   Making a mathematical table for the sine function

You now have all the basic building blocks to repeat what Charles Babbage's Difference Engine did: calculating mathematical tables. To keep things simple let's begin by printing out angles, as follows.

Listing 3.3   A loop printing out angles in increments of 15

```
angle = 0
while angle <= 90
    println(angle)
    angle = angle + 15
end
```

You could copy and paste this code into your Julia REPL, and you would get this result printed out:

```
0
15
30
45
60
75
90
```

Before calculating the sine of these angles you need to convert them to radians, as sine, cosine, and tangent functions generally don't work with degrees from 0° to 360° but rather radians from 0 to 2π. The illustrations in figure 3.6 show how 1 radian is

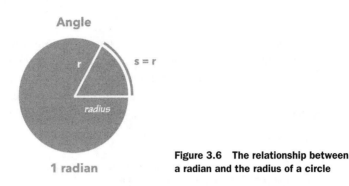

Figure 3.6   The relationship between a radian and the radius of a circle

defined. If you have a circle with radius *r* and draw an arch *s* of length *r* along the perimeter of the circle, then the pie slice has an angle equal to 1 radian.

The circumference *C* and arc length *s* of a circle are defined as the following:

$$C = 2\pi r \qquad\qquad \theta = \frac{s}{2\pi r}$$

From this you can derive a function deg2rad to convert from degrees to radians.

Listing 3.4   Converting degrees to radians

```
deg2rad(θ)  =  (θ/360)*2π
```

In fact you don't have to write this function because Julia already comes with it in its standard library. With this function you can modify the code in listing 3.3 and create a small program that produces a table of sine values, as follows.

Listing 3.5   Loop printing out a sine table

```
angle = 0
while angle <= 90
    rad = deg2rad(angle)
    x = sin(rad)
    println(x)
    angle = angle + 15
end
```

When you run this you will get the following output:

```
0.0
0.25881904510252074
0.49999999999999994
0.7071067811865475
0.8660254037844386
0.9659258262890683
1.0
```

3.3.3   *Range objects*

When reading normal Julia code you will find that looping based on conditions is, in fact, not the normal approach. Instead loops tend to be defined using range objects; ranges are constructed with the : operator. You can do a number of things with ranges, such as checking whether a particular value is within the given range. In this example you will get the first and last part of a range, before querying whether a particular number is within a given range:

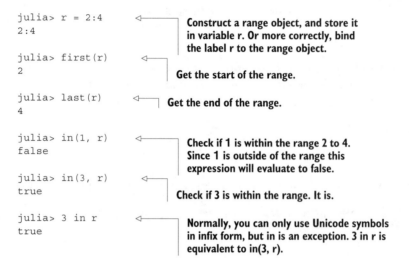

```
julia> r = 2:4
2:4
```
Construct a range object, and store it in variable r. Or more correctly, bind the label r to the range object.

```
julia> first(r)
2
```
Get the start of the range.

```
julia> last(r)
4
```
Get the end of the range.

```
julia> in(1, r)
false
```
Check if 1 is within the range 2 to 4. Since 1 is outside of the range this expression will evaluate to false.

```
julia> in(3, r)
true
```
Check if 3 is within the range. It is.

```
julia> 3 in r
true
```
Normally, you can only use Unicode symbols in infix form, but in is an exception. 3 in r is equivalent to in(3, r).

3.3.4   *For loops*

Range objects are commonly used in for loops, but before showing a for loop example let me just show you how you might use it in a while loop. The loop is repeated as long as the i in 0:4 condition remains true, as follows.

Listing 3.6   While loop using a range

```
i = 0
while i in 0:4
    println(i)
    i = i + 1
end
```

This is such a common and useful idiom that for loops are made to remove a lot of the boilerplate. The following code is equivalent in behavior.

Listing 3.7   For loop over a range

```
for i in 0:4
    println(i)
end
```

What about cases when you don't want to increment by 1 on each iteration? When you calculated angles you did it in increments of 15. Is that possible to do with a for loop? No problem; ranges allow you to define a step size, as in the following listing.

Listing 3.8   For loop with stepped range

```
for angle in 0:15:90
    println(angle)
end
```

When you run this code you get the following output:

```
0
15
30
45
60
75
90
```

Objects you can use in a for loop, such as range objects, are referred to as *iterable*. There are many different iterable objects in Julia, which we will explore in later chapters.

3.4   *Multiline functions*

The functions you have used until now have been defined on a single line. That is quite limiting. More complex problems require multiple lines of code. How do you do that? You need a way to mark the beginning and end of the code that should be included in the function. The for loop and while loop may already give you a hint at how you to do that. A multiline function starts with the keyword function and ends with the keyword end. In the following example code you use a loop to print out the sine value for all angles from 0 to max_angle with an angle increment.

Listing 3.9   Code for creating a sine table stored in a function

```
function print_sin_table(increment, max_angle)
    angle = 0
    while angle <= max_angle
        rad = deg2rad(angle)
        x = sin(rad)
        println(x)
        angle = angle + increment
    end
end
```

Notice how listing 3.9 modifies previous code listing 3.5 to use function arguments increment and max_angle instead of hard coding 15- and 90-degree angles. Thus users can easily change the table they produce. For example, users can produce sine values with 1-degree increments, with print_sin_table(1, 90).

So how does this relate to the Difference Engine made by Charles Babbage? Babbage's equivalent of `println` would not have written numbers on a computer screen but to a sort of printer. The Difference Engine was meant to be attached to a machine that would imprint numbers on metal plates. These could then be used for printing number tables in books. You could also send the numbers you produce to other devices, but this will be covered in later chapters on input and output.

3.4.1   *Implementing the sine trigonometric function*

Now that you have learned to use loops and multiline functions, you actually have all the building blocks necessary to build your own `sin` function, meaning you can replicate what a calculator does. Review the Taylor series used to calculate the *sin(x)* function:

$$\sin(x) = \frac{x}{1!} - \frac{x^3}{3!} + \frac{x^5}{5!} - \cdots$$

This function can be written as a summation:

$$\sin(x) = \sum_{i=0}^{\infty} (-1)^i \frac{x^{2i+1}}{(2i+1)!}$$

I will not prove mathematically how to arrive at this definition; your interest here is demonstrating how computers can be used to solve such problems. Computing by hand became a real problem in the 1800s, as the importance of mathematics and science expanded.

If you are unfamiliar with mathematical notation, let me demonstrate in code how the Σ operator works. Let's start with a simple case:

$$f(n) = \sum_{x=1}^{n} 2x + 1$$

The bottom and top half of the Σ symbol basically define a range. You are stating that you will iterate over the variable *x* from 1 to *n*. You can think of the Σ operator as performing a loop; it iterates across a range and adds up values of the expression it iterates over. You can mimic this behavior with a for loop, as follows.

Listing 3.10   How the sum operator works

```
function f(n)
    total = 0          ⟵──  For storing the
    for x in 1:n            total sum
        total += 2x + 1  ⟵──  A shorthand for total =
    end                       total + 2x + 1
    total   ⟵──  Return value
end
```

A function evaluates to the value of its last expression. In many other languages this is called the *return value*, and the last expression would have been written as

```
return total
```

This is also valid in Julia, but it is only used when you need to exit a function early. Otherwise return is usually omitted in Julia functions. The following listing should help you understand how you can use the Taylor series to implement a sine function.

Listing 3.11 Sine implemented using the Taylor series

```
function sine(x)
    n = 5
    total = 0
    for i in 0:n
        total += (-1)^i*x^(2i+1)/factorial(2i + 1)
    end
    total
end
```

Placing this function in a separate file (e.g., trig.jl) along with other trigonometric functions you implement is a good exercise for the reader. Implement cosine and tangent as well; you can perform an internet search to find their Taylor series definition. You can then load this file into Julia and compare with the built-in sin function:

```
julia> sine(0.5)
0.4794255386041834

julia> sin(0.5)
0.479425538604203

julia> sine(1.0)
0.841470984648068

julia> sin(1.0)
0.8414709848078965
```

You can see that the results are quite similar despite the fact that you only iterate up to n = 5. The accurate definition implies that n = ∞, which is impractical to implement in code. Try with different values of n to see if you can get as accurate result as the built-in sin function.

3.5 Implementing factorial

Your custom sine function uses the built-in factorial function. The factorial of a number *n* means multiplying every number from 1 up to *n*. So the factorial of five would be $5 \times 4 \times 3 \times 2 \times 1$. How would you implement this yourself? There are many approaches. We will look at some of them in this section:

  1 Using the built-in prod function.
  2 Using a while loop to perform multiple multiplications.
  3 Multiplying repeatedly by combining recursion with an if statement.

The prod function is able to multiply all the numbers in a range:

```
julia> fac(n) = prod(1:n)                    ◁────┐  Define your own factorial function
                                                   │  named fac, implemented with prod.
julia> fac(5)                    ◁─────────────────┐
120                                                │  Check that fac and factorial
                                                   │  give the same result.
julia> factorial(5)          ◁─────────────────────┘
 120
```

Experiment with both of these functions to make sure you get the same result. You could do this by using a loop as before.

> **Listing 3.12   Factorial implemented using a loop**

```
function fac(n)
    prod = 1
    while n >= 1
        prod *= n
        n -= 1
    end
    prod
end
```

On each iteration in the loop you decrease the value of n by 1 until the condition n >= 1 no longer holds true and exit with the product[2] of all numbers in the range n to 1.

3.6   *Factorial with recursion*

There is another way you can achieve looping without using the while and for loops, called *recursion*. Check out the following code.

> **Listing 3.13   Broken factorial function implemented using recursion**

```
fac(n) = n*fac(n-1)
```

Try running this. It doesn't quite work. You get the following error message:

```
ERROR: StackOverflowError:
Stacktrace:
 [1] fac(n::Int64) (repeats 79984 times)
```

This is because the fac function keeps calling fac indefinitely. Or more specifically, it calls fac 79,984 times in my example, until it blows up by running out of memory.

---

[2] Product is the result of multiplying numbers, in contrast to sum which is the result of addition.

This produces a *stackoverflow* error message. This is because you keep calling fac, even when the n argument has become less than 1. Somehow you need to check whether n has become less than 1 and exit. You are lucky because Julia's if statement can help you do that.

3.7 *If statements*

Now rewrite your recursive fac function using an if statement. The following code is the first attempt. You will expand on this code until the factorial function handles all edge cases, such as fac(0).

Listing 3.14   Almost-working factorial function implemented using recursion

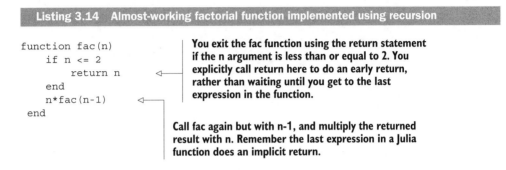

```
function fac(n)
    if n <= 2
        return n
    end
    n*fac(n-1)
end
```

You exit the fac function using the return statement if the n argument is less than or equal to 2. You explicitly call return here to do an early return, rather than waiting until you get to the last expression in the function.

Call fac again but with n-1, and multiply the returned result with n. Remember the last expression in a Julia function does an implicit return.

3.7.1 *If-else statements*

Instead of using the return statement to exit the function early, you can choose between two different blocks of code to execute by adding an else clause, as in the following listing.

Listing 3.15   If–else statement

```
function fac(n)
    if n <= 2
        n
    else
        n*fac(n-1)
    end
end
```

If the n <= 2 condition is not true, you will evaluate the code between the else-end block. The whole if-else statement, like all other statements in Julia, is an expression that evaluates to a value. The statement evaluates to the value of the code block that was evaluated. You can try this out in the Julia REPL yourself. Experiment with different values for x, and see how the value of y changes:

```
julia> x = 4
4
```

```
julia> y = if x > 3
            6
       else
            4
       end
6

julia> y
6
```

However your `fac` function doesn't actually work correctly yet:

```
julia> factorial(0)
1

julia> factorial(-1)
ERROR: DomainError with -1:
`n` must not be negative.

julia> fac(0)
0

julia> fac(-1)
-1
```

`fac(0)` returns 0, but it should return 1. Also, `fac(n)` with n < 0 should not even be allowed. Thus you need to handle the case in which n == 0 and n < 0 differently.

3.7.2   *Elseif clause*

In this scenario the `elseif` clause comes to the rescue. You can add several of these clauses to any if statement. You have done just that in the following listing to handle all the unique cases. Go ahead and test in the REPL whether `fac(0)` and `fac(-1)` behave correctly with this update.

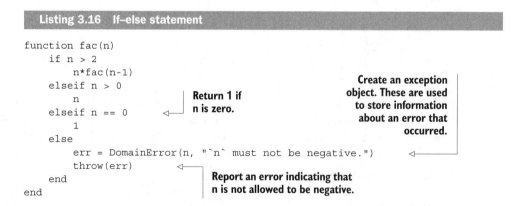

Listing 3.16 If–else statement

```
function fac(n)
    if n > 2
        n*fac(n-1)
    elseif n > 0
        n
    elseif n == 0
        1
    else
        err = DomainError(n, "`n` must not be negative.")
        throw(err)
    end
end
```

Return 1 if n is zero.

Create an exception object. These are used to store information about an error that occurred.

Report an error indicating that n is not allowed to be negative.

Each `elseif` clause adds another condition check. First check if n > 2, then check if it is n > 0. Continue performing every `elseif` check, until you hit a condition that evaluates to `true`. If no condition is true, evaluate the `else` clause that reports an error (figure 3.7).

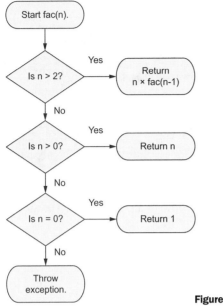

Figure 3.7   If statement with elseif and else

Before discussing error handling further, I will conclude by clarifying the rules for writing an if statement:

1   There must be exactly one `if` keyword used, and it has to be at the start.
2   `else` is optional, but it can only be used once and only at the very end.
3   You can write any number of `elseif` clauses, but they have to come after the `if` clause.

3.8   *Throwing exceptions to handle errors*

In programming speak, functions `return` values but `throw` exceptions. In Julia this is used to handle programmer mistakes. As a programmer you should not provide negative numbers to `fac`. However, mistakes happen, and have to be dealt with. The idea is to report a problem as early as possible—as soon as you have discovered it. This makes it easier to diagnose problems when you are developing and testing your software.

How is throwing an exception different from returning a value? Let me explain with an example (figure 3.8).

If function `alpha` calls `beta` which calls `gamma`, then you get what is called a *call stack*. The call stack is a place in memory storing the location of function calls. This is necessary because when your CPU finishes processing instructions in `gamma`, it needs

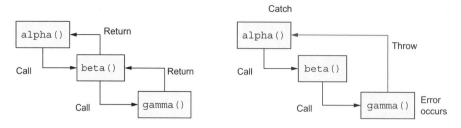

Figure 3.8   Difference between regular returns and throwing exceptions

to get back to the location in `beta` where `gamma` was called initially. This location is stored in memory. You call it the *return address*. Likewise you need to remember how to return to `alpha` from `beta`. These nested function calls create a stack of return addresses. This is the *call stack*.

As figure 3.8 shows, `return` carries you back the same way you came. `throw` is different; it allows you to skip many steps in the call stack. `throw` skips every function called until it reaches a point where there is a `catch` defined:

```
function alpha()          Defines a block of code, where somewhere
    try               ◁── in the callstack an exception may occur
        beta()
    catch e       ◁─┐    If an exception does occur it will be
        # handle exception   caught, and this block of code is meant
    end               │    to clean up or handle the exception.
end
```

Information about the error is stored in an exception object, which was passed to the `throw` function. The variable `e` gets set to this object; thus the `catch` block is able to access information about the error that occurred. At this point we cannot discuss exceptions in great detail, as this requires a firmer understanding of the Julia type system. You can, however, experiment with this in the REPL yourself to get a feel for how exceptions break the normal flow of control:

```
julia> y = try
           fac(3)
       catch e
           42
       end
6

julia> y = try
           fac(-3)
       catch e
           42
       end
42
```

```
julia> fac(-3)
ERROR: DomainError with -3:
`n` must not be negative.
```

Remember, almost everything in Julia is an expression, including try-catch blocks.

3.9 *Control flow vs. data flow*

Now that you have looked at different forms of control flow, we'll discuss the meaning of *control flow* in greater depth. Comparing control flow with data flow may help you better grasp the concept. Consider this simple code snippet:

```
alice = encrypt(bob)
```

There are two different perspectives when looking at this code: a message stored in bob flows *into* the encrypt function, and a cipher text object flows *out* of the function (figure 3.9).

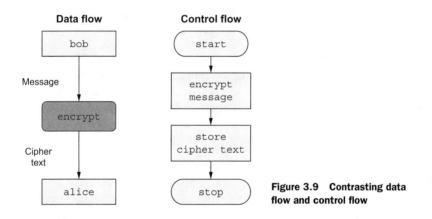

Figure 3.9 Contrasting data flow and control flow

With data flow, data is flowing along the arrow between the boxes. In figure 3.9 the light boxes are sources and sinks, and the dark box is a filter. It transforms incoming data into another type of data.

In a control flow diagram (e.g., a flowchart), arrows don't represent movement of data, but transition of control. Control flow is about how control flows from one box to the other and how that flow can be altered and redirected:

```
y = gamma(beta(alpha(x)))
```

In this example, you can think of how control is passed from the alpha function to the beta function and finally to the gamma function: there is a flow of control. From a data flow perspective, we think of data flowing into alpha, out of it, and then into beta.

When analyzing complex code, sketching out a data flow diagram can be useful. By labeling arrows with the type of data going in and out of functions (filters) you can get a better overview of complex data flows through your code.

3.10   *Counting rabbits*

In many programming books you will find an implementation of the `fib` function, which is short for *Fibonacci*. Why is this function so popular in programming? And why should you care? Consider the following reasons:

1 It is a simple way of demonstrating transformation of a mathematical definition into code.

2 Implementing it allows you to contrast solving problems through *recursion* and *iteration* (loops).

3 Fibonacci numbers pop up in all sorts of real-life circumstances: in the number of flower petals, spirals on a sunflower or nautilus shell, and fractions that appear in phyllotaxis.

4 It is a simple demonstration of how you build models of real-world phenomena.

This is what the number sequence looks like. The sequence goes on towards infinity:

$$0, 1, 1, 2, 3, 5, 8, 13, 21, 34, 55, 89, 1444, \ldots$$

Each of the numbers in this sequence is called a *Fibonacci number*. Mathematicians like to refer to each of these numbers using the letter *F*. The first number in the sequence is F_0, the second is F_1 and so on. In other words, the indexing starts at 0. Mathematically, Fibonacci numbers are defined as follows:

$$F_0 = 0, F_1 = 1$$
$$F_n = F_{n-1} + F_{n-2}, n > 1$$

This may seem as enlightening as a Wikipedia page (i.e., not very), so I'll try to provide some intuition behind this mathematical definition with a concrete example: the growth of a rabbit population. In fact, this is how Fibonacci numbers were discovered. Leonardo of Pisa, also known as Fibonacci, was wondering some 800 years ago how a rabbit population would grow each month. He asked the following hypothetical question:

> *If we have one pair of rabbits at the start of the year, how many will there be at the end of the year?*

To answer this question, you need to build models of reality. When building models, try to extract the most important features of the specific traits you are trying to model. For instance, you don't care about how the rabbits spread out, what they look like, what they eat, or how they obtain food. Your model is only concerned with how their population grows. All models are built for a particular purpose; if you want to check how well a new cellphone will fit in somebody's pocket, then the model doesn't need to be anything more advanced than a block of wood. The only thing you need to mimic is the physical dimensions of the phone, not the color of the exterior or crispness of the screen.

Models, thus, always involve major *simplifications* of reality. In Fibonacci's model of rabbit growth, you deal with immortal rabbits. They never actually die. They are born, and a month after birth they start reproducing. You always model them as pairs. One pair of rabbits produces another pair of rabbits every month as soon as they reach reproductive age (figure 3.10).

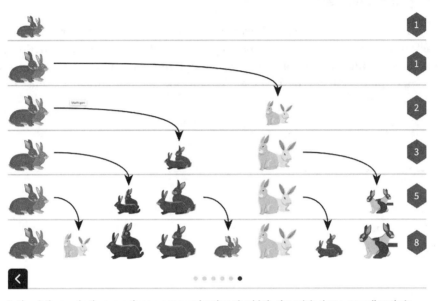

In the sixth month, there are three more couples that give birth: the original one, as well as their first two pairs or kids.

Figure 3.10   Rabbit population growth each month, as illustrated by Mathigon

Mathigon (https://mathigon.org/course/sequences/fibonacci) is an excellent online source demonstrating interactively how rabbit populations grow according to the Fibonacci number sequence. The hexagons in the screenshot show how many rabbit pairs exist for a given month. In the first month you only have 1 pair, while in the sixth month you have 8 pairs. When you implement the `fib` function (listing 3.17) to calculate Fibonacci numbers, it works like this: `fib(1)` is the same as F_1; `fib(n)` corresponds to F_n.

Listing 3.17   Calculating a Fibonacci number

```
function fib(n)
    if n == 0
        0
    elseif n == 1
        1
    else
```

⊲――┐ **The mathematical definition**
⊲――┘ **says $F_0 = 0$, $F_1 = 1$, which is expressed here.**

```
      fib(n-1) + fib(n-2)
  end
end
```

> For all other values of n, they are equal to the two preceding Fibonacci numbers. This expresses a recursion. The fib function is calling itself with another argument.

Let's try to walk through how this function works in practice. What happens when you try to evaluate fib(3)? This sets n = 3. Whenever n > 1 the following line is evaluated:

```
fib(n-1) + fib(n-2)
```

This will get evaluated over and over again, but the argument n is reduced by 1 and 2 each time, meaning sooner or later the first conditions of the fib function becomes true. The result then bubbles back up, completing earlier requests. Thus you have a sort of double recursion in this case. These REPL examples provide a sense of how the Fibonacci function works:

```
julia> fib(3) == fib(2) + fib(1)
true

julia> fib(4) == fib(3) + fib(2)
true

julia> n = 5
5

julia> fib(n) == fib(n-1) + fib(n-2)
true
```

3.10.1 *Base case*

To avoid the recursion running until you consume all your stack memory, you need to define the *base case*. This is the if statement that lets you exit the recursion at some point.

Listing 3.18 Calculating a Fibonacci number

```
function fib(n)
    if 0 <= n <= 1
        n
    else
        fib(n-1) + fib(n-2)
    end
end
```

> Check if n is within the range of 0 to 1. Is it equal to or greater than zero as well as smaller or equal to one?

The 0 <= n <= 1 condition defines the base condition or exist point. You need something similar for every recursive function. A recursive function is a function that calls itself.

3.10.2 *Iteration vs. recursion*

Earlier you demonstrated that recursion is just one of many ways of solving a problem; it is never a requirement. A recursion can always be replaced by an iteration. By iteration I mean looping (e.g., using a for loop or while loop). For example, with the following code you are *iterating* over the range 0 to 4:

```
for i in 0:4
    println(i)
end
```

If you can solve the same problem with iteration, then why use recursion? Let's look at the iteration solution to discuss its pros and cons.

Listing 3.19 Calculating a Fibonacci number using iteration

```
function fibi(n)
    if 0 <= n <= 1
        return n
    end

    prev = 0
    x    = 1
    for i in 2:n
        tmp = x
        x += prev
        prev = tmp
    end
    x
end
```

Early exit; to avoid deep nesting you use the return keyword to exit the function immediately with the value n.

prev is used to represent fib(n-2).

To hold the final result fib(n)

This is shorthand for x = x + prev, which is equivalent to the fib(n-1) + fib(n-2) calculation.

While this code may be easier conceptually, you may notice that iteration makes everything a lot messier. You get a lot more bookkeeping, meaning we have more variables to maintain and update properly. I spent markedly longer time creating this example code, while making several mistakes in the initial version. The recursive variant, in contrast, I wrote correctly on my first attempt.

Thus while recursion may take some time getting accustomed to, it frequently makes your code much simpler. One downside is that recursion is often slower. Thus, often you will implement your solution through recursion first, and if it turns out to be too slow, you rewrite it using iteration.

3.10.3 *To return or not return*

The last example used a `return` statement to perform an early exit from the function. This is also optional, but as you can see, writing the code without `return` can make it harder to read. This is because you can end up with deep nesting of control-flow statements, as seen in the following listing.

Listing 3.20 Calculating a Fibonacci number without early return

```
function fibi(n)
    if 0 <= n <= 1
        n
    else
        prev = 0
        x    = 1
        for i in 2:n
```

```
            tmp = x
            x += prev
            prev = tmp
        end
        x
    end
end
```

There are no hard rules here. You will just have to use common sense and rely on your own sense of good taste. As a rule of thumb, I try to avoid nesting deeper than three levels; however, avoid creating strict rules. An obsession with rules carved in stone has always plagued the software industry. It is better to be flexible and use common sense. Julia itself is a language that tries to be pragmatic.

Summary

- Control-flow statements use conditions composed using Boolean expressions. Loops repeat as long as condition remains true.
- Even control-flow statements are expressions in Julia, meaning they evaluate to a value. In Julia, even nothing is a value.
- Computers' ability to repeat similar calculations a large number of times makes them suited for computations that are hard to do by hand, such as calculating trigonometric functions.
- A recursive function is a function that calls itself. Recursive functions must have a *base case*, or they will never terminate execution.
- Recursion and iteration can solve the same problems. Recursion often makes the code easier to write, while iteration usually provides better performance.

Julia as a spreadsheet

This chapter covers

- Working with collections of numbers using the `Array` and `Tuple` types
- Useful types to put into collections, such as numbers, characters, and text strings
- Performing statistics
- Transforming lists of numbers with `map`
- Using predicates with the `filter` function

In the second chapter we discussed how to work with Julia as a calculator. However, people working with numbers today don't usually use desk calculators; they use spreadsheet tools, such as Microsoft Excel or Apple Numbers (figure 4.1).

In these applications, numbers are stored in tables. All serious scientific work involves working with large tables of data, including whole columns of numbers. Scientists and data analysts get survey data or measurements they want to analyze. Julia is excellent for this type of work. You are not literally working with a graphical spreadsheet tool, but you are manipulating data in table form, much like a modern spreadsheet application.

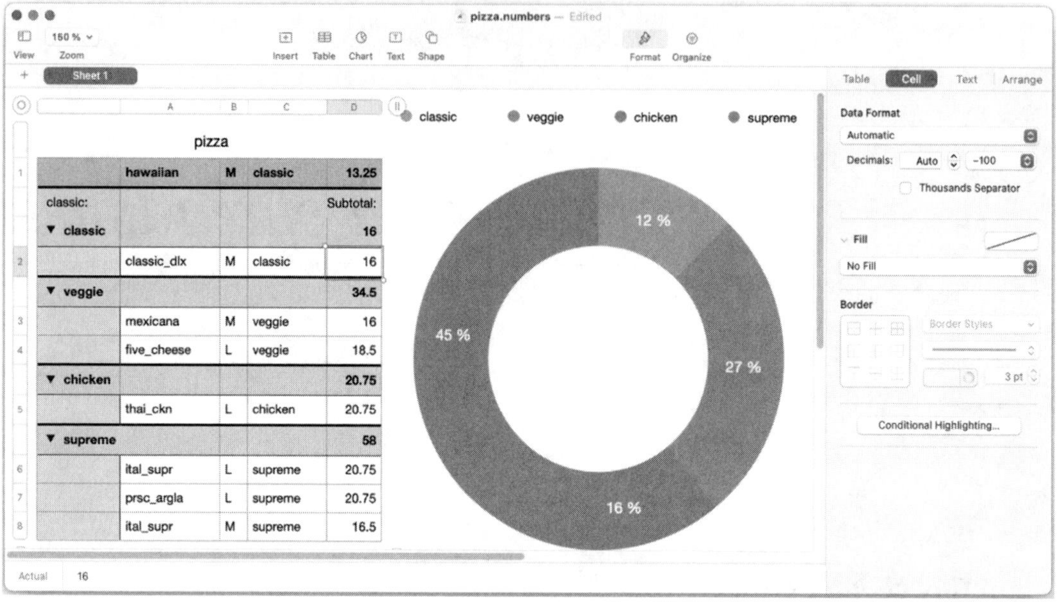

Figure 4.1 Apple Numbers is a spreadsheet application for working with rows and columns of numbers.

You will only scratch the surface of what is possible in this chapter. Instead, the main purpose is introducing the `Array` and `Tuple` datatypes. Because these are containers for other values, you will also touch upon the `Char` (character) and `String` (text string) types to have something interesting to put in your arrays and tuples. In fact, you will put numbers, characters, text strings, and Boolean values into these two collection types.

4.1   Analyzing pizza sales

To better understand the purpose of different `Array` operations, I will use an example of pizza sales. Table 4.1 shows different types of pizza sold in different amounts and at different prices. You will explore how Julia code can be used to answer questions such as the following:

- How many pizzas were sold in total?
- How much revenue did you get in total from your pizza sales?
- What was the average price of pizzas sold?
- What was the average number of pizzas sold in each category?

Table 4.1   Pizza sales data, where each row says how many pizzas of each type were sold

Pizza	Amount	Price
Pepperoni	4	15.0
Margherita	1	11.5

Table 4.1 Pizza sales data, where each row says how many pizzas of each type were sold *(continued)*

Pizza	Amount	Price
BBQ Chicken	5	13.0
Hawaiian	3	12.75
Prosciutto	2	14.25

4.2 *Different types of arrays*

An array in Julia can represent a row, column, or table of numbers. In fact, arrays can contain any type of element, not just numbers. You could have arrays of Booleans, characters, or text strings (e.g., elements in an array are ordered). You can ask for elements at a specific position, such as, "Give me the third element in array A."

Let's create a column of numbers containing the number of pizzas sold. Notice how the numbers are listed vertically. This is Julia's way of telling you that you just made a *column vector*. When creating a column vector, separate each element with a comma:

```
julia> amounts = [4, 1, 5, 3, 2]
5-element Vector{Int64}:
 4
 1
 5
 3
 2
```

It is also possible to create a *row vector* instead by separating each element with a space:

```
julia> row = [4 1 5 3 2]
1×5 Matrix{Int64}:
 4  1  5  3  2
```

Each of the values in the vector has an associated *element index*, as illustrated in figure 4.2. The index of the first element is 1.

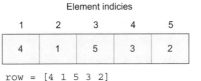

Figure 4.2 Illustration of how elements are organized in a row vector

The word *vector* is commonly used to refer to one-dimensional arrays, while a two-dimensional array is called a *matrix*. You can think of a matrix as the same as a table in a spreadsheet application. In Julia, you can construct tables by stacking row vectors on top of each other.

Notice how each row is separated with a semicolon. Here you have a table with the amounts and prices columns:

```
julia> pizzas = [4 15.0;
                 1 11.5;
                 5 13.0;
                 3 12.75;
                 2 14.25]
5×2 Matrix{Float64}:
 4.0   15.0
 1.0   11.5
 5.0   13.0
 3.0   12.75
 2.0   14.25
```

The new lines are not required; they just make it easier to read the code. You would have gotten exactly the same matrix by writing the following:

```
pizzas = [4 15.0; 1 11.5; 5 13.0; 3 12.75; 2 14.25]
```

To conceptualize how columns and matrices are organized, you can look at the following illustration (figure 4.3). With one-dimensional vectors we normally talk about element indices, but for a matrix, both the rows and the columns are numbered.

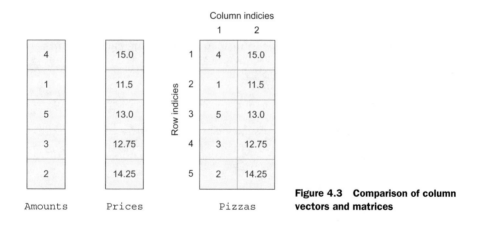

Figure 4.3   Comparison of column vectors and matrices

In this chapter, however, you will focus primarily on column vectors. They correspond most closely to what are called *arrays* in other languages. Multidimensional arrays are not a central feature in other languages like they are in Julia.

4.3   Performing operations on arrays

Lists of numbers aren't very interesting, unless they allow you to do something useful. Fortunately, many functions operate on arrays. For instance, Julia's sum function can be used to add up all the elements in an array. Here you calculate the total number of pizzas sold:

```
julia> no_pizzas_sold = sum(amounts)
15
```

If you want to find out how many elements there are in amounts, you can use length. This also allows you to calculate the average number of pizzas sold of each type:

```
julia> length(amounts)
5

julia> avg = sum(amounts) / length(amounts)
3.0
```

Let's put the prices in a variable to have something to experiment with:

```
julia> prices = [15.0, 11.5, 13.0, 12.75, 14.25]
5-element Vector{Float64}:
 15.0
 11.5
 13.0
 12.75
 14.25
```

To make it easier to get an overview of the different prices you have, you can sort them:

```
julia> sorted = sort(prices)          Sorted prices
5-element Vector{Float64}:            stored in sorted
 11.5
 12.75
 13.0
 14.25
 15.0

julia> prices            sort did not
5-element Vector{Float64}:   modify prices.
 15.0
 11.5
 13.0
 12.75
 14.25
```

When you call sort, you create a new vector. The prices vector is not modified. By convention, Julia functions never modify any of their inputs. Sometimes it is necessary to modify inputs to a function. Julia developers have established the convention of tacking on an exclamation mark (!) to the name of any function which modifies its input. Hence, many Julia functions that don't modify their inputs have sibling functions

that do. For instance, the sort! function will sort its input vector rather than returning a new sorted version:

```julia
julia> sort!(prices)
5-element Vector{Float64}:
 11.5
 12.75
 13.0
 14.25
 15.0

julia> prices
5-element Vector{Float64}:
 11.5
 12.75
 13.0
 14.25
 15.0
```

**Prices were
modified by sort!**

What if you live in a country with value-added tax? To figure out the sticker price on
your pizzas, you need to add the sales tax. If you live in Norway, the value added tax is
25%. Let's calculate new prices with taxes:

```julia
julia> prices = [15.0, 11.5, 13.0, 12.75, 14.25];
julia> prices_with_tax = prices * 1.25
5-element Vector{Float64}:
 18.75
 14.375
 16.25
 15.9375
 17.8125
```

But what if you want to find out how much money you made on each type of pizza?
You could try to multiply the amounts with the prices:

```julia
julia> amounts * prices
ERROR: MethodError: no method matching *(::Vector{Int64}, ::Vector{Float64})
```

Don't worry about the error message. I will explain the concepts you need to grasp to
read it in later chapters.

  For now, what you need to know is that there is no obvious definition of what a
multiplication between two columns of numbers should produce. One can imagine
numerous ways of interpreting this. Thus you have to explicitly tell Julia that you want
elementwise operations. You can achieve this by adding a dot to the mathematical
operator. +, -, *, and / are for performing arithmetic on individual numbers (scalars).
To perform elementwise operations on arrays of numbers you need to use the .+, .-,
.*, and ./ operators:

```julia
julia> amounts .* prices
5-element Vector{Float64}:
```

```
60.0
11.5
65.0
38.25
28.5
```

You can feed this result to the sum function to compute your total profit from selling pizza:

```
julia> sum(amounts .* prices)
203.25
```

4.4 Working with the statistics module

Professionals doing statistics and data analysis usually work with tables of data; you can easily implement your own functions to perform statistics on individual columns of data. Following is a basic example of an average function.

Listing 4.1 Calculating arithmetic mean

```
average(A) = sum(A) / length(A)
```

Instead of reinventing the wheel, you can use ready-made statistical functions. These are bundled with Julia but placed in the Statistics module (see https://docs.julialang .org/en/v1/stdlib/Statistics/). Modules will be covered more extensively later, but you can think of them as bundles of premade functionality that you can use in your programs. To use a module, write

```
using Statistics
```

This will cause the functions, types, and constants defined in the module to be loaded and made available to you. It will also make documentation available for the module. Remember, you can enter Julia's documentation mode by writing a question mark (?) at the beginning of the line:

```
julia> using Statistics

help?> Statistics
search: Statistics

  Statistics


  Standard library module for basic statistics functionality.

help?> middle(3, 4)
  middle(x, y)


  Compute the middle of two numbers x and y, which is equivalent in both
  value and type to computing their mean ((x + y) / 2).
```

To get an overview of what types and functions exist in the module, write the module name and a dot, and then press the Tab key twice. This will show all possible completions (I have edited out some of the results for clarity):

```
julia> Statistics.
corm            mean            realXcY
corzm           mean!           sqrt!
cov             median          std
cov2cor!        median!         stdm
covm            middle          unscaled_covzm
covzm           quantile        var
eval            quantile!       varm
include         range_varm      varm!
```

Let's explore some of the statistics functions in the REPL:

```
julia> mean(amounts)
3.0
```
Compute the arithmetic mean of amounts.

```
julia> mean(prices)
13.3
```

```
julia> median(amounts)
3.0
```
The middle value when values are sorted

```
julia> median(prices)
13.0
```

```
julia> std(amounts)
1.5811388300841898
```
Standard deviation

```
julia> std([3, 3, 3])
0.0
```

mean and median are both used to compute averages, but work slightly differently. With mean you add up all the values and divide by the number of values. If there are a few extreme values, the average can be heavily skewed. Thus, when, for instance, calculating the average income of a family, you usually use the median. Median income is calculated by sorting all the household incomes and then picking the income in the middle of the sorted list. That way, a few ultra-rich families will not skew the result.

With the std function, you find the standard deviation in a collection of values. The standard deviation is a measure of how much values differ. If every element is the same, then the standard deviation will be zero. Thus far, you have looked at dealing with arrays as a whole, but to be able to build your own functionality processing arrays, you need to know how to access individual elements in the array.

4.5   *Accessing elements*

Every element in a Julia array is numbered starting from 1. This is called 1-based indexing and is very common in numerical and mathematically oriented languages. However,
mainstream languages, such as Python, C, C++, and Java, use 0-based indexing.

> **1-based vs. 0-based indexing**
>
> The best way to index arrays is a topic developers love to argue about. In mathemat-
> ics, it is a common convention to number elements, rows, and columns using 1-based
> indexing. When discussing hardware details, such as computer memory addresses,
> it is more common to use 0-based indexing. Thus, languages with a numerical focus
> have tended to use 1-based indexing, while languages closer to the hardware, such
> as C, have used 0-based indexing.

Use square brackets to define array literals as well as to access individual elements
by index:

```
julia> amounts = [4, 1, 5, 3, 2]
5-element Vector{Int64}:
 4
 1
 5
 3
 2

julia> amounts[1]          Access the first
4                          element in the
                           amounts array.

julia> amounts[2]
1                          Get the fifth (last)
                           element in the
julia> amounts[5]          amounts array.
2
```

Use square brackets both to define an array literal and to access individual elements.
Of course you also want to be able to change individual elements. This is done in
identical fashion:

```
julia> xs = [2, 3]
2-element Vector{Int64}:
 2
 3

julia> xs[1] = 42
42

julia> xs
2-element Vector{Int64}:
 42
  3
```

```
julia> xs[2] = 12
12

julia> xs
2-element Vector{Int64}:
 42
 12
```

Each time you change an element, you can print it out to show what the array currently looks like. All these examples are neat and tidy. What happens if you try to access an element with an invalid index?

> **The array xs has only two values, so you cannot attempt to set the third element. Julia checks if you use valid indices.**

```
julia> xs[3] = 5
ERROR: BoundsError: attempt to access 2-element Vector{Int64} at index [3]

julia> xs[0]
ERROR: BoundsError: attempt to access 2-element Vector{Int64} at index [0]
```

**Elements start at index 1.
There are no values at index 0.**

The behavior you see here is common across most mainstream languages. However, some older popular langauges allow you to set elements at any index, regardless of how large you made the array in advance.

There are some challenges with the way you have accessed elements in these examples:

1 You don't always know the index of the last element, as arrays can have different sizes and can be grown.
2 While 1-based indexing is the standard, it is possible to construct 0-based arrays in Julia.

To deal with the fact that you cannot always know where an array starts or ends, use the begin and end keywords to access the first and last element, respectively:

```
julia> amounts[1]
4

julia> amounts[begin]
4
```

> **Access the first element.
> [1] and [begin] are identical.**

```
julia> amounts[5]
2

julia> amounts[end]
2
```

> **Access the last element.
> [5] and [end] are the same.**

```
julia> amounts[4]
3

julia> amounts[end-1]
3
```

> **By subtracting, you can do things like access the second-last element.**

4.6   *Creating arrays*

Thus far, you have created arrays using array literals. An *array literal* means you literally list each element an array is composed of. For example, [4, 8, 1] and [false, false, true] are both examples of array literals. The variable xs may refer to an array, but it is not an array literal. However, array literals are not very effective at creating large arrays. You have a number of functions, such as zeros, ones, fill, and rand, which makes it easier to quickly create arrays containing particular values.

For instance, what if you want an array containing 50 elements, all with the value 0? For this you can use the zeros function:

```
julia> xs = zeros(50)
50-element Vector{Float64}:
 0.0
 0.0
 0.0
 ⋮
 0.0
 0.0
 0.0
 0.0

julia> length(xs)
50
```

It is so common to initialize vectors elements to 1 that there is a function, ones, to do that explicitly. The function creates an array of specified length with every element set to the value 1:

```
julia> ones(5)
5-element Vector{Float64}:
 1.0
 1.0
 1.0
 1.0
 1.0
```

But it is possible to fill a large array with any value using the fill function. Here you create an array with six elements, each set to the value 42:

```
julia> fill(42, 6)
6-element Vector{Int64}:
 42
 42
 42
 42
 42
 42
```

In many situations you need arrays with large number of random values. rand(n) creates a vector holding n random numbers between 0 and 1:

```
julia> rand(3)
3-element Vector{Float64}:
 0.5862914538673218
 0.8917281248249265
 0.37928032685681234
```

When you create arrays, the description of the array made in the Julia REPL will look something like this:

```
5-element Vector{Float64}
```

This says that the vector you have made contains five elements, and each of those elements is of type `Float64`. But what if you want elements of a different type? Say you want 8-bit signed integers instead. How do you do that? The `ones`, `zeros`, and `rand` functions allow you to specify element type. Here are some examples:

```
julia> ones(Int8, 5)
5-element Vector{Int8}:
 1
 1
 1
 1
 1
```

Make an array containing signed 8-bit integers with the value 1. Notice the description of the vector says Vector{Int8}.

```
julia> zeros(UInt8, 4)
4-element Vector{UInt8}:
 0x00
 0x00
 0x00
 0x00
```

Create four zeros of type unsigned 8-bit. Notice how zero is written in hexadecimal form, as that is the default way of formatting unsigned integers in Julia.

```
julia> rand(Int8, 3)
3-element Vector{Int8}:
 -50
 125
  58
```

Create three random 8-bit signed integer values. The values will be randomly picked from the full range: -128 to 127.

Even array literals allow you to specify the element type. Thus, you can indicate that you want a vector of 8-bit signed integers:

```
julia> xs = Int8[72, 69, 76, 76, 79]
5-element Vector{Int8}:
 72
 69
 76
 76
 79
```

The array literal is prefixed with the type you want for each element—`Int8` in this case. If you don't prefix with the type, Julia will infer the element type. The details of how that works will become apparent when I discuss types in chapter 7. If you want to check what type each element in an array is, you can use the eltype (short for element type) function:

```
julia> eltype(xs)
Int8

julia> eltype([3, 4, 5])
Int64

julia> eltype([true, false])
Bool
```

4.7 Mapping values in an array

You can do more than simply adding and multiplying values. Across all programming languages that support functional style programming, you will find a trio of functions called map, reduce, and filter. Let's explore the map function first by revisiting your earlier sine table calculations. Do you remember this function?

Listing 4.2   Code for creating a sine table stored in a function

```
function print_sin_table(increment, max_angle)
    angle = 0
    while angle <= max_angle
        rad = deg2rad(angle)
        x = sin(rad)
        println(x)
        angle = angle + increment
    end
end
```

However, instead of printing out the table of sine values, you can create an array of all the sine values. For this you use the map function, which is designed to transform a collection of values into another array of values. Here an array of degrees is transformed to an array of radians using map. map applies the deg2rad function to every element in the input arrays:

```
julia> degs = [0, 15, 30, 45, 60];

julia> rads = map(deg2rad, degs)
5-element Vector{Float64}:
 0.0
 0.2617993877991494
 0.5235987755982988
 0.7853981633974483
 1.0471975511965976
```

map is referred to as a *higher order function*. These are functions that take other functions as arguments and/or return functions. This is different from the functions you have seen thus far, which take numbers as arguments exclusively. The basic form of map takes a function f as first argument and applies that function to every element in a collection, xs, producing a new collection, ys, as output:

```
ys = map(f, xs)
```

The second argument, representing a collection, does not need to be an actual array. It could be anything one can iterate over and get multiple elements; thus you can also use a range object. Here you use a range from 0 to 90, with 15 degrees as a step value:

```
julia> map(deg2rad, 0:15:90)
7-element Vector{Float64}:
 0.0
 0.2617993877991494
 0.5235987755982988
 0.7853981633974483
 1.0471975511965976
 1.3089969389957472
 1.5707963267948966
```

You can combine this to create a sine table:

```
julia> map(sin, map(deg2rad, 0:15:90))
7-element Vector{Float64}:
 0.0
 0.25881904510252074
 0.49999999999999994
 0.7071067811865475
 0.8660254037844386
 0.9659258262890683
 1.0
```

However, this is not normally how you do it. Instead, you collect all transformations you want to do into a single function. This is more memory efficient, as every call to map produces a new array. Another solution is to preallocate an array of the same size as the output and use this array in repeated mappings. The mutating map! function allows you to do just that.

It writes its outputs straight to the array given as the second argument. The third argument is the input, which will not be modified by the map! function.

However, if the input is of the same type and length as required by the output, then you can reuse the input argument as your output argument:

```
result = zeros(Float64, length(0:15:90))      ◁── Allocate array
map!(deg2rad, result, 0:15:90)                       to hold results.
 map!(sin, result, result)                    ◁── The input and destination
                                                   array must have equal length.
```

However, this is not an elegant way of writing the code, and mutating function calls are best avoided, as they make analyzing data flow much more difficult. Thus, you collect all transformations into one function, which reduces the number of memory allocations the code has to do and is often easier to read:

```
degsin(deg) = sin(deg2rad(deg))
map(degsin, 0:15:90)
```

The first line is just a one-liner function definition. You could have used a multiline definition instead, but it would take more space:

```
function degsin(deg)
    sin(deg2rad(deg))
end

map(degsin, 0:15:90)
```

A great way of understanding built-in functions is implementing them yourself. To better understand map, create your own map function called transform. It contains new concepts, which we will discuss in more detail.

Listing 4.3   Knock-off version of the built-in map function

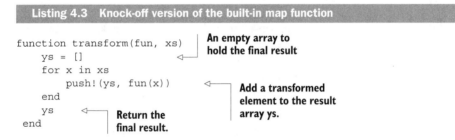

```
function transform(fun, xs)
    ys = []                         ⟵  An empty array to
    for x in xs                         hold the final result
        push!(ys, fun(x))           ⟵  Add a transformed
    end                                 element to the result
    ys          ⟵  Return the           array ys.
end                 final result.
```

transform takes two arguments, fun and xs, where the former is a function, and the latter is an array or other iterable collection object. Functions can be stored in variables and used. The following is a simple demonstration:

```
julia> sin(1.0)
0.8414709848078965

julia> g = sin
sin (generic function with 13 methods)

julia> g(1.0)         ⟵  Calling the sin
0.8414709848078965        function

julia> add = +                    ⟵  Remember the plus
+ (generic function with 190 methods)   operator in Julia is
                                        a function.
julia> add(2, 3)
5
```

This is why you can use fun as a function and call it, despite it being an argument to the transform function. The next part that needs some further explanation is

```
push!(xs, x)
```

This function adds the element x to the array xs. Remember, the exclamation mark warns you that the push! function potentially alters its inputs. In this case, the xs argument is modified.

You must add the exclamation mark to call the right function; the exclamation mark is part of the function name, so push and push! would count as two different function names. In Julia, there is no function named push. If it had existed, you could imagine it would have returned a new array with an extra element.

There is no requirement to add the exclamation mark to functions you define, but you should get in the habit of doing it to aid fellow developers reading your code. This way, it is easy to see where a variable is potentially modified (mutated).

> **TIP** To a beginner, mutating functions may not seem like a big deal. However, when writing larger programs you will start to notice that functions that mutate inputs often make programs harder to read and follow. The exclamation mark helps reduce mental load when reading source code. Without it, every function call could potentially modify its input, making code analysis much more difficult.

The following is a simple demonstration of how push! works. You create an empty array ys and add numbers to it. Each time you can see how the array grows larger:

```
julia> ys = []          ⟵┐   Create an
Any[]                     │   empty array.

julia> push!(ys, 3)     ⟵┐   Add the number
1-element Vector{Any}:    │   3 to the array.
 3

julia> push!(ys, 8)
2-element Vector{Any}:
 3
 8

julia> push!(ys, 2)
3-element Vector{Any}:
 3
 8
 2
```

4.8 *Introducing characters and strings*

Thus far, you have worked almost exclusively with numbers, but your pizza table contains more than just numbers. The table contains text as well, such as the names of the pizzas. How do you work with text in Julia?

Let's start with the most basic building block. Text is made up of characters, and a single character is represented by the Char type in Julia. In computer memory, everything is a number, including characters. Here is a little challenge: look at the following example, and see if you can make sense of it:

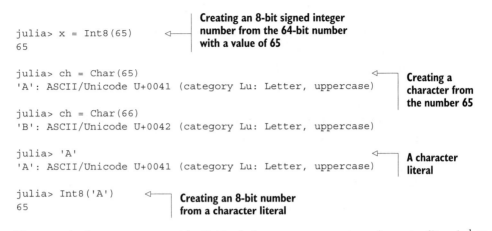

```
julia> x = Int8(65)
65
```
Creating an 8-bit signed integer number from the 64-bit number with a value of 65

```
julia> ch = Char(65)
'A': ASCII/Unicode U+0041 (category Lu: Letter, uppercase)
```
Creating a character from the number 65

```
julia> ch = Char(66)
'B': ASCII/Unicode U+0042 (category Lu: Letter, uppercase)
```

```
julia> 'A'
'A': ASCII/Unicode U+0041 (category Lu: Letter, uppercase)
```
A character literal

```
julia> Int8('A')
65
```
Creating an 8-bit number from a character literal

You put single quotes around individual characters to create a character literals.[1] 'A' and 'Y' are both character literals.

This code example shows that characters in Julia are just numbers with a different type. Remember how an UInt8 and Int8 consume the same number of bits and can hold the same data but interpret it differently? The same thing holds true for characters. While in memory they look the same, the type determines what you can do with them. For instance, you cannot add two characters, but you can add a number to a character:

```
julia> 'A' + 'B'
ERROR: MethodError: no method matching +(::Char, ::Char)
```

```
julia> 'A' + 3
'D': ASCII/Unicode U+0044 (category Lu: Letter, uppercase)
```

You can create arrays of characters, just like you can create arrays of numbers or Booleans:

```
julia> chars = ['H', 'E', 'L', 'L', 'O']
5-element Vector{Char}:
 'H': ASCII/Unicode U+0048
 'E': ASCII/Unicode U+0045
 'L': ASCII/Unicode U+004C
 'L': ASCII/Unicode U+004C
 'O': ASCII/Unicode U+004F
```

> **NOTE**   To improve readability and clarity, I occasionally edit the REPL output. For example, I remove the (category Lu: Letter, uppercase) description tacked on characters, as it creates a lot of visual noise.

---

[1] A character literally is a character from A to Z rather than, for example, a variable or constant containing a character.

A text string is just characters joined together. Notice from the output that text strings are identified with double quotes, while individual characters are identified with single quotes:

```
julia> join(chars)
"HELLO"
```

join can take any iterable object (objects you can use in a for loop) as input. Hence you can provide a range of characters as well:

```
julia> join('A':'G')
"ABCDEFG"
```

Skip every other character by using a step size of '2' in the range object:

```
julia> join('A':2:'G')
"ACEG"
```

You can collect the individual characters in a text string, so you can get back an array of characters:

```
julia> collect("HELLO")
5-element Vector{Char}:
 'H': ASCII/Unicode U+0048
 'E': ASCII/Unicode U+0045
 'L': ASCII/Unicode U+004C
 'L': ASCII/Unicode U+004C
 'O': ASCII/Unicode U+004F
```

collect is a versatile function; it can turn any object that allows iterating over many values into an array. Thus you can collect ranges as well:

```
julia> collect(2:5)
4-element Vector{Int64}:
 2
 3
 4
 5

 julia> collect('B':'D')
3-element Vector{Char}:
 'B': ASCII/Unicode U+0042
 'C': ASCII/Unicode U+0043
 'D': ASCII/Unicode U+0044
```

Strings and characters are very useful for representing pizza data. Let's a look at how you can bundle together information about each pizza.

4.9 *Storing pizza data in tuples*

To do this you will use a close sibling of arrays called tuples. To write them, replace the square brackets [] with parentheses (). Below is an example of a tuple describing sales info about pepperoni pizza. It says a small (S) Hawaiian pizza was sold for $10.50:

```
pizza_tuple = ("hawaiian", 'S', 10.5)
```

Since a number of popular languages, such as Python and JavaScript, use both single quotes and double quotes to denote strings, it is worth reminding the reader that in this example 'S' denotes a character and not a string. You cannot write strings in Julia using single quotes:

```
julia> 'hawaiian'
ERROR: syntax: character literal contains multiple characters
```

Thus there is an important distinction between 'S' and "S". The latter is a string, which you must think of as a collection of characters. The difference is similar to the difference between the number 42 and the array [42]. Instead of writing a tuple to contain pizza data you could use an array:

```
pizza_array = ["hawaiian", 'S', 10.5]
```

So what exactly is the difference? Arrays are meant for homogenous data. Every element has to be of the same type. But clearly, in this case they are *not* of the same type. The result is that the element type of the array becomes the Any type:

```
julia> pizza = ["hawaiian", 'S', 10.5]
3-element Vector{Any}:
   "hawaiian"
    'S': ASCII/Unicode U+0053
 10.5

julia> eltype(pizza)
Any
```

You will explore the Julia type system in greater detail later. For now you can think of Any as meaning that anything goes. You can put any kind of value into the array. This would not have worked if the element type was more specific, such as an Int64:

```
julia> xs = [4, 5, 3]
3-element Vector{Int64}:        Julia infers that
   4                            each element is
   5                            of type Int64.
   3
                                                Julia doesn't know
julia> xs[1] = "hi"                             how to turn a string
ERROR: MethodError: Cannot `convert` an object of type String to an object     into a number.
of type Int64
```

Pizza arrays, in contrast, are completely indiscriminate, meaning they don't care about the object type. You can assign anything to the individual elements because the element type of the pizza array is Any:

```
julia> pizza[3] = true
true

julia> pizza[1] = 42
42

julia> pizza
3-element Vector{Any}:
    42
       'S': ASCII/Unicode U+0053
  true
```

Tuples, on the other hand, are much stricter. A tuple keeps track of the type of every element; you can see this if you perform a typeof on a tuple:

```
julia> pza = ("hawaiian", 'S', 10.5)
("hawaiian", 'S', 10.5)

julia> typeof(pza)
Tuple{String, Char, Float64}
```

Secondly, tuples are *immutable*, meaning they cannot be changed. You can only read values from them; you cannot change the values.

```
julia> pza[1]
"hawaiian"

julia> pza[1] = "pepperoni"
ERROR: MethodError: no method matching
   setindex!(::Tuple{String, Char, Float64}, ::String, ::Int64)
```

In other aspects, tuples are very similar to arrays. You can loop over a tuple just like an array or range:

```
julia> for item in pza
            println(item)
        end
hawaiian
S
10.5
```

You can pass them to functions such as sum, median, and mean, given they actually contain numbers:

```
julia> nums = (3, 4, 1)
(3, 4, 1)
```

```
julia> sum(nums)
8

julia> median(nums)
3.0
```

You can look at how to create a list of pizza sales data (table 4.2) by combining tuples and arrays. This is the data you want to store in Julia.

Table 4.2 Pizza sales data, where each row is a sold pizza

Pizza	Size	Price
Hawaiian	S	10.5
Sicilian	S	12.25
Hawaiian	L	16.5
BBQ chicken	L	20.75
BBQ chicken	M	16.75

You want to be able to process this data and find out information such as how much you made in total or how many large pizzas you sold. You can represent this in Julia in the following manner:

```
julia> sales = [
          ("hawaiian", 'S', 10.5),
          ("sicilian", 'S', 12.25),
          ("hawaiian", 'L', 16.5),
          ("bbq chicken", 'L', 20.75),
          ("bbq chicken", 'M', 16.75)
      ]
```

You are using floating-point numbers to represent currency data, which is a bad choice. If you build software for customers handling currency data, you should always use fixed-point numbers,[2] but I am keeping things simple for educational purposes.

To make it easier to process pizza data, you will define *accessor* functions[3] for different properties. You will call the accessor for pizza size portion because Julia already has a function called size in the standard library:

```
name(pizza)    = pizza[1]
portion(pizza) = pizza[2]
price(pizza)   = pizza[3]
```

---

[2] Look up the FixedPointDecimals.jl or CurrenciesBase.jl to work with currency data.
[3] Functions used to set and get values within a more complex data structure are referred to as *accessor functions*, or simply *accessors*.

These are just regular functions. Here I use the Julia one-liner syntax for function definitions, but I could have used the multiline definition as well:

```
function price(pizza)
    pizza[3]
end
```

Remember that the last expression in a Julia function is the return value. You don't have to write return pizza[3].

What type are these pizza arguments? Are they tuples or arrays? Actually, it doesn't matter what they are because index access works on both in identical fashion. These accessor functions are useful with map because they allow you to do things like getting the names of all the pizzas:

```
julia> map(name, sales)
5-element Vector{String}:
 "hawaiian"
 "sicilian"
 "hawaiian"
 "bbq chicken"
 "bbq chicken"
```

The preceding code snippet simply applied the name function to every element in the sales array and collected all the result values into a new array.

4.10 *Filtering pizzas based on predicates*

With some useful data to work with, I can introduce you to the next higher-order function:

```
ys = filter(p, xs)
```

The filter function takes a collection of values, xs, and returns a subset, ys, of those values. The specific values from xs that are included in the resulting ys are determined by the predicate p. What is a predicate you ask?

> **DEFINITION**   A *predicate* is a function that takes some value and always returns a Boolean value, such as true or false.

Julia has a number of predicate functions bundled with its standard library. Here are some examples:

```
julia> iseven(3)          ⟵┐   Check if numbers
false                          are even (dividable
                               by two).
julia> iseven(2)          ⟵┘
true

julia> isodd(3)           ⟵┐   Check if numbers are
true                           odd (not dividable
                               by two).
julia> isodd(4)           ⟵┘
false
```

Predicates are not limited to numbers. There are also predicates for characters:

```
julia> isuppercase('A')
true
```

Is the provided character an uppercase letter?

```
julia> isuppercase('a')
false
```

```
julia> isspace(' ')
true
```

Is the character a space? For example, x is a letter, not a blank space.

```
julia> isspace('X')
false
```

Predicates are very useful with the `filter` function. The following is an example of getting even numbers from a range:

```
julia> filter(iseven, 1:10)
5-element Vector{Int64}:
  2
  4
  6
  8
 10
```

But to work with the pizza data you will need to define your own predicates, which allows us to retrieve sales of a particular pizza size or type:

```
issmall(pizza)  = portion(pizza) == 'S'
islarge(pizza)  = portion(pizza) == 'L'
isbbq(pizza)    = name(pizza) == "bbq chicken"
```

4.10.1 Combining higher-order functions

You can use the following approach to combine map, accessors, `filter`, and predicates to find out how much money you made selling large pizzas or BBQ chicken pizzas, for example. First, find the large pizzas:

```
julia> filter(islarge, sales)
2-element Vector{Tuple{String, Char, Float64}}:
 ("hawaiian", 'L', 16.5)
 ("bbq chicken", 'L', 20.75)
```

Next, you get the price of the large pizzas:

```
julia> map(price, filter(islarge, sales))
2-element Vector{Float64}:
 16.5
 20.75
```

Using sum, you can figure out how much money you made selling large pizzas:

```
julia> sum(map(price, filter(islarge, sales)))
37.25
```

In the final example, you determine how much money was made selling BBQ chicken pizzas:

```
julia> bbq_sales = filter(isbbq, sales)
2-element Vector{Tuple{String, Char, Float64}}:
 ("bbq chicken", 'L', 20.75)
 ("bbq chicken", 'M', 16.75)

julia> sum(map(price, bbq_sales))
37.5
```

It turns out that in programming, mapping many values to another set of values and then reducing all these values to 1 is such a common practice that it has its own name: mapreduce. In the last case, you were mapping BBQ chicken sales items to sales prices and then adding them up. Adding up all the numbers is, in functional programming speak, called a *reduction*.

4.11   *Mapping and reducing an array*

With the mapreduce function you could have written the last part as a single function call:

```
julia> mapreduce(price, +, bbq_sales)
37.5
```

mapreduce is composed of two higher-order functions: map and reduce. To demonstrate how this works, create your own variant of mapreduce, called mapcompress, to avoid a naming conflict:

```
mapcompress(f, g, xs) = reduce(g, map(f, xs))
```

Let me clarify how reduce works: it takes some binary function, g, as the first argument, and then uses this function to combine the elements in the collection, xs, provided as the second argument.

```
g(x, y) = ...
y = reduce(g, xs)
```

Unlike map, reduce requires an input function taking *two* arguments. That is why it is called a *binary* function. Regular mathematical operators, such as +, - and *, are binary functions in Julia. Thus you can use them with reduce to perform the equivalent of sum and factorial:

```
julia> sum(2:4)
9

julia> reduce(+, 2:4)
9
```

```
julia> factorial(4)
24

julia> reduce(*, 1:4)
24
```

NOTE Many developers find the naming of the function `reduce` unintuitive. Potentially better names would have been *accumulate, aggregate,* or *compress.* In some languages it is called `inject`.

4.11.1 Sine table with map and reduce

The sine function itself is, in fact, a classic case of mapping and reducing. For each argument to `sin(x)` you get an infinite sequence of numbers, which you reduce to one value by adding. This is how you implemented your own sine function, called sine, without conflicting with the built-in sin function.

Listing 4.4 Sine function implemented using the Taylor series

```
function sine(x)
    n = 5
    total = 0
    for i in 0:n
        total += (-1)^i*x^(2i+1)/factorial(2i + 1)
    end
    total
end
```

You can express this calculation more elegantly using the `mapreduce` higher-order function.

Listing 4.5 Sine function through `mapreduce` on a Taylor's series

```
function sinus(x)
    n = 5
    taylor(i) = (-1)^i*x^(2i+1)/factorial(2i + 1)
    mapreduce(taylor, +, 0:n)
end
```

Here you are doing something new: inside the `sinus` function you are defining a new function called `taylor`, which takes a single argument `i`. The function is used to calculate a term in the Taylor series, meaning one of the numbers in the Taylor series that gets added up. It is perfectly possible to define a function inside other functions.

But why not define this function outside? This is because it uses the x variable, and the value of x would not be known outside of the `sinus` function definition. If this makes your head spin, don't worry. These concepts will be revisited many times later in the book and will likely make more sense at that point.

mapreduce(taylor, +, 0:n) will first apply the taylor function to every value in the range 0:n. This will produce an array of values, which will then be combined with the + operator, which is the second argument to the mapreduce function.

4.12 Counting matches with Boolean arrays

In chapter 3, I mentioned it can be useful to treat Boolean values as integers 0 or 1. Now that you have been exposed to array we will explore a concrete example.

> **Listing 4.6 Counting pizzas matching predicates**

```
julia> matches = map(islarge, sales)
5-element Vector{Bool}:
 0
 0
 1
 1
 0

julia> sum(matches)
2
```

Since you are combining a map and sum higher-order function you could replace this with a single call to mapreduce. However, adding elements after mapping is so common that Julia's sum function allows mapping and adding. This gives you an elegant way to calculate the number of large pizzas, how many are BBQ chicken, and so on:

```
julia> sum(islarge, sales)
2

julia> sum(isbbq, sales)
2
```

sum will transform all the pizza sales into Boolean values by applying the first argument as a predicate. That will produce an array of zeros and ones, which are added up by sum.

After reading this chapter you have managed to learn about the most fundamental concepts in programming. Without control flow and collections of data, programming wouldn't be very useful. The ability to easily work with multiple elements of data is what makes computers so versatile and powerful.

Summary

- Julia supports many different kinds of arrays. A *vector* is a one-dimensional array, while a *matrix* is a two-dimensional array.
- Both in mathematics and in Julia, one distinguishes between *column vectors* and *row vectors*. Column vectors most closely resemble what are called arrays in other programming languages.

- Julia represents row vectors as matrices with only one row, which is why row vectors are very different from one-dimensional arrays in other languages.
- Arrays in Julia default to 1-based indexing. That means the first element starts at index 1.
- Mathematical operation can be performed on whole arrays on every element. To do this, prefix the normal math operators with a dot: `.+`, `.-`, `.*`, and `./`.
- Operations on arrays can be described as either a mapping, filtering, or reduction (e.g., `sum` and `mean` perform a reduction, since multiple values are reduced to one).
- The functions `zeros`, `ones`, `fill`, and `rand` make it easy to create arrays with a large number of elements.
- An array of `Char` objects is not quite the same as a `String`. Characters must be joined together to form a string. However, strings behave similarly to arrays.
- Tuples have similar behavior to arrays but are immutable, meaning you cannot change them.

Working with text

This chapter covers

- Representing text with the `String` type
- Formatting text with `lpad` and `rpad`
- Reading text from a keyboard or file
- Writing text to the screen or a file
- Creating a simple interactive program

This chapter will focus on practical aspects of working with text in Julia, such as how to show text on the screen and read or write it to a file. You will also look at a simple interactive application where the user writes responses to questions.

However, first I will focus on different ways of displaying text on the screen, revisiting your pizza sales and sine table examples. The tables you created before were not very readable. How about creating a neat display like the one in figure 5.1?

Here sine and cosine values are neatly arranged in separate columns. Likewise, would it not be better to neatly organize information about pizza sales into clearly separated columns, as seen in figure 5.2?

You will use the `printstyled` function for coloring your text and the `rpad` and `lpad` functions for formatting the output. You will use the `^` operator to repeat characters. Next you will use the `open` function to allow you to use `print` and

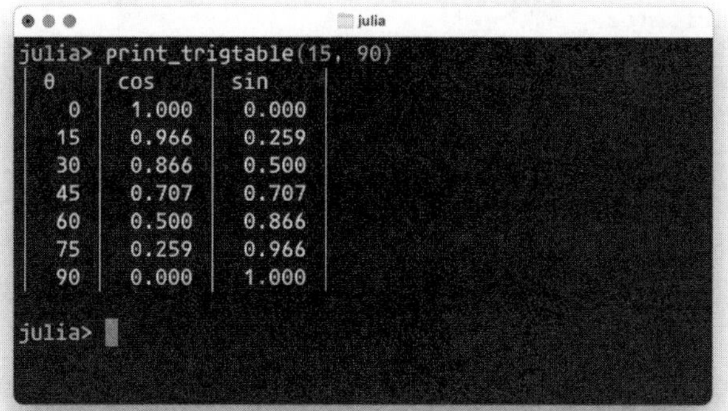

Figure 5.1 Neatly formatted display of a cosine and sine table

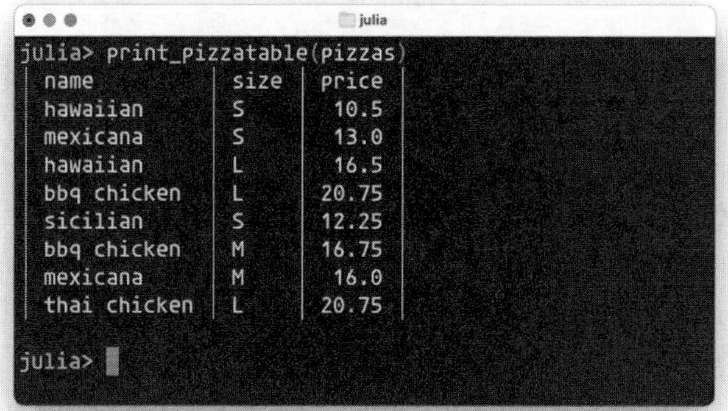

Figure 5.2 Formatted display of pizza sales using alignment and colors in a Unix terminal window

println for writing text output to files. To read and process input you will use the readline, split, and parse functions.

5.1 Making a pretty pizza sales table

You will start by looking at the final result, the code you want to write, and then working your way backward to explain how you got there. The code should not be entirely alien, but there are some new concepts I will explain.

Listing 5.1 Creating a pretty table of pizza sales

```
function print_pizzatable(pizzas)
    print("| ")
    printstyled(rpad("name", 12), color=:cyan)
    print(" | ")
    printstyled("size", color=:cyan)
    print(" | ")
    printstyled(rpad("price", 5), color=:cyan)
    println(" |")

    for pz in pizzas
        print("| ",  rpad(name(pz), 12))
```

```
        print(" | ", rpad(portion(pz), 4), " | ")
        println(lpad(price(pz), 5), " |")
    end
end
```

You have new functions—printstyled, rpad, and lpad—which need further explora-
tion and explanation. To get the print_pizzatable function to work, you also need
the *accessor* functions you defined in chapter 4. All of these functions take a pizza
tuple, such as ("bbq chicken", 'L', 20.75), as an argument and return one of the
elements in the tuple.

Listing 5.2   Pizza tuple accessor functions

```
name(pizza)    = pizza[1]
portion(pizza) = pizza[2]
price(pizza)   = pizza[3]
```

I will cover each function used inside print_pizzatable in more detail with some
simple examples. I only briefly covered print and println in past chapters, so let's
cover the details.

5.1.1   *Print, println, and printstyled*

These are versatile functions that can be used to write text to your screen or even files
or a network connection (see chapter 18 for greater detail). Let's look at some simple
examples to demonstrate how these functions work:

```
julia> println("hello world")
hello world
julia> print("hello world")
hello world
```

Huh? Are they not doing the exact same thing? No, but it isn't easy to tell with this
example. Instead you will use a semicolon ; to separate statements on a single line.
That will help make the difference clearer:

```
julia> println("hello"); println("world")
hello
world

julia> print("hello"); print("world")
helloworld
julia> print("hello\n"); print("world\n")
hello
world
```

This code shows you that println is just short for print, with a newline character \n
added to the end. Julia, like many other languages, allows you to express nonvisible
control characters, like a newline, by using a backslash with different letter combinations. Table 5.1 shows some of the more common control characters you can use in
Julia to influence how text is written to a Unix terminal window.

Table 5.1   Escape sequences to write common control characters used in Unix terminals

Escape sequence	Hex value	Effect
\n	0x0A	Newline
\t	0x09	Horizontal tab
\v	0x0B	Vertical tab
\r	0x0D	Carriage return
\b	0x08	Backspace
\\	0x5C	Backslash
\"	0x22	Double quotation marks

The double quotation mark is not a control character, but since you use it to mark the start and end a string, you need to use an escape sequence to represent it. But what is the utility of knowing the hex value? You can use this directly to create characters. Here, a new line is created with the 0x0a hex value:

```
julia> newln = Char(0x0a)
'\n': ASCII/Unicode U+000A

julia> print("hi"); print(newln); print("world")
hi
world
```

Let's look at more examples of the effect of using these different escape sequences combined with regular text:

```
julia> println("hello \v world")
hello
        world
```
This uses a vertical tab \v as opposed to the more widely known horizontal tab \t.

```
julia> println("hello \n world")
hello
 world
```

```
julia> println("hello \r world")
 world
```
The carriage return moves the cursor to the start of the line. Hence the word, world, overwrites hello, written initially.

```
julia> println("ABC\n\tABC\n\tABC")
ABC
    ABC
    ABC
```

This requires some context. Why do characters in your text strings cause the cursor to move around? It has to do with the history of the text printing system you have today. When the Unix operating system was first developed, there were no electronic displays, like the ones you use today. Instead, computer users used electro-mechanical devices called *teletypes* (figure 5.3). A teletype is very similar to an old-fashioned typewriter in operation.

Figure 5.3   Teletype Type 68D from Siemens (Norsk Teknisk Museum)

These also served as your screen. If the computer wanted to give you some information, it had to send characters to your typewriter, which would cause it to print the characters sent onto paper. This created a need for control characters, meaning characters that bossed around your teletype, telling it to create a new line and move the caret down or back.

The terminal applications you use today are simulators of these old teletypes. This was so programs written to work with teletypes could still work. Unix commands such as ls, cp, cat, and echo have no idea they are running on modern computers with electronic displays. As far as they are concerned, they are interacting with a good old teletype.

Eventually, these paper-based terminals were replaced by electronic terminals. At this point one expanded the control characters with new ones to represent colors. For instance, when an electronic terminal would receive the escape sequence \u001b[33m it would switch to writing yellow letters. If it got \u001b[31m, it would write red letters. So to write hello world in yellow letters, you can write the following:

```
julia> print("\u001b[33m hello world")
hello world
```

However, remembering these escape sequences for different colors is cumbersome. Thus, Julia provides the printstyled function, which lets you specify a color to use by name. The color is specified using the *keyword argument* color:

```
julia> printstyled("hello world", color = :cyan)
hello world
```

This statement produces hello world in cyan color. You can look up the help for printstyled to get overview of what colors you can use. Just move the text cursor to the beginning of the line (Ctrl-A) and press ? to go into help mode:

```
help?> printstyled("hello world", color = :cyan)
  printstyled([io], xs...; bold=false, color=:normal)

  Print xs in a color specified as a symbol or integer,
  optionally in bold.

  color may take any of the values :normal, :default,
  :bold, :black, :blink, :blue, :cyan, :green, :hidden,
  :light_black, :light_blue, :light_cyan, :light_green,
  :light_magenta, :light_red, :light_yellow, :magenta,
  :nothing, :red, :reverse, :underline, :white, or :yellow
  or an integer between 0 and 255 inclusive. Note that not
  all terminals support 256 colors. If the keyword bold is
  given as true, the result will be printed in bold
```

All the colors are given as *symbols*. A symbol is very similar to a text string. It is often used for text strings, which only matter to programmers and not users of your program. You can programmatically create symbol objects:

```
julia> sym = Symbol("hello")
:hello
```

```
julia> sym == :hello
true
```

5.1.2 Printing multiple elements

All the print functions are quite versatile in what they allow you to print and how many elements you can print:

```
julia> print("abc", 42, true, "xyz")
abc42truexyz
```

Numbers and Boolean values get converted to text strings when passed as arguments to the various print functions. It is worth knowing that the string function works exactly the same way, except it returns a String instead of printing to the screen:

```
julia> string("abc", 42, true, "xyz")
"abc42truexyz"
```

This allows you to use a single `println` statement to display information about one pizza. Notice the use of accessor functions defined earlier:

```
julia> pizza = ("hawaiian", 'S', 10.5)
("hawaiian", 'S', 10.5)

julia> println(name(pizza), " ", portion(pizza), " ", price(pizza))
hawaiian S 10.5
```

5.1.3   *Printing multiple pizzas*

You can use this functionality to write out a simple table regarding pizza sales.

Listing 5.3   Primitive pizza table printing

```
pizzas = [
    ("hawaiian", 'S', 10.5),
    ("mexicana", 'S', 13.0),
    ("hawaiian", 'L', 16.5),
    ("bbq chicken", 'L', 20.75),
    ("sicilian", 'S', 12.25),
    ("bbq chicken", 'M', 16.75),
    ("mexicana", 'M', 16.0),
    ("thai chicken", 'L', 20.75),
]

for pz in pizzas
    println(name(pz), " ", portion(pz), " ", price(pz))
end
```

The problem with this code is that the name, size, and price columns don't get aligned, but end up like this:

```
hawaiian S 10.5
mexicana S 13.0
hawaiian L 16.5
bbq chicken L 20.75
sicilian S 12.25
bbq chicken M 16.75
mexicana M 16.0
thai chicken L 20.75
```

To perform alignment you need to add left padding and right padding using the `lpad` and `rpad` functions.

5.1.4   *Align with lpad and rpad*

With the Julia padding functions you can specify that a text string should always be of a given length. If the text you supply is smaller, it will get padded with a chosen character. If no character is specified, the padding character defaults to space.

```
julia> lpad("ABC", 6, '-')          ◁──┐  Padding on the left
"---ABC"
```

```
julia> rpad("ABC", 6, '-')        ◁——┐ Right-side padding
"ABC---"
```

First, you pad with the - character on the left side, until the whole string is 6 characters long. The second example is identical, except you pad on the right side with the - character.

With lpad and rpad you can define how wide each column in your table should be and add padding, such as spaces, wherever the supplied text string is shorter. In this example, you'll keep it simple and check what width the widest strings in each column would be:

```
julia> length("thai chicken")    ◁——┐ Width for pizza
12                                    name column

julia> length("size")      ◁——┐ Width for
4                              size column        ┌ Width for
                                                  │ price column
julia> max(length("16.75"), length("price"))  ◁——┘
5
```

Let's modify the initial code to use padding. You could just paste this code into your terminal or store it in a file you load into the terminal with, for example, include. Notice in the code that you don't specify the padding character. If you don't specify, it will default to a space.

Listing 5.4 Simple aligned pizza table

```
function simple_pizzatable(pizzas)
    pname  = rpad("name", 12)
    psize  = rpad("size", 4)
    pprice = rpad("price", 5)

    printstyled(pname, " ",
                psize, " ",          You use cyan color for
                pprice,              the header describing
                color=:cyan)    ◁——┘ each column.
    println()

    for pz in pizzas
        pname  = rpad(name(pz), 12)      Numbers are padded
        psize  = rpad(portion(pz), 4)    on the left, so the
        pprice = lpad(price(pz), 5)  ◁——┘ decimals align.
        println(pname, " ", psize, " ", pprice)
    end
end
```

You can test this in the terminal:

```
julia> simple_pizzatable(pizzas)
name         size price
hawaiian      S    10.5
```

```
mexicana       S      13.0
hawaiian       L      16.5
bbq chicken  L      20.75
sicilian       S      12.25
bbq chicken  M      16.75
mexicana       M      16.0
thai chicken L      20.75
```

Notice how the points are not aligned. There are many ways to solve that, but in the next example with trigonometric tables, you will make sure each number has the same number of decimals after the point.

5.1.5   *Adding lines*

Adding separating lines is actually quite simple. You simply use the symbol for a long vertical line: '│':

```
julia> '│'
'│': Unicode U+2502 (category So: Symbol, other)
```

This is Julia's way of telling you that this character is represented by the hexadecimal value 0x2502. Thus, you could get this character in two different ways:

```
julia> Char(0x2502)
'│': Unicode U+2502
```

```
julia> '\U2502'
'│': Unicode U+2502
```

In fact, there are many useful characters for making tables:

```
julia> collect("─├┼┤")
3-element Vector{Char}:
 '├': Unicode U+251C
 '─': Unicode U+2500
 '┼': Unicode U+253C
 '┤': Unicode U+2524
```

To draw lines, it is useful to know how to easily repeat characters. In Julia, the exponent ^ operator is used to repeat characters:

```
julia> "A2"^3
"A2A2A2"
```

```
julia> "-"^4
"----"
```

```
julia> "─"^2
"──"
```

5.2 Printing a trigonometric table

You can reuse what you've learned to create a trigonometry table. This code uses many of the same functions as you have seen already: `print`, `printstyled`, `lpad`, and `rpad`. Don't try to run this function yet; I am just giving you an overview.

Listing 5.5 Creating a trigometric table

```
function print_trigtable(inc, maxangle)
    print("| ")
    printstyled("θ  ", color=:cyan)
    print(" | ")
    printstyled(rpad("cos", n),           Write out the header
            color=:cyan)                  for each column of
    print(" | ")                          numbers.
    printstyled(rpad("sin", n),
            color=:cyan)
    println(" |")
    angle = 0
    while angle <= maxangle
        rad  = deg2rad(angle)
        cosx = format(cos(rad))
        sinx = format(sin(rad))
        print("| ")                       Write out row
        print(lpad(angle, 3), " | ",      of trig values for
            lpad(cosx, 6),   " | ",       each angle.
            lpad(sinx, 6))
        println(" |")
        angle += inc
    end
end
```

There are not a lot of new ideas in this code; I covered the core logic in chapter 3. However, numbers need special handling to align the decimal point. You need an equal number of digits after the point on every number, and you don't want numbers that are too long. If you use the results as they are, you get way too many digits:

```
julia> rads = map(deg2rad, 0:15:90);

julia> map(sin, rads)
7-element Vector{Float64}:
 0.0
 0.25881904510252074
 0.49999999999999994
 0.7071067811865475
 0.8660254037844386
 0.9659258262890683
 1.0
```

Instead you want something like this:

```
julia> print_trigtable(15, 180)
| θ   | cos    | sin   |
|   0 | 1.000  | 0.000 |
|  15 | 0.966  | 0.259 |
|  30 | 0.866  | 0.500 |
|  45 | 0.707  | 0.707 |
|  60 | 0.500  | 0.866 |
|  75 | 0.259  | 0.966 |
|  90 | 0.000  | 1.000 |
| 105 | -0.259 | 0.966 |
| 120 | -0.500 | 0.866 |
| 135 | -0.707 | 0.707 |
| 150 | -0.866 | 0.500 |
| 165 | -0.966 | 0.259 |
| 180 | -1.000 | 0.000 |
```

To achieve this, you have a helper function you can see in the main code listing: `format`.

Listing 5.6   Helper function for formating numbers

```
n = length("-0.966")

function format(x)                        Round down to
    x = round(x, digits=3)    ◁────────   three decimals.
    if x < 0
        rpad(x, n, '0')       ◁────────   If you have a negative number
    else                                  you must allow for an extra
        rpad(x, n-1, '0')                 character for the - sign.
    end
end
```

n stores the maximum character width of a number. I am basically using a worst-case scenario, such as a negative number to get the maximum characters needed for the number string:

```
julia> format(3.1)
"3.100"

julia> format(-3.1)
"-3.100"
```

You can see in the preceding example that when you use negative numbers you must allow more characters. Later you will print with `lpad` using spaces, which means the total width doesn't change, whether the number is negative or not:

```
julia> lpad(format(4.2), 6)
" 4.200"

julia> lpad(format(-4.2), 6)
"-4.200"
```

5.3 Reading and writing pizza sales to CSV files

The data you have been dealing with thus far is in table format, which is exactly what a spreadsheet application has been designed to deal with. A very common file format for exchanging data between various types of spreadsheet applications and scientific applications is called CSV, which is short for *comma separated values*. You will implement a `store_pizzatable` function to write pizza data in CSV format to a file and a `load_pizzatable` function to read the same CSV file. The following is an example of the pizza data CSV file format both functions will work with:

```
name,size,price
hawaiian,S,10.5
mexicana,S,13.0
hawaiian,L,16.5
bbq chicken,L,20.75
sicilian,S,12.25
bbq chicken,M,16.75
mexicana,M,16.0
thai chicken,L,20.75
```

The first line is referred to as the *header*. It gives a name to each column in the file. For each row you separate each value with a comma. Figure 5.4 is an example of loading such a CSV file into Apple Numbers.

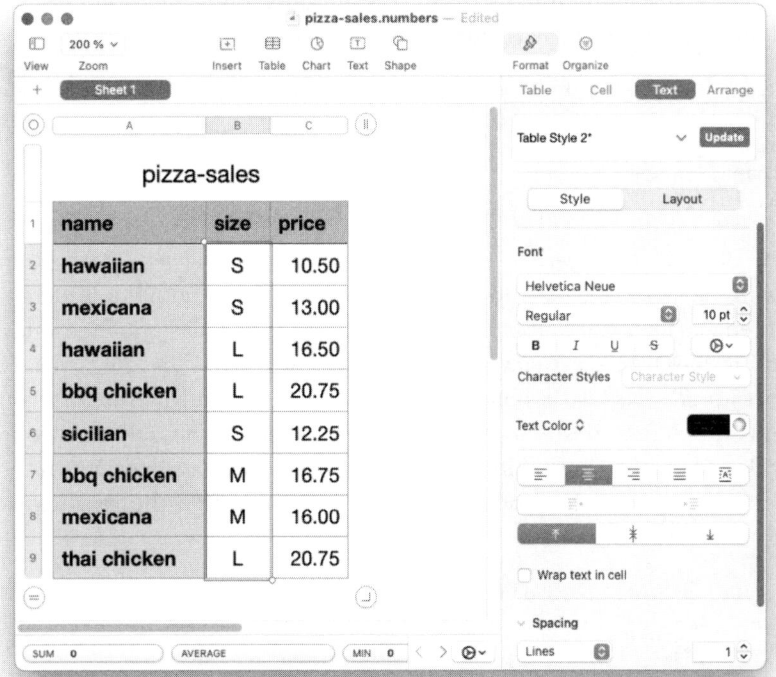

Figure 5.4 Pizza sales data loaded into the Apple Numbers spreadsheet application

Say you produce lots of useful calculations you want to share, examine in a table, or plot graphically; exporting to CSV format helps. Julia already has built-in functions for this and very good external libraries, such as CSV.jl at csv.juliadata.org. However, your focus will be on learning the basics of reading and writing to files; thus you will not be using external packages or functions.

5.3.1   *Writing pizza sales to a file*

You will define a simple function, `store_pizzatable`, which outputs pizza sales data as comma separated values.

Listing 5.7   Function for exporting pizza sales data as comma separated values

```
function store_pizzatable(io, pizzas)
    println(io, "name,size,price")          ◁──┐   Write out the
                                                │   CSV header.
    for pz in pizzas                    ◁───────
        println(io, name(pz), ",",
                    portion(pz), ",",       A line for each
                    price(pz))              pizza sold
    end
end
```

This function should look familiar to you. What is new is that the `println` function is taking a new first argument named `io`. This presents some common pitfalls, so let me use this function incorrectly at first:

```
julia> store_pizzatable("-->", pizzas[1:3])
-->name,size,price
-->hawaiian,S,10.5
-->mexicana,S,13.0
-->hawaiian,L,16.5
```

This is predictable. It just writes out the `io` object as a regular text string. But if the first argument is of a special type—not a string, not a number, and not a Boolean but an `IO` object, then you alter where the `print` and `println` functions write their output.

`println("hello")` is actually short for `println(stdout, "hello")`. What is `stdout`? It is short for *standard out*, which represents a destination for your printing. `stdout` represents the default destination for anything printed. The default is your terminal window; however, the destination could be a file or even a network connection. You can try using `stdout` instead of the string `"--->"`, although the result will be rather boring:

```
julia> store_pizzatable(stdout, pizzas[1:3])
name,size,price
hawaiian,S,10.5
mexicana,S,13.0
hawaiian,L,16.5
```

It gets more interesting when you provide a file as a destination. To do that you need to create an IO object representing a file.

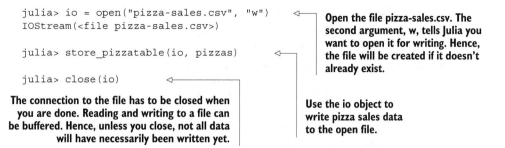

```
julia> io = open("pizza-sales.csv", "w")
IOStream(<file pizza-sales.csv>)

julia> store_pizzatable(io, pizzas)

julia> close(io)
```

Open the file pizza-sales.csv. The second argument, w, tells Julia you want to open it for writing. Hence, the file will be created if it doesn't already exist.

The connection to the file has to be closed when you are done. Reading and writing to a file can be buffered. Hence, unless you close, not all data will have necessarily been written yet.

Use the io object to write pizza sales data to the open file.

You can go into shell mode by writing a semicolon ; at the beginning of the line. Whenever you want to go back to the Julia mode, you can press Backspace at the start of the line. Go into shell mode, and look at the file you created by using the Unix cat command:

```
shell> cat pizza-sales.csv
name,size,price
hawaiian,S,10.5
mexicana,S,13.0
hawaiian,L,16.5
bbq chicken,L,20.75
sicilian,S,12.25
bbq chicken,M,16.75
mexicana,M,16.0
thai chicken,L,20.75
```

5.3.2   Reading pizza sales from a file

You may commonly download a CSV file from the internet that you want to read from. Statistical data for anything from school results to unemployment numbers to GDP per capita can be downloaded as a CSV file.

You can open the pizza-sales.csv file and try to read from it. There are lots of clever ways of doing this, which I will cover in greater detail in chapter 17. This example keeps it simple using the readline function; it reads one line at a time:

```
julia> io = open("pizza-sales.csv")
IOStream(<file pizza-sales.csv>)

julia> line = readline(io)
"name,size,price"

julia> line = readline(io)
"hawaiian,S,10.5"
```

The source it reads from doesn't need to be a file. As we discussed earlier, your terminal window is treated as an IO object called stdout. There is a corresponding IO object representing your keyboard called stdin. This gives you a way of reading keyboard inputs:

```
julia> s = readline(stdin)
hello                                    The text you wrote, which
"hello"                                  got captured by readline

julia> print(s)        The value stored in s. Notice the
hello                  use of quotation marks to
                       indicate this value is a string.
```

To get a feel for how it works, it is best to try another example. You will make a simple application that utilizes this shortly.

Anyway, let's get back to the pizzas. How do you turn a comma-separated string into a pizza tuple or array? For this you can use the split function. It allows you to split a string into multiple parts and collect the parts into an array:

```
julia> pizza = split(line, ',')
3-element Vector{SubString{String}}:
 "hawaiian"
 "S"
 "10.5"
```

There are, however, a number of problems with treating this as a pizza. Say you want to add a value-added tax of 25%. That will not work:

```
julia> p = price(pizza)
"10.5"

julia> p*1.25
ERROR: MethodError: no method matching *(::SubString{String}, ::Float64)
```

This problem exists because the price, p, isn't actually a number but a string (or, more specifically, a substring, but let's not get bogged down in details):

```
julia> typeof(p)
SubString{String}
```

This applies to anything you read from a file; Julia will treat it as text. It cannot know that you might want part of the file to be represented as numbers, Boolean values, or something else. However Julia has a function called parse, which allows you to convert a text string to anything else. In the following snippet you can see the conversion to a number:

```
julia> parse(Int, "42")
42

julia> parse(Float64, "42")
42.0
```

```
julia> parse(Bool, "true")
true

julia> parse(Bool, "1")
true
```

Here the number 42 is parsed twice. In the first case it is turned into a integer, while in the second case it is turned into a floating-point number. Thus the same text can be interpreted in many different ways. It is your choice how to interpret it.

There are also entirely different text strings that can be interpreted as the same object. For example, both "true" and "1" can be parsed as the Boolean value true. With these building blocks you can put together a pizza loading function.

> **Listing 5.8   Loading pizza sales data**

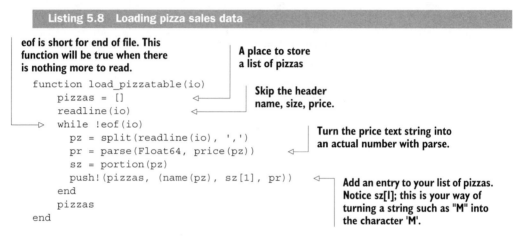

eof is short for end of file. This function will be true when there is nothing more to read.

A place to store a list of pizzas

```
function load_pizzatable(io)
    pizzas = []
    readline(io)
    while !eof(io)
        pz = split(readline(io), ',')
        pr = parse(Float64, price(pz))
        sz = portion(pz)
        push!(pizzas, (name(pz), sz[1], pr))
    end
    pizzas
end
```

Skip the header name, size, price.

Turn the price text string into an actual number with parse.

Add an entry to your list of pizzas. Notice sz[I]; this is your way of turning a string such as "M" into the character 'M'.

If you try this function in the REPL you should get a result similar to this:

```
julia> io = open("pizza-sales.csv");

julia> pizzas = load_pizzatable(io)
8-element Vector{Any}:
 ("hawaiian", 'S', 10.5)
 ("mexicana", 'S', 13.0)
 ("hawaiian", 'L', 16.5)
 ("bbq chicken", 'L', 20.75)
 ("sicilian", 'S', 12.25)
 ("bbq chicken", 'M', 16.75)
 ("mexicana", 'M', 16.0)
 ("thai chicken", 'L', 20.75)

julia> close(io)
```

5.4   *Interacting with the user*

Let's make an interactive application demonstrating the utility of being able to read user input through stdin. This one was inspired by a simple application I made to help my children practice their multiplication tables (figure 5.5).

Figure 5.5   Running the multiplication testing application

The app repeatedly asks the user to multiply two numbers and checks the answer. At the end you get a summary of how many correct answers you got. Let's look at the implementation of the practice function.

Listing 5.9   Practice multiplication: Asks user to write n answers

```
function practice(n)
    correct = 0                    ◁─── Keep track of how many
    for i in 1:n                        answers the user got right.
        x = rand(2:9)              ◁─┐ Random numbers
        y = rand(2:9)                │ in the range 2 to 9
        print(x, " * ", y, " = ")
        answer = readline(stdin)        Convert the number the
        z = parse(Int, answer)     ◁─── user wrote to an integer.
        if z == x*y                ◁─┐ Check if the user got
            correct += 1              │ the answer right.
        else
            printstyled("Wrong, it is ", x*y, color = :red)
            println()
        end
    end
    println("Correct: ", correct, " of ", n)
end
```

You can start this program by invoking the practice function from the REPL. Say you want to practice on eight different multiplications. You would write the following:

```
julia> practice(8)
```

Whenever you deal with more complex functions you are trying to understand, you can explore how they work by simply copying and pasting lines of code like this:

```
julia> x = rand(2:9)
3

julia> y = rand(2:9)
6
```

```
julia> print(x, " * ", y, " = ")
3 * 6 =
julia> answer = readline(stdin)
18
"18"
```

The benefit is that you can see the value of every expression. This allows you to see how a value gets transformed in multiple steps. For example, you can explore why comparing the answer directly doesn't work:

```
julia> z = parse(Int, answer)
18

julia> answer == x*y
false

julia> z == x*y
true
```

To cement your understanding you can experiment with improving this program. Here are some ideas: Time yourself. Record how long you spend answering the questions. You can use the `time()` function for this purpose. Record the time before asking questions and after you are done. Look at the difference. You might want to round to nearest second with the `round()` function. Use the Julia help system to see how to best use these functions.

You might also want to provide the range used with `rand` as an argument to the `practice` function. There might be a particular range of numbers you want to practice more on. It could also be fun experimenting with creating nice tables using the ─, ├, ┤, and ┼ symbols.

Summary

- `print`, `println`, and `printstyled` can all be used to send text to a destination such as a terminal window or a file.
- In a terminal, one can use special control character sequences to write colored text. `printstyled` simplifies this task, so you only have to remember the names of different colors.
- To write to files or read from them, you need to `open` them. When you are done, you need to `close` them.
- While reading a file, you can check if you are done with `eof`.
- The `lpad` and `rpad` functions help you align text in columns. This is done by padding with a chosen character either on the left or right side until the desired string width is achieved.
- Text can be written or read from `IO` objects. `IO` objects are placeholders for real physical things, such as files on a hard drive, a keyboard, a network connection, or a terminal window—or even a teletype.
- Text strings can be converted to a variety of objects using the `parse` function.

Storing data
in dictionaries

This chapter covers

- Storing values on keys in dictionaries
- Working with pair objects
- Using tuples to create dictionaries
- Comparing dictionaries and arrays
- Comparing named tuples and dictionaries

This chapter introduces a new data type called a *dictionary*. In some other languages this datatype is also referred to as a *map*. In dictionaries, values are looked up by keys, as opposed to being looked up exclusively using integer indices, like in an array. The code example illustrates the difference. Each line performs the following operations:

1. Looking up the 42nd value x in array xs. Values in arrays are ordered. However, xs could have been a dictionary as well, since dictionary keys can be anything, including integers.
2. Looking up a value y in dictionary ys with the key "foo".
3. Using a character 'D' rather than a string as the key in the dictionary zs to lookup value z.

```
x = xs[42]
y = ys["foo"]
z = zs['D']
```

You will discover the utility of dictionaries by working through a code example involving the conversion of Roman numerals to decimal values and back. A dictionary will be used to keep track of what value a letter such as I, V, or X corresponds to in the decimal system.

6.1 *Parsing Roman numerals*

While Roman numerals are not very practical to use today, they are useful to learn about for understanding number systems. In particular, when programming, you will encounter various number systems.

Both Roman numerals and binary—the system used by computers—may seem very cumbersome to use. However it often appears that way because you don't use the numbers as they were intended.

It is hard to make calculations using Roman numerals with pen and paper compared to Arabic numerals (which is what you typically use for numerals). However, the Romans did not use pen and paper to perform calculations. Rather they performed their calculations using a Roman abacus (figure 6.1).

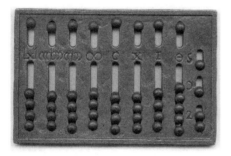

Figure 6.1   A Roman abacus with pebbles representing different values. The column decides how much value each pebble is given.

It is divided into multiple columns. Going from right to left, you can see columns of pebbles marked as I, X, and C; they each contain four pebbles. Each of these pebbles represents a different value, depending on what column they are in:

- In the I column every pebble represents 1.
- In the X column, every pebble represents 10.
- In the C column, every pebble represents 100.

These columns contain a single pebble each. They are called V, L, and D and represent the values 5, 50, and 500. (On a Roman abacus you cannot actually see the VLD letters.)

NOTE The beauty of the Roman system is that you can quickly write down exactly what the pebbles on the abacus say. Likewise, it is quick to arrange pebbles on a Roman abacus to match a Roman numeral you have read. For this reason Roman numerals were used all the way into the 1500s in Europe, long after Arabic numerals had been introduced.

Let's look at how you can use this knowledge to parse Roman numerals and turn them into Arabic numerals. Put the following code into a text file, and save it. Don't worry about the new syntax; we will cover that.

Listing 6.1   Parsing and converting Roman numerals to decimal numbers

```
roman_numerals =
    Dict('I' => 1, 'X' => 10, 'C' => 100,
         'V' => 5, 'L' => 50, 'D' => 500,
         'M' => 1000)

function parse_roman(s)
    s = reverse(uppercase(s))
    vals = [roman_numerals[ch] for ch in s]
    result = 0
    for (i, val) in enumerate(vals)
        if i > 1 && val < vals[i - 1]
            result -= val
        else
            result += val
        end
    end
    result
end
```

Load this file into the Julia REPL environment to test it out. This is an example of using parse_roman with different Roman numerals as input:

```
julia> parse_roman("II")
2

julia> parse_roman("IV")
4

julia> parse_roman("VI")
6

julia> parse_roman("IX")
9

julia> parse_roman("XI")
11
```

Let's go through how the code works.

6.2   *Using the Dict type*

You map or translate the Roman letters I, V, X, and so on to numbers using what is called a *dictionary*. A dictionary is made up of multiple pairs; pairs are constructed using the arrow operator, =>. You cannot use the equals operator, =, because it is used for assignment. x = y assigns the value of y to variable x, while x => y creates a pair of the values in x and y:

```
julia> 'X' => 10                    ⟵        A pair of the letter X
'X' => 10                                    and the number 10

julia> pair = 'X' => 10             ⟵
'X' => 10                                    Pairs can be stored in a
                                             variable and examined later.

julia> dump(pair)                   ⟵
Pair{Char,Int64}                             dump allows you to look at
   first: Char 'X'                           the fields of any value.
   second: Int64 10
                                             Extracting the first
                                             value in the pair
julia> pair.first                   ⟵
'X': ASCII/Unicode U+0058 (category Lu: Letter, uppercase)

julia> pair.second
10
```

Pairs are composite objects with the fields `first` and `second`. These fields allow you to access both values given when the pair was constructed. However, you should consider that an implementation detail and access the fields of pairs with `first` and `last` accessor functions. This behavior makes pairs very similar to range objects covered in chapter 3 and tuples covered in chapter 4:

```
julia> range = 2:4
2:4

julia> pair = 8=>9
8 => 9

julia> tuple = (3, 'B')
(3, 'B')

julia> first(range), first(pair), first(tuple)
(2, 8, 3)

julia> last(range), last(pair), last(tuple)
(4, 9, 'B')
```

In this code example I accessed several values in one line by separating them with a comma. That produced a tuple with three values.

It may seem confusing that the `second` field of a pair is accessed with the function `last`. The reason is that last element also exists for arrays and tuples. Hence `last` generalizes better across multiple collection types.

> **NOTE**   Out of curiosity you may try to use the `dump` function on a dictionary object. It has fields such as `slots`, `idxfloor`, `maxprobe`, and so on, which likely won't make much sense. That is because `dump` exposes implementation details. As a user of a datatype, you should not need to know what fields it has, only which function you can use to operate on it.

You provide a list of these pairs to create a dictionary. The following code shows how to create a dictionary to map letters used by Roman numerals to their corresponding decimal value.

```
julia> roman_numerals =
          Dict('I' => 1, 'X' => 10, 'C' => 100,
                'V' => 5, 'L' => 50, 'D' => 500,
                'M' => 1000)
Dict{Char,Int64} with 7 entries:
  'M' => 1000
  'D' => 500
  'I' => 1
  'L' => 50
  'V' => 5
  'X' => 10
  'C' => 100
```

When used in a dictionary, you refer to the first values in each pair as the *keys* in the dictionary. The second values in each pair form the *values* of the dictionary. So I, X, and C are keys, while 1, 10, and 100 are values.

You can ask a dictionary for the value corresponding to a key. This takes a Roman letter and returns the corresponding value:

```
julia> roman_numerals['C']
100
```

```
julia> roman_numerals['M']
1000
```

6.3   *Looping over characters*

You can use this dictionary to help you convert Roman letters to corresponding values. At line 8 in the parse_roman function, you do this conversion with what is called an *array comprehension*. You iterate over every character, ch, in the string, s. On each iteration, you evaluate roman_numerals[ch], and all of these values get collected into an array:

```
vals = [roman_numerals[ch] for ch in s]
```

A comprehension is like a for-loop, where a value is evaluated on each iteration and added to a collection. You can create a comprehension for any collection, including dictionaries:

```
julia> Dict('A'+i=>i for i in 1:4)
Dict{Char, Int64} with 4 entries:
  'C' => 2
  'D' => 3
  'E' => 4
  'B' => 1
```

But in the Roman-numeral code the comprehension for loop is used to build an array. To better understand how an *array comprehension* works let's look at a regular for loop doing the exact same thing. In this example, you start with Roman numerals "XIV", which you want to convert:

```
julia> s = "XIV"
"XIV"

julia> vals = Int8[]
Int8[]

julia> for ch in s
           push!(vals, roman_numerals[ch])
       end

julia> vals
3-element Vector{Int8}:
 10
  1
  5
```

"XIV" is turned into the array of values [10, 1, 5], named vals. However, the job is not quite done. Later, you need to combine these values into one number.

Before converting input strings, the code sets every letter in uppercase. "xiv" would not get processed correctly because all the keys to the dictionary are uppercase.

I will walk you through the mechanics of the process and save the explanation for why you perform these steps for last. Reverse the order of the letters, so you can process numerals conveniently from right to left in a loop:

```
julia> s = "xiv"
"xiv"

julia> s = reverse(uppercase(s))
"VIX"
```

6.4 Enumerating values and indices

When processing a value, val, in the loop, you want to be able to compare with the preceding value. You could have accomplished that with a variable, say prev, store value from the previous iteration. Instead, you will use the enumerate function to get the index, i, of each value, val, being processed. The value preceding val is then simply vals[i-1]:

```
for (i, val) in enumerate(vals)
    if i > 1 && val < vals[i - 1]
        result -= val
    else
        result += val
    end
end
```

To better understand how enumerate works, let's use some examples focused exclusively on enumerate:

```
julia> enumerate([4, 6, 8])
enumerate([4, 6, 8])
```

That output wasn't very useful at all. The reason is that enumerate is *lazy*. You don't get any values out because this expression doesn't actually need any values to be evaluated. But you can use the collect function to collect all the values enumerate would have produced into an array. The following is a simple example of collecting a range:

```
julia> collect(2:3:11)
4-element Vector{Int64}:
  2
  5
  8
 11
```

More interesting is how you collect values from an enumeration:

```
julia> collect(enumerate(2:3:11))
4-element Vector{Tuple{Int64, Int64}}:
 (1, 2)
 (2, 5)
 (3, 8)
 (4, 11)

julia> collect(enumerate([4, 6, 8]))
3-element Vector{Tuple{Int64, Int64}}:
 (1, 4)
 (2, 6)
 (3, 8)
```

The collect function will simulate looping over something, just like a for loop, except it will *collect* all the values encountered into an array, which it returns. So you can see with enumerate you get a pair of values upon each iteration: an integer index and the value at that index.

6.5 *Explaining the conversion process*

You cannot simply add up the individual Roman letters converted to their corresponding values. Consider the Roman number XVI. It turns into [10, 5, 1]. You could add up the elements and get the correct result: 16. However, XIV is supposed to mean 14 because when a smaller Roman numeral is in front of a larger one, such as in *IV*, you subtract the smaller value from the larger.

You cannot just sum up the corresponding array [10, 1, 5]. Instead, you reverse it to work your way backwards through the values. At every index you ask if the current value is lower than the previous one. If it is, you subtract from the result; otherwise you add the following:

```
if i > 1 && val < vals[i - 1]
    result -= val
else
    result += val
end
```

That is what val < vals[i - 1] does. It compares the current value, val, to the previous value, vals[i -1]. result is used to accumulate the value of all the individual Roman letters.

6.6   *Using dictionaries*

Now that you have looked at a practical code example utilizing the dictionary type Dict in Julia, let's explore some more ways of interacting with a dictionary.

6.6.1   *Creating dictionaries*

There are a multitude of ways to create a dictionary. In this section, I'll discuss some examples, starting with multiple arguments, where each argument is a pair object:

```
julia> Dict("two" => 2, "four" => 4)
Dict{String,Int64} with 2 entries:
  "two"  => 2
  "four" => 4
```

Pass an array of pairs to the dictionary constructor (a function named the same as the type it makes instances of):

```
julia> pairs = ["two" => 2, "four" => 4]
2-element Vector{Pair{String, Int64}}:
  "two" => 2
  "four" => 4

julia> Dict(pairs)
Dict{String,Int64} with 2 entries:
  "two"  => 2
  "four" => 4
```

Pass an array of tuples to the dictionary constructor. Unlike pairs, tuples may contain more than two values. For dictionaries they must only contain a key and a value though:

```
julia> tuples = [("two", 2), ("four", 4)]
2-element Vector{Tuple{String, Int64}}:
 ("two", 2)
 ("four", 4)

julia> Dict(tuples)
Dict{String,Int64} with 2 entries:
  "two"  => 2
  "four" => 4
```

How do you know which variant to use? That depends on the problem you are trying to solve. For instance, when you read pizza data in chapter 5, you got an array of tuples back:

```
pizzas = [
    ("mexicana",  13.0),
    ("hawaiian",  16.5),
    ("bbq chicken", 20.75),
    ("sicilian", 12.25),
 ]
```

You might want to put this data into a dictionary to quickly look up the price for a given pizza:

```
julia> pizza_dict = Dict(pizzas)
Dict{String, Float64} with 4 entries:
  "sicilian"    => 12.25
  "bbq chicken" => 20.75
  "mexicana"    => 13.0
  "hawaiian"    => 16.5

julia> pizza_dict["mexicana"]
13.0
```

However, if keeping pizza data in order is not important, you could define this dictionary directly instead:

```
Dict(
   "sicilian"    => 12.25,
   "bbq chicken" => 20.75,
   "mexicana"    => 13.0,
   "hawaiian"    => 16.5)
```

Sometimes you need an empty dictionary, which you later fill up. One example would be loading from file straight into a dictionary. Instead of appending values to the end of an array, you could insert them into a dictionary:

```
julia>  d = Dict()
Dict{Any, Any}()
```

Notice the {Any, Any} part. This describes what Julia has inferred is the type of key and value in the dictionary. However, when you created your pizza dictionary, you would have noticed that Julia described it as having the Dict{String, Float64} type. String refers to the type of keys in the dictionary, and Float64 refers to the type of values. You can, however, specify the types of keys and values for an empty dictionary as well:

```
julia> d = Dict{String, Float64}()
Dict{String,Int64} with 0 entries

julia> d["hawaiian"] = 16.5
16.5
```

The benefit of specifying the type of the key and value is that it is easier to catch wrong usage of the dictionary at runtime. If you try to use values of the wrong type for key and value, Julia will throw an exception to indicate an error (chapter 6 covers different types in greater depth). In this case you are trying to use an integer 5 as a key when a text string key is expected:

```
julia> d[5] = "five"
ERROR: MethodError: Cannot `convert` an object of type Int64
to an object of type String
```

Sometimes you get keys and values in separate arrays. However you can still combine them into pairs to create dictionaries using the zip function.

```
julia> words = ["one", "two"]
2-element Vector{String}:
 "one"
 "two"

julia> nums = [1, 2]
2-element Vector{Int64}:
 1
 2

julia> collect(zip(words, nums))
2-element Vector{Tuple{String,Int64}}:
 ("one", 1)
 ("two", 2)

julia> Dict(zip(words, nums))
Dict{String,Int64} with 2 entries:
  "two" => 2
  "one" => 1
```

6.6.2 *Element access*

You have already looked at one way of getting and setting dictionary elements. But what happens if you try to retrieve a value for a key that does not exist, such as "seven"?

```
julia> d["hawaiian"]
16.5

julia> d["seven"]
ERROR: KeyError: key "seven" not found
```

You get an error. You can, of course, simply add it:

```
julia> d["seven"] = 7;

julia> d["seven"]
7.0
```

But how do you avoid producing an error when you are not sure a key exists? One solution is the get() function. If the key does not exist, a sentinel value is returned instead. The sentinel can be anything.

> **NOTE**   In computer programming, a *sentinel value* (also referred to as a *flag value*, a *trip value*, a *rogue value*, a *signal value*, or dummy data) is a special value in the context of an algorithm that uses its presence as a condition of termination, typically in a loop or recursive algorithm.

This is a strategy used in many programming languages when working with dictionaries. The following example uses -1 as a sentinel value:

```
julia> get(d, "eight", -1)
-1
```

Or you could simply ask the dictionary if it has the key:

```
julia> haskey(d, "eight")
false

julia> d["eight"] = 8
8

julia> haskey(d, "eight")
true
```

6.7   Why use a dictionary?

In principle, you could use an array to do the conversion of Roman numerals to decimal numbers. Here is an example of how you could do that.

Listing 6.2   Look up a value by key in an array of key–value pairs

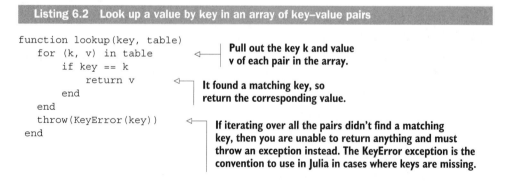

```
function lookup(key, table)
    for (k, v) in table          ◁——  Pull out the key k and value
        if key == k                    v of each pair in the array.
            return v         ◁—  It found a matching key, so
        end                      return the corresponding value.
    end
    throw(KeyError(key))   ◁—  If iterating over all the pairs didn't find a matching
end                            key, then you are unable to return anything and must
                               throw an exception instead. The KeyError exception is the
                               convention to use in Julia in cases where keys are missing.
```

You could define the lookup table as an array of pairs instead of a dictionary:

```
numerals = ['I' => 1, 'X' => 10, 'C' => 100,
            'V' => 5, 'L' => 50, 'D' => 500,
                                 'M' => 1000]
```

With this you could do lookup of values based on keys in a similar fashion to a dictionary.

```
julia> lookup('X', roman_numerals)
10

julia> lookup('D', roman_numerals)
500

julia> lookup('S', roman_numerals)
 ERROR: KeyError: key 'S' not found
```

A demonstration of looking
up a key that doesn't exist,
producing an exception

Avoid arrays when doing key-based lookup because the time to perform a lookup grows linearly with the size of the array. Looking up an element among 30 entries takes, on average, three times as long as looking up an entry among 10 elements. It is not hard to see how this does not scale well with large arrays. Looking for one element among 1 million elements will take 1,000 times longer than locating it among 1,000 elements.

Dictionaries, in contrast, are made so that the lookup time is *independent* of how many elements the dictionary contains. Looking up 1 element among 100 is similar to doing it among 1 million.

Why are dictionary lookups so fast?
Why dictionaries allow fast lookup of a value given a key is outside the scope of this book. Books about data structures and algorithms usually cover this topic in detail, and a dictionary refers more to the interface to the data than the actual data structure used to achieve fast lookups. In Julia, *hash tables* are used to allow fast lookups, but it is also possible to implement a dictionary using a *binary search tree* data structure.

But don't discount arrays. Short arrays are very fast to search—faster than a dictionary of comparable size. Thus, while the number of elements is less than 100, arrays are still a viable choice. In fact, the Roman-numeral code example used a dictionary because dictionaries are convenient to work with when dealing with key-based lookup, and you never have to worry about performance taking a nosedive because you added too many elements.

However, there are special cases in which using an array can work really well (e.g., if you never modify the array). If elements are never added or removed you can simply keep the array sorted. A sorted array can be searched very quickly using Julia's `searchsortedfirst` function. In fact, the Roman numeral code example is well suited for this approach, since the mapping between numerals and decimal values is fixed. You can do this by keeping the keys and values in separate arrays sorted by the key values.

Listing 6.3 Array of sorted keys with a matching array of values

```
keys = ['C', 'D', 'I', 'L', 'M', 'V', 'X']
vals = [100, 500, 1, 50, 1000, 5, 10]
```

With `searchsortedfirst` you can find the index of a particular key.

```julia
julia> i = searchsortedfirst(keys, 'I')
3
```

Make sure the value for key `I` is located at the same index `i` in the `vals` array:

```julia
julia> vals[i]
1
```

Here's another example:

```julia
julia> j = searchsortedfirst(keys, 'V')
6

julia> vals[j]
5
```

6.8   *Using named tuples as dictionaries*

Before rounding off this chapter, I want to show you another neat trick that allows you to write more-readable code with better performance. You have already seen tuples where you can access elements by index. What you have not seen is accessing tuple values by key, just like a dictionary.

Remember you created a pizza tuple like this: `("hawaiian", 'S', 10.5)`. It is possible to give names to each value; the names you give will not be text strings but Julia *symbols* (built-in Julia type to represent identifiers). In chapter 5, you used symbols such as `:cyan`, `:green`, and `:red` to specify color of printed text. Similarly, you can access individual values in the pizza tuple using symbols such as `:name` and `:price`:

```julia
julia> pizza = (name = "hawaiian", size = 'S', price = 10.5)
(name = "hawaiian", size = 'S', price = 10.5)

julia> pizza[:name]
"hawaiian"

julia> pizza[:price]
10.5

julia> pizza.name
"hawaiian"

julia> pizza.size
'S': ASCII/Unicode U+0053
```

Notice how you use a shortcut in the last two expressions; `pizza[:price]` is equivalent to writing `pizza.price`. This way of working with data will look familiar to JavaScript developers.

Keep in mind that symbols are a lot more limited in functionality than strings. In most cases they are treated as atomic values. You cannot access individual characters in a symbol or combine and manipulate them like strings. Fortunately, it is easy to convert back and forth between keys and strings:

```
julia> s = "price"; t = :name;

julia> Symbol(s)          ◄─┐   Create a symbol from a string.
:price

julia> string(t)          ◄─┘   Create a string from a symbol.
 "name"
```

With this knowledge you can rewrite your parse_roman function from listing 6.1 to use a named tuple instead of a dictionary. Observe that you have to change the lookup roman_numerals[ch] to roman_numerals[Symbol(ch)] because roman_numerals no longer have characters as keys but symbols.

Listing 6.4   Parsing Roman numerals using named tuples

```
roman_numerals =                ◄─┐   Changed from
        (I = 1, X = 10, C = 100,      dictionary to
         V = 5, L = 50, D = 500,      named tuple
         M = 1000)

function parse_roman(s)
    s = reverse(uppercase(s))
    vals = [roman_numerals[Symbol(ch)] for ch in s]   ◄─┐  Lookup with
    result = 0                                            Symbol(ch)
    for (i, val) in enumerate(vals)                       instead of ch
        if i > 1 && val < vals[i - 1]
            result -= val
        else
            result += val
        end
    end
    result
end
```

6.8.1 *When do you use a named tuple?*

Named tuples look very similar to dictionaries, so what is the point of having them? All types of tuples are immutable, meaning you cannot change them. You cannot add values to a tuple after you have created it, nor can you modify existing values. In contrast, both arrays and dictionaries allow you to add values. Dictionaries give you a wider selection of types which can by used as keys. A named tuple only allows you to use symbols as keys.

The benefit of any tuple type over an array or a dictionary is that the Julia JIT compiler will know exactly which elements will be in the tuple at any given time, which allows for more aggressive optimizations. Thus you can assume a tuple will generally give you equal or better performance compared to an array or a dictionary.

While only using symbols as keys is a limitation, it also allows named tuples to offer more convenient syntax for accessing values. For example, pizza.name is easier to write and read than pizza[:name].

6.8.2   *Tying it all together*

This chapter has covered all the key types any programmer should know. With numbers, ranges, strings, arrays, tuples, and dictionaries you can do almost anything. However, I have not yet said much about *what* a type actually is or how you can make your own custom types. This is crucial for facilitating the construction of larger, more feature-rich applications. That will be the focus of the next two chapters.

Summary

- Dictionaries hold key–value pairs, where the key has to be unique.
- Key–value pairs can quickly be looked up, added, or removed from a dictionary. This differs from large arrays, which may require time-consuming searches.
- Arrays offer better performance when the number of elements is small or when you can do index-based rather than key-based accessing of elements.
- In Julia, keys and values are typed. Hence, Julia is able to catch the usage of keys of the wrong type as well as attempts at inserting values of the wrong type.
- Named tuples work like an immutable version of dictionaries. You can look up values, but you cannot modify them or add new entries.

Part 2

Types

In part 1, Basics, you looked at types in a superficial manner. Part 2 discusses the Julia type system in greater detail by building up various examples, such as a recurring rocket example, that demonstrate how the type system works and what benefits it offers.

This part introduces what makes Julia special. The greater depth of coverage of the type system in this part also allows me to cover how functions and methods work in Julia. In particular, it allows a proper explanation of multiple dispatch, which is the killer feature in Julia. Multiple dispatch is at the heart of what makes Julia such an expressive and high-performance language, despite being dynamically typed.

Understanding types

This chapter covers

- Understanding type hierarchies
- Differences between abstract and concrete types
- Combining primitive types to make composite types
- Harnessing the power of multiple dispatch to solve complex tasks elegantly
- How multiple dispatch differs from single dispatch in object-oriented languages[1]

All objects in Julia are of a particular type. Remember, you can use `typeof` to discover the type of any object:

```
julia> typeof(42)
Int64

julia> typeof('A')
Char
```

---

[1] Most mainstream languages today are object oriented. They are designed to couple behavior to types and reuse functionality through what we call *inheritance*.

```
julia> typeof("hello")
String
```

The type decides what you can do with an object. For example, a dictionary allows you to look up a value by key, while an array stores elements in order. An expression evaluating to a `Bool` value, such as `true` or `false`, can be used in an if statement and while loops, while expressions evaluating to a floating-point value can't:

```
julia> if 2.5
           print("this should not be possible")
       end
ERROR: TypeError: non-boolean (Float64) used in boolean context
```

Thus, if you want to create objects with different behavior and features, you need to define new types. In programming, we often try to mimic the real world:

- Banking apps have types representing bank accounts, customers, and transactions.
- Video games have objects representing monsters, heroes, weapons, spaceships, traps, and so on.
- Graphical user interfaces have objects representing buttons, menu entries, pop-up menus, and radio buttons.
- Drawing applications have objects representing different shapes, strokes, colors, and drawing tools.

So whatever type of application you want to make, you will need to know how to create relevant types to the application. This chapter and the next one will define types relevant to model behavior in a video game and rocket simulator.

7.1 Creating composite types from primitive types

Let's start with the basics: Integers, characters, and floating-point numbers are all examples of primitive types. You cannot break them further down into smaller parts. In some languages, such as LISP, these are aptly named *atoms*. With the `isprimitive-type` you can check whether a type is *primitive*:

```
julia> isprimitivetype(Int8)
true

julia> isprimitivetype(Char)
true

julia> isprimitivetype(String)
false
```

You can combine primitive types to create *composite types*. Composite types can even be made out of other composite types. For example, a string is a composite type made up of multiple characters, which are primitive types. Let's demonstrate this with a concrete example by defining a composite type that could be useful in a video game to represent an archer shooting arrows at opponents.

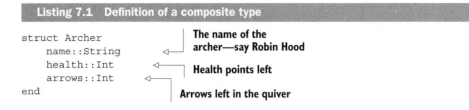

Listing 7.1   Definition of a composite type

```
struct Archer                    The name of the
    name::String                 archer—say Robin Hood
    health::Int                  Health points left
    arrows::Int
end                              Arrows left in the quiver
```

Think of types as templates or cookie cutters, which you use to stamp out multiple objects. The objects you make from a type are called *instances*.

> **WARNING**   Julia composite types may look very similar to classes in Java, C++, or Python, but they are not the same thing. They don't support implementation inheritance and don't have methods attached.

The following snippet shows the creation of instances of the Archer type. You may also hear people use phrases such as, "Instantiate an Archer object."

```
julia> robin = Archer("Robin Hood", 30, 24)
Archer("Robin Hood", 30, 24)

julia> william = Archer("William Tell", 28, 1)
Archer("William Tell", 28, 1)

julia> robin.name              Access the name field
"Robin Hood"                   of the robin object.

julia> robin.arrows            Access the arrows field
 24                            of the robin object.
```

The definition of a composite type has some similarities with using a dictionary. For example, you define fields for storing values that can be accessed through their field name. However, unlike a dictionary, you can specify a different type for each field using a *type annotation*.

> **IMPORTANT**   In Julia the :: is used to annotate variables and expressions with their type. x::T means variable x should have type T. It helps Julia figure out how many bytes are needed to hold all fields in a struct.

To clarify this point, define a dictionary to hold information about an archer.

Listing 7.2   Using a dictionary to store information about an archer

```
julia> robin = Dict("name"    => "Robin Hood",
                    "health"  => 30,            Dictionary with String
                    "arrows"  => 24)            key and where the
Dict{String, Any} with 3 entries:              value is of type Any
  "name"    => "Robin Hood"
```

```
    "health" => 30
    "arrows" => 24
                                    Accessing
                                    value stored
                                    for name key
julia> robin["name"]        ⊲──┘
"Robin Hood"

julia> robin["arrows"]
24
```

A problem with using a dictionary is that it requires every value to be of the same type. But wait a minute, how can this be the case? name and arrows are entirely different types?

The short answer is that the values in the dictionary are of type Any. That means you can store values of any type. The keys are more restrictive, as they are defined to be of type String. But to really understand how this works you need to explore Julia type hierarchies.

7.2   *Exploring type hierarchies*

If you are familiar with object-oriented languages, then you should be familiar with class[2] inheritance hierarchies. In Julia, you also have type hierarchies, but a significant difference is that these hierarchies also exist for primitive types. For example, in a language such as Java or C++, an integer or floating-point number is just one concrete type. However, in Julia, even numbers, collections, and strings are part of deeper type hierarchies (figure 7.1).

You can explore these hierarchies with the supertype and subtypes functions. You can recreate the type hierarchy for numbers in figure 7.1 by starting at the top of the type hierarchy and working your way downward, using the subtypes function to find subtypes, which can then be explored further:

```
julia> subtypes(Number)        ⊲───┐  Find immediate
2-element Vector{Any}:                subtypes of the
 Complex                              Number type.
 Real

julia> subtypes(Real)          ⊲───┐  Discover
4-element Vector{Any}:                subtypes of
 AbstractFloat                        real numbers.
 AbstractIrrational
 Integer
 Rational

julia> subtypes(Integer)       ⊲───┐  Integers can
3-element Vector{Any}:                be signed or
 Bool                                 unsigned.
 Signed
 Unsigned
```

---

[2] A *class* in object-oriented programming is a type that can be part of a type hierarchy and has associated functions called *methods*.

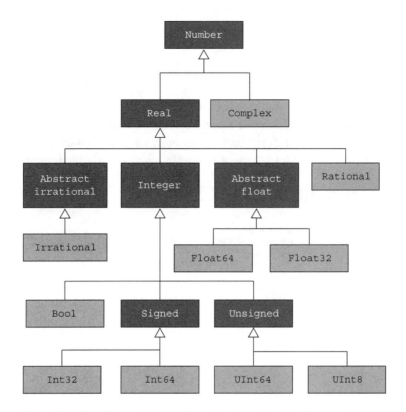

Figure 7.1   Type hierarchy for numbers, showing abstract and concrete types in dark and light shaded boxes

But how do you know that the root of the number hierarchy is the Number type? You could work your way upward from number types you already know:

```
julia> T = typeof(42)
Int64
```
◁─── **Store the type of 42 in variable T.**

```
julia> T = supertype(T)
Signed
```
◁─── **Look up supertype Int64, and store it in T.**

```
julia> T = supertype(T)
Integer

julia> T = supertype(T)
Real

julia> T = supertype(T)
Number
```

You can even continue to pass the root of the number hierarchy, until you get to the root of the whole Julia type hierarchy. Once you reach Any, you know you have reached the top of the type hierarchy because the supertype of Any is also Any:

```
julia> T = supertype(T)
Any

julia> T = supertype(T)
Any
```

It is essential to realize that Julia's types are first-class objects that you can pass around as arguments or store in variables. For example, here you are storing the type of the integer 42 in a variable called T. It is a convention in many languages to use T as a name for an arbitrary type. Let's explore the type hierarchy with some simple functions.

Listing 7.3   Finding the root of the type hierarchy

```
function findroot(T)
    T2 = supertype(T)        ┐  Check if the
    println(T)               │  supertype of T is
    if T2 != T        ◁──────┘  the same as T.
        findroot(T2)
    end
end
```

This is a recursive[3] function, which you can use to find the top of the type hierarchy:

```
julia> findroot(typeof(42))
Int64
Signed
Integer
Real
Number
Any

julia> supertype(Any)
Any
```

You can see that the type hierarchy stops at Any, since the supertype of Any is Any. So what is the significance of these type of hierarchies? How do they help you as a programmer? Let me give you this example in the REPL to give you a hint:

```
julia> anything = Any[42, 8]     ◁──┐  Define an array
2-element Vector{Any}:              │  that can hold
 42                                 │  Any value.
  8
```

```
julia> integers = Integer[42, 8]   ◁──┐  Define an array
2-element Vector{Integer}:            │  to hold Integer
 42                                   │  values.
  8
```

---

[3] A *recursive function* is a function that calls itself as opposed to using a loop.

```
julia> anything[2] = "hello"
"hello"
```
← Putting a string into anything array works fine.

```
julia> integers[2] = "hello"
ERROR: MethodError: Cannot `convert` an object
       of type String to an object of type Integer
```

The integers array will not accept strings.

Since every object in Julia conforms to the Any type, you can put any object into an array where you have specified that each element must be of type Any. However, not every Julia object is of type Integer. Thus, putting a text string such as "hello" into an array where each element must be of type Integer will not work.

How do you know what types are compatible? The value you try to store has to be of a type that is a subtype of the allowed element type. It turns out you can check this programmatically with the <: operator.

> **Listing 7.4   Examining which types are subtypes of each other**

```
julia> String <: Any
true

julia> String <: Integer
false
```
← A string is not a kind of integer.

```
julia> Int8 <: Integer
true

julia> Float64 <: Integer
 false
```
← Float64 is a number but not an integer.

You can see from this example that types cannot be merely somewhat related (e.g., floating-point numbers and integers). For example, 4.5 is a floating-point number but not an integer. However both Int8(4) and Int32(5) are integer numbers; they are subtypes of Integer.

That should give you a hint about the advantages of defining composite types to hold related data over using a dictionary. Each field can have a different type. That provides better type checking at runtime.

7.3   *Creating a battle simulator*

To further explore these concepts, you will develop a simple simulator of battles between different warriors, as is frequently done in board games, card games, and video games.

Many computer games work on the rock-paper-scissors principle. Let me clarify: there are archers, knights, and pikemen in your game, which you would set up so that

- archers beat pikemen,
- knights beat archers, and
- pikemen beat knights.

That is roughly how these units worked historically. Archers would fire arrows at slow-moving pikemen and beat them before they could get close enough to attack the archers. This strategy would fail with knights who could ride up to the archers before they managed to loosen many arrows and cut them down. However, the knights could not use this strategy against pikemen, as a wall of spears would prevent the knights from charging the pikemen, lest they get skewered.

You will be implementing the following in code:

- An abstract type `Warrior` for all warrior types
- Concrete warrior types `Archer`, `Pikeman`, and `Knight`
- An explanation of the relation between concrete and abstract types
- Behavior for each warrior type by defining functions such as `shoot!` and `mount!`
- An `attack!` function to simulate one warrior attacking another
- A `battle!` function to simulate two warriors repeatedly attacking each other until one is victorious or both perish

7.3.1   *Defining warrior types*

Make a file named `warriors.jl` to store the code you will develop. Start with a definition of the types you will use.

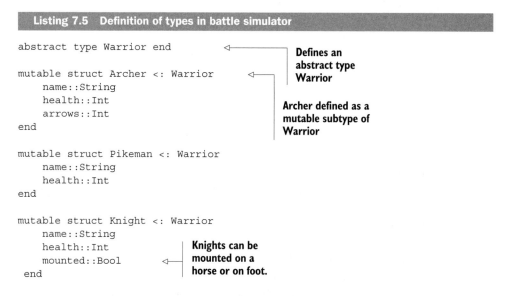

Listing 7.5   Definition of types in battle simulator

```
abstract type Warrior end                              ◁──────  Defines an
                                                                abstract type
mutable struct Archer <: Warrior           ◁──                 Warrior
    name::String
    health::Int                                                Archer defined as a
    arrows::Int                                                mutable subtype of
end                                                            Warrior

mutable struct Pikeman <: Warrior
    name::String
    health::Int
end


mutable struct Knight <: Warrior
    name::String
    health::Int           Knights can be
    mounted::Bool     ◁── mounted on a
  end                     horse or on foot.
```

The code in listing 7.5 is creating a type hierarchy illustrated below. In these hierarchies you make distinctions between abstract and concrete types. `Archer`, `Pikeman`, and `Knight` are examples of concrete types, while `Warrior` is an example of an abstract type. You can create objects of a concrete type but not of an abstract type:

```
julia> robin = Archer("Robin Hood", 34, 24)
Archer("Robin Hood", 34, 24)
```

```
julia> Warrior()
ERROR: MethodError: no constructors have been defined for Warrior
```

The purpose of abstract types is to facilitate the construction of type hierarchies.

In figure 7.2, I have added `name` and `health` to the `Warrior` type box. However, this is just to clarify that all subtypes are required to have these fields. Julia offers no syntax to enforce this. Instead, this is something you do by convention.

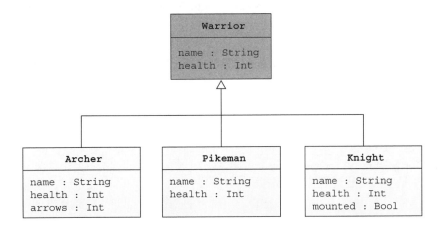

Figure 7.2   Warrior type hierarchy. The dark box is abstract and light boxes are concrete types.

In Julia, if you define a type as `abstract type` it cannot have any fields. Only concrete types can have fields or a value. A *composite type* is a concrete type with fields, while a *primitive type* is a concrete type with a single value.

The subtype operator `<:` is not only used to check if a type is a subtype of another but also to define a type as subtype:

```
struct B <: A
  ...
end
```

This code snippet defines type `B` as a subtype of type `A`. In Julia, you cannot subtype concrete types. If you have used popular object-oriented languages such as Java, C++, C#, Python, or Ruby this will likely come as a surprise to you. If you consider the number hierarchy we have just covered this makes sense. You know how much space an `Int32` or `Float64` needs, but how many bytes of storage would you need to hold an `Integer` or `Real` number? You cannot know that. That is why most of the number types are abstract.

7.3.2   *Adding behavior to warriors*

Warriors containing only data isn't exciting. So you will add behavior to them by defining several functions with accompanying methods. Add these to the `warrior.jl` source code file (listing 7.6).

All these functions have an exclamation mark in their name because they modify a field (remember, this is only a convention). That's why the composite types have the `mutable` keyword added to their definitions. If a `struct` type is not defined as *mutable*, it will not support functions that modify a field. Without the `mutable` keyword, a composite type will default to being *immutable*.

Listing 7.6   Adding behavior to warrior types

```
function shoot!(archer::Archer)
    if archer.arrows > 0
        archer.arrows -= 1
    end
end

function resupply!(archer::Archer)
    archer.arrows = 24
end

function mount!(knight::Knight)
    knight.mounted = true
end

function dismount!(k::Knight)
    knight.mounted = false
end
```

Here is a short description of what each function does:

- `shoot!`—An archer shoots an arrow. Deplete the number of arrows by one.
- `resupply!`—Simulate that archer gets a resupply of 24 arrows.
- `mount!`—Change the state of the knight to be mounted on a horse.
- `dismount!`—Dismount the knight to make ready for foot combat.

Mutable vs. immutable types

The following is an important insight developed within the functional programming community: if objects cannot be modified, your program will be less likely to have bugs. Objects that cannot be modified are called *immutable*. If they can be modified, they are referred to as *mutable*.

In older languages, objects have tended to be mutable by default. Julia follows a modern trend: making objects *immutable* unless explicitly marked as *mutable*.

With the `shoot!` function you can simulate how the archer will spend arrows in battle. Usually a medieval archer would have 24 arrows in a quiver. When those had been spent, the archer would need to resupply:

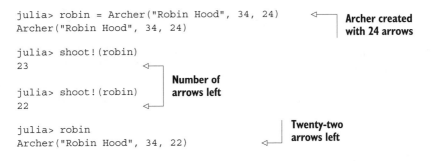

```
julia> robin = Archer("Robin Hood", 34, 24)          ⊲─┐ Archer created
Archer("Robin Hood", 34, 24)                              │ with 24 arrows

julia> shoot!(robin)
23                                        ⊲──┐
                                              │  Number of
julia> shoot!(robin)                          │  arrows left
22                                        ⊲──┘

julia> robin                                     ┐ Twenty-two
Archer("Robin Hood", 34, 22)             ⊲──────┘ arrows left
```

You can improve the `shoot!` function with a trick I use frequently when developing Julia software: I return the object that is most useful to see displayed when running a function in the REPL (see listing 7.7). When calling functions that modify an object, it is very useful to see what that object looks like after the modification. Thus, it is a good habit to return the modified object in mutating functions.

Listing 7.7 Modifying mutating functions to be REPL-friendly

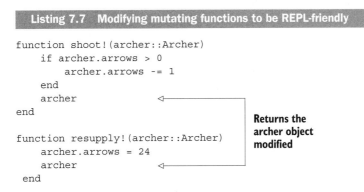

```
function shoot!(archer::Archer)
    if archer.arrows > 0
        archer.arrows -= 1
    end
    archer              ⊲───────────┐
end                                  │  Returns the
                                     │  archer object
function resupply!(archer::Archer)   │  modified
    archer.arrows = 24               │
    archer              ⊲───────────┘
 end
```

This makes testing functions you are developing, and checking whether they perform the correct operations, much simpler:

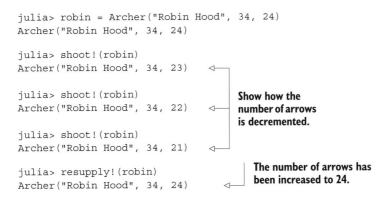

```
julia> robin = Archer("Robin Hood", 34, 24)
Archer("Robin Hood", 34, 24)

julia> shoot!(robin)
Archer("Robin Hood", 34, 23)     ⊲──┐

julia> shoot!(robin)                 │  Show how the
Archer("Robin Hood", 34, 22)     ⊲──┤  number of arrows
                                     │  is decremented.
julia> shoot!(robin)                 │
Archer("Robin Hood", 34, 21)     ⊲──┘

julia> resupply!(robin)              ┐ The number of arrows has
Archer("Robin Hood", 34, 24)     ⊲──┘ been increased to 24.
```

You can use these functions to construct new functions to simulate a warrior attacking another. Again, add this code to the `warriors.jl` file. It looks as if you defined `attack!` twice. How is that possible?

Listing 7.8   Two methods for simulating battle between archers and knights

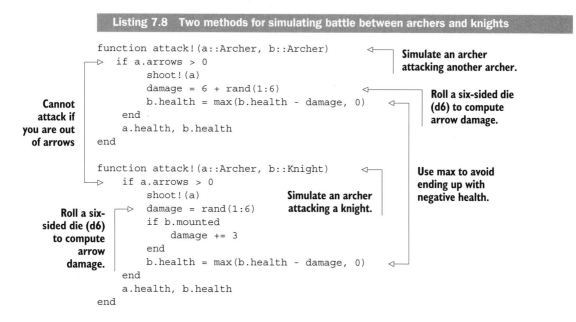

```
function attack!(a::Archer, b::Archer)
    if a.arrows > 0
        shoot!(a)
        damage = 6 + rand(1:6)
        b.health = max(b.health - damage, 0)
    end
    a.health, b.health
end

function attack!(a::Archer, b::Knight)
    if a.arrows > 0
        shoot!(a)
        damage = rand(1:6)
        if b.mounted
            damage += 3
        end
        b.health = max(b.health - damage, 0)
    end
    a.health, b.health
end
```

Cannot attack if you are out of arrows

Simulate an archer attacking another archer.

Roll a six-sided die (d6) to compute arrow damage.

Roll a six-sided die (d6) to compute arrow damage.

Simulate an archer attacking a knight.

Use max to avoid ending up with negative health.

If this was a regular dynamic language, such as JavaScript, Python, Ruby, or Lua, the last definition of `attack!` would have overwritten the first one. If this was a statically typed language, such as Java, C#, or C++, you would have created something called *function overloading*[4]. But in Julia, something entirely different happens.

7.3.3   *Using multiple dispatch to invoke methods*

In Julia, you are not actually defining two functions but rather two *methods* attached to the `attack!` function. I know this sounds confusing, so let me break it down in more detail. In Julia, you actually define functions as shown in the following listing.

Listing 7.9   Function definitions in Julia without methods

```
function shoot! end
function resupply! end
function attack! end
```

Functions are just names. Unless you attach methods to them, they cannot do anything. Start up a fresh Julia REPL, and paste the following function definitions along with the definitions of the `Warrior`, `Archer`, and `Knight` types (see listing 7.5), and create some objects to work with:

---

[4] *Function overloading* is a feature of many statically typed languages. It allows defining the same function multiple times with arguments of different types. When the code gets compiled, the compiler picks the right function.

```
julia> robin = Archer("Robin Hood", 34, 24)
Archer("Robin Hood", 34, 24)

julia> white = Knight("Lancelot", 34, true)
Knight("Lancelot", 34, true)
```

Now you can try to do things with these objects and see what happens:

Trying to call a function with no defined methods

```
julia> attack!(robin, white)
ERROR: MethodError: no method matching attack!(::Archer, ::Knight)

julia> shoot!(robin)
ERROR: MethodError: no method matching shoot!(::Archer)

julia> mount!(white)
 ERROR: UndefVarError: mount! not defined
```
Attempting to call an undefined function

You can see from these errors that Julia distinguishes between functions you have not defined at all, such as mount!, and functions that are defined but have no methods, such as shoot! and attack!. But how do you know they don't have any methods? Julia has a function called methods, which allows you to inspect how many methods are attached to a function:

Show that attack! is a function with no methods.

```
julia> methods(attack!)
# 0 methods for generic function "attack!":

julia> methods(mount!)
 ERROR: UndefVarError: mount! not defined
```
mount! cannot be found by Julia.

You can see that Julia reports that attack! doesn't have any methods. Let's compare this result with loading the warriors.jl file into the REPL.

```
julia> include("warriors.jl")
```
Loads the code into the Julia REPL

```
julia> methods(shoot!)
# 1 method for generic function "shoot!":
[1] shoot!(archer::Archer)

julia> methods(attack!)
# 2 methods for generic function "attack!":
[1] attack!(a::Archer, b::Archer)
[2] attack!(a::Archer, b::Knight)

julia> methods(mount!)
# 1 method for generic function "mount!":
[1] mount!(knight::Knight)
```

Figure 7.3 illustrates what you see in the REPL. Internally, Julia has a list of functions. Every function enters another list containing the methods for the corresponding

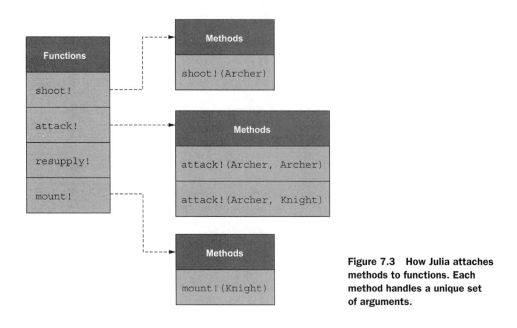

Figure 7.3 **How Julia attaches methods to functions. Each method handles a unique set of arguments.**

function entry. Methods can span different types, as they are not attached to types but to functions. Nothing prevents you from adding a shoot! method, which operates on a dictionary or array type.

Let's create some objects that allow you to play around a bit:

```
julia> robin = Archer("Robin Hood", 34, 24)
Archer("Robin Hood", 34, 24)

julia> tell = Archer("William Tell", 30, 20)
Archer("William Tell", 30, 20)

julia> white = Knight("Lancelot", 34, true)
Knight("Lancelot", 34, true)

julia> black = Knight("Morien", 35, true)
Knight("Morien", 35, true)
```

With some objects, you can experiment with using objects of different type when invoking the attack! function:

Health points left for attacker and defender

```
julia> attack!(robin, white)
(34, 30)
```
Attack a knight with an archer.

```
julia> attack!(robin, white)
(34, 26)
```

```
julia> attack!(tell, robin)
(30, 22)
```
Let an archer attack another archer.

Let a knight attack a knight.

```
julia> attack!(black, white)
ERROR: MethodError: no method matching attack!(::Knight, ::Knight)
Closest candidates are:
    attack!(::Archer, ::Knight)
```
Method with closest match to the attempted call

I advise you to experiment a bit with this yourself. You can look at how health points get depreciated with different attacks. To make it easier to keep track of how health points change, each method is set up to return a tuple with the health points of the attacker and defender at the end of the fight.

The interesting point here is the last part, when you try to have a battle between two knights. You might have noticed that we have not yet added a method for dealing with a fight between two knights. We add one in the following listing.

Listing 7.10 Method for simulating an attack by a knight against another knight

```
function attack!(a::Knight, b::Knight)
    a.health = max(a.health - rand(1:6), 0)
    b.health = max(b.health - rand(1:6), 0)
    a.health, b.health
end
```

You can add this method to the warriors.jl file and reload it. Instead of reloading everything, you could just paste the definition into the REPL. Afterward, you will notice that having the black knight Sir Morien attack the white knight Sir Lancelot works fine:

```
julia> attack!(black, white)
(33, 22)
```

And you will notice that Julia reports that the attack! function has three methods now:

```
julia> methods(attack!)
# 3 methods for generic function "attack!":
[1] attack!(a::Archer, b::Archer)
[2] attack!(a::Archer, b::Knight)
[3] attack!(a::Knight, b::Knight)
```

Let's add another attack! method to allow archers to attack pikemen. Then you can see for yourself how the number of methods has changed.

Listing 7.11 Archer attacking pikeman

```
function attack!(a::Archer, b::Pikeman)
    if a.arrows > 0
        shoot!(a)
        damage = 4 + rand(1:6)
        b.health = max(b.health - damage, 0)
    end
```
Only allow an attack if an archer has greater than zero arrows.

```
        a.health, b.health
end
```

7.4   *How Julia selects method to call*

When you invoke `attack!(a, b)`, Julia will find the type of every argument to find a tuple of all the argument types:

```
argtypes = (typeof(a), typeof(b))
```

Julia will use this tuple of argument types to look through the list of all methods to find the one matching. Remember, functions don't have code in Julia; methods have code. If a function doesn't have any methods, you cannot run that function. This process is illustrated in figure 7.4.

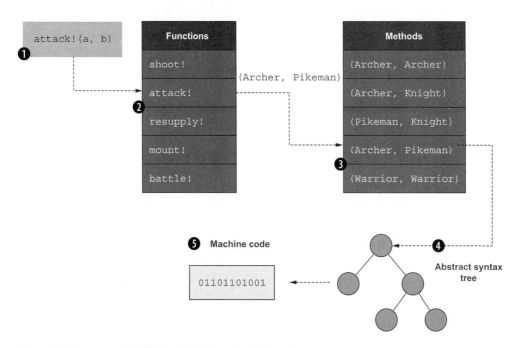

Figure 7.4   How a method is invoked using multiple-dispatch

We assume in this example that an archer is attacking a pikeman, so the `a` is an `Archer`, and the `b` is a `Pikeman`. Let's look at what happens step by step:

1 Julia tries to evaluate (execute) the `attack!(a, b)` expression in your program.
2 It takes the name of the function `attack!` and looks through a table of all functions, until it finds the entry for `attack!`.
3 Julia does the equivalent of `(typeof(a), typeof(b))` to get the tuple (Archer, Pikeman). Julia scans the list of methods stored on the `attack!` function from top to bottom, until it finds a match at the 4th entry.

4 Julia locates the method. The method is encoded as an abstract syntax tree (AST). This is a common data structure[5] in dynamic languages[6] for representing functions and methods at runtime.

5 The Julia JIT compiler converts the AST to machine code,[7] which gets executed. The compiled machine code gets stored in the methods table, so next time the `attack(Archer, Pikeman)` gets looked up, it can just execute cached machine code.

Understanding all of this fully would require a deep dive into compiler and interpreter theory, which would be outside the scope of this book. Thus, the best way for you to think about this is that you are done at step 4. Somehow you find a representation of your method you can run. The last steps are useful mainly to those interested in understanding why Julia has such high performance compared to other languages.

ASTs for the curious

This is not a book about compiler concepts, such as ASTs. But I will offer a little bit of information about them to help you understand Julia. Consider an expression such as

```
y = 4*(2 + x)
```

When a compiler or interpreter reads such code it will usually turn it into a tree structure called an AST, like in the following figure:

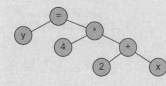

AST of the expression `y = 4*(2 + x)`

In Julia, every method is turned into such a tree structure. The methods table for each function keeps track of each of these tree structures. The Julia compiler uses these to create actual machine code that the computer understands.

---

[5] A *data structure* is a particular way of organizing data in a computer program. Arrays, strings, binary trees, linked lists, and hash tables are examples of data structures. But almost any composite type could be thought of as defining a data structure.

[6] In a dynamic language, you don't have a compiler analyzing type correctness before a program is allowed to run. Julia has a compiler, but it is invoked at runtime.

[7] A microprocessor doesn't understand programming languages such as Julia or Java. It only understands machine code.

7.4.1   *Contrasting Julia's multiple dispatch with object-oriented languages*

Multiple dispatch is often confusing to developers with a background in object-oriented programming languages. Thus I will try to contrast the Julia approach with how object-oriented languages work. In an object-oriented language method, implementations to execute are picked based on a single argument type. That is why we call the approach *single dispatch*. In an object-oriented language, you would not write attack!(archer, knight) but the code in the following listing.

> **Listing 7.12   Syntax if Julia was an object-oriented language**

```
archer.attack!(knight)
archer.shoot!()
knight.mount!()
```

While you cannot write Julia code like that, you can simulate this behavior in Julia.

> **Listing 7.13   Single dispatch in Julia**

```
function attack(archer::Archer, opponent)          Handle all the cases
    if typeof(opponent) == Archer                  where the attacker
        ...                                         is an Archer.
    elseif typeof(opponent) == Knight
        ...
    elseif typeof(opponent) == Pikeman

    end
end

function attack(knight::Knight, opponent)          Handle all the cases
    if typeof(opponent) == Archer                  where the attacker
        ...                                         is a Knight.
    elseif typeof(opponent) == Knight
        ...
    elseif typeof(opponent) == Pikeman

    end
end
```

That illustrates the limitations of single dispatch. Because attack! methods can only be picked based on the first argument type, you need a long list of if-else statements to deal with opponents of different types. Let me clarify how single dispatch works with a step-by-step explanation (figure 7.5).

1 When a.attack!(b) is evaluated, lookup the object referred to by a.
2 On this archer object, there is a hidden field, isa, which points to the type of the archer object.
3 The type Archer is an object itself with various fields. It has fields for each method: shoot!, attack!, and so on. It is like a dictionary, where you use the function name attack! to look up the correct method.
4 The method is an AST, which you can evaluate.

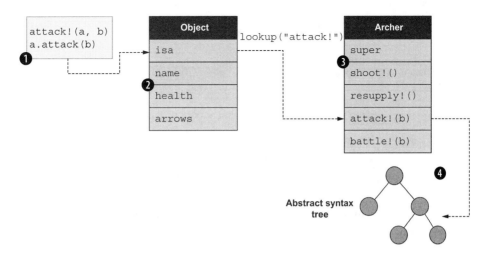

Figure 7.5   How a method is invoked using single dispatch

So the key difference to realize with Julia is that in most mainstream languages, methods are stored on the type of an object, while in Julia methods are stored on functions.

7.4.2   How is multiple dispatch different from function overloading?

Statically typed languages, such as Java, C#, and C++, have something called function overloading, which looks superficially the same as multiple dispatch. The key difference is that with function overloading, the correct method to call is decided at compilation time, which means a method like the one shown in the following listing isn't possible in a statically typed language.

Listing 7.14   Writing out the outcome of a battle between two warriors

```
function battle!(a::Warrior, b::Warrior)          Both a and b must be subtypes
   attack!(a, b)                                   of the Warrior type.
      if a.health == 0 && b.health == 0
         println(a.name, " and ", b.name, " destroyed each other")
      elseif a.health == 0
         println(b.name, " defeated ", a.name)
      elseif b.health == 0
         println(a.name, " defeated ", b.name)
      else
         println(b.name, " survived attack from ", a.name)
      end
end
```

Add this method to your warriors.jl source code file. Reload everything, and recreate the usual suspects, white and robin, to test out battle! in the REPL. Robin Hood attacks Sir Lancelot multiple times, until the health points of Lancelot drop low enough that battle! prints out that he has been defeated:

```
julia> battle!(robin, white)
Lancelot survived attack from Robin Hood

julia> battle!(robin, white)
Lancelot survived attack from Robin Hood

julia> battle!(robin, white)
Robin Hood defeated Lancelot
```

When you call `battle!(robin, white)`, Julia will look for a method with the signature `battle!(a::Archer, b::Knight)`, but this cannot be found. However `battle!(a::Warrior, b::Warrior)` is a valid match, because both `Knight` and `Archer` are subtypes of `Warrior`.

When the Julia compiler compiles the `battle!` method, it cannot know what concrete type argument a and b will have. It can only know they are some subtype of `Warrior`. Thus the *compiler* cannot pick the correct `attack!` method to call. This decision can only be made at runtime. That is what makes this different from function overloading. Function overloading, as found in Java and C++, relies on the compiler being able to pick the correct method.

Summary

- Numbers in Julia are part of an elaborate type hierarchy.
- In a type hierarchy, only the leaf nodes can be concrete types. All other types are abstract.
- The `typeof`, `supertype`, and `subtypes` functions can be used to explore type hierarchies.
- A function is just a name. Without attached methods, they cannot do anything. Code is always stored inside methods. The type of the arguments determines which method will get executed at runtime.
- Object-oriented languages use single dispatch, meaning only the type of the first function argument decides what method is selected. Julia is multiple dispatch, meaning *all* arguments influence which method gets selected.
- A composite type, unlike a primitive type, is composed of zero or more fields. The `struct` keyword is used to define a composite type.
- By adding the `mutable` keyword to a `struct` definition, you allow individual fields in the composite to be modified at runtime.

Building a rocket 8

This chapter covers

- Building complex data structures made up of many different objects of different types
- Abstracting away differences between different but related types

In the last chapter, you made some simple composite types to represent different types of warriors. However, in more realistic applications, you will have to combine many different types of objects into more complex data structures.

To explore this topic, you will be building a rocket in code. Why a rocket? Because rockets are made up of many different parts. That gives you an opportunity to build composite types out of other composite types and show different ways in which abstract types can be used in Julia to facilitate the construction of complex data structures. This rocket example will be used to explore many other topics later in the book, such as how Julia represents collections of objects.

The code example will start by defining a simple rocket of type `Rocket`, consisting of a `Payload`, a `Tank`, and an `Engine` object. Later you will modify the simple type definition to create a more complex multistage rocket made up of multiple `StagedRocket` objects. Next you will modify the code further to add a type `Cluster`, representing a cluster of rocket engines, which can be attached to any rocket

141

stage. At the end you will define the function `launch!` to simulate the launch of a multistage rocket.

8.1   *Building a simple rocket*

Let's start by modeling a simple space rocket in code. This is a single-stage rocket made up of the following parts from bottom to top (see figure 8.1):

- *Rocket engine*—Providing propulsion
- *Propellant tank*—Containing matter expelled by the engine
- *Payload*—Such as a capsule or satellite

The payload is the useful stuff you want to move around in space. It could be a crew module for astronauts or a probe with instruments to explore other planets.

Such a rocket could be defined by a composite type (listing 8.1). But don't type this out yet; this is just to get you to think about the types you will need to define. You will implement different types for tanks and engines. Then you will add different attributes and behavior, such as refilling tanks and consuming propellant.

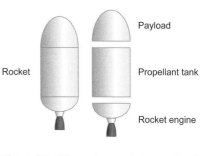

Figure 8.1   **The parts a rocket is made of**

Listing 8.1   The first definition of a simple rocket

```
struct Rocket
    payload::Payload
    tank::Tank
    engine::Engine
end
```

Instead you will focus your attention on the propellant tank. Propellant is the matter a rocket engine expels to move forward. In its simplest form, it is a compressed gas being released. In real space rockets, however, it is a combination of a fuel such as kerosene or hydrogen and an oxidizer such as liquid oxygen (LOX). However, these are details you don't have to include in your model. Instead, consider the following:

- *Dry mass*—Mass of an empty tank
- *Total mass*—Mass of a full tank
- *Propellant mass*—Propellant currently left in the tank
- *Mass*—Dry mass plus propellant currently left

I will show some different way of modeling this in Julia and talk about pros and cons of these different approaches.

To make it easier to organize the code you write in this chapter, you can spread it over multiple files and then have one file (e.g., Rockets.jl), which includes all of them.

That way, you can load just this file into your REPL to get all the code imported. Listing 8.2 assumes you have already made the tanks.jl, engines.jl, and payloads.jl files and want to load all of them in one go.

Listing 8.2 Rockets.jl

```
include("tanks.jl")
include("engines.jl")
include("payloads.jl")
```

This is just a suggestion. You can dump all the code into one file if you find that more practical.

> **IMPORTANT** When changing the definition of a type in your source code, you will need to restart your Julia REPL completely and load your code anew. Changing functions, however, only requires pasting the new code into the REPL to take effect.

To allow a rocket to contain many different types of tanks, make `Tank` an abstract type. Since the medium and large tanks defined in the following listing are subtypes of `Tank`, they can be inserted into any field expecting a `Tank` object.

Listing 8.3 Defining different propellant tanks with fixed capacity

```
abstract type Tank end          ⟵──┤ Make Tank an
                                     abstract type.

mutable struct SmallTank <: Tank   ⟵─┐
    propellant::Float64
end
                                       Mutable to allow
mutable struct MediumTank <: Tank   ⟵─ propellant mass
    propellant::Float64                to change
end

mutable struct LargeTank <: Tank    ⟵─┘
    propellant::Float64
end

# Accessor functions (getters)
drymass(::SmallTank) = 40.0
drymass(::MediumTank) = 250.0
drymass(::LargeTank) = 950.0        drymass and
                                     totalmass are
totalmass(::SmallTank) = 410.0      not stored.
totalmass(::MediumTank) = 2300.0
totalmass(::LargeTank) = 10200.0
```

The dry mass and total mass of these tanks is tied to their type. However, you could also make a flexible tank, where you can set dry mass and total mass to whatever you like, as in the following listing.

Listing 8.4   Propellant tank with flexible capacity

```
mutable struct FlexiTank <: Tank
    drymass::Float64
    totalmass::Float64
    propellant::Float64
end


# Accessors (getters)
drymass(tank::FlexiTank) = tank.drymass
totalmass(tank::FlexiTank) = tank.totalmass
```

At the moment, your tanks are just dumb containers of information. They don't do anything useful, so let's add useful behavior.

Listing 8.5   Adding propellant tank abilities and behavior

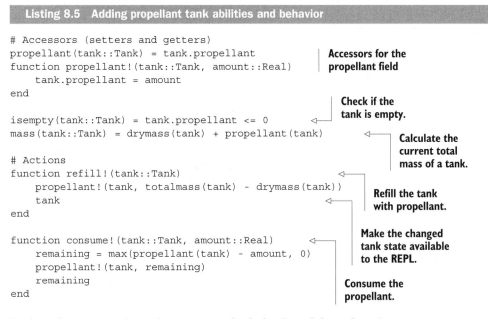

```
# Accessors (setters and getters)
propellant(tank::Tank) = tank.propellant              Accessors for the
function propellant!(tank::Tank, amount::Real)        propellant field
    tank.propellant = amount
end
                                                       Check if the
                                                       tank is empty.
isempty(tank::Tank) = tank.propellant <= 0
mass(tank::Tank) = drymass(tank) + propellant(tank)
                                                       Calculate the
                                                       current total
# Actions                                              mass of a tank.
function refill!(tank::Tank)
    propellant!(tank, totalmass(tank) - drymass(tank))
    tank                                               Refill the tank
end                                                    with propellant.

                                                       Make the changed
function consume!(tank::Tank, amount::Real)            tank state available
    remaining = max(propellant(tank) - amount, 0)      to the REPL.
    propellant!(tank, remaining)
    remaining                                          Consume the
end                                                    propellant.
```

Let's make some tanks to demonstrate the behavior of these functions:

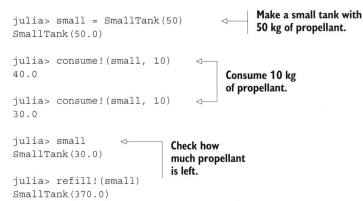

```
julia> small = SmallTank(50)          Make a small tank with
SmallTank(50.0)                        50 kg of propellant.

julia> consume!(small, 10)
40.0
                                       Consume 10 kg
                                       of propellant.
julia> consume!(small, 10)
30.0

julia> small                           Check how
SmallTank(30.0)                        much propellant
                                       is left.
julia> refill!(small)
SmallTank(370.0)
```

```
julia> flexi = FlexiTank(5, 50, 0)
FlexiTank(5.0, 50.0, 0.0)

julia> refill!(flexi)
FlexiTank(5.0, 50.0, 45.0)
```

◁—— **5 kg dry mass, 50 kg total mass, and 0 kg propellant**

In the code example, you are using two different tanks: a small tank and a flexi tank. Although consume! and refill! have only been written to deal with the Tank type, you can use these functions for both SmallTank and FlexiTank because you have implemented drymass and totalmass for all concrete subtypes of Tank.

   propellant and propellant! are implemented on the assumption that all Tank subtypes have a propellant field. That may not always be the case. However, this is not a problem. If you define propellant accessor functions for a concrete Tank subtype, these will always take precedence. When Julia searches through the method list of a function, it always looks for the methods with the most concrete argument types.

> **NOTE**   In object-oriented languages, accessor functions, also known as setters and getters, are important. For instance, in Java, if a type has the propellant field, you might write a GetPropellant and SetPropellant method. In Julia, the equivalent is propellant for getting a value and propellant! for setting a value. However, Julia is not an object-oriented language, so avoid overusing this pattern.

You can use the refill! methods to have tanks automatically filled to the max when constructed.

Listing 8.6   Extra constructors, making it easy to create full tanks

```
function SmallTank()
    refill!(SmallTank(0))
end

function MediumTank()
    refill!(MediumTank(0))
end

function LargeTank()
    refill!(LargeTank(0))
end
```

The code examples have shown there are different ways of modeling a propellant tank. How do you decide which approach to use in your own code? The first approach of having specific types for each capacity, such as having a SmallTank, MediumTank, and LargeTank, potentially saves memory if you are creating a lot of these objects. The number of bytes an object requires to be stored in memory is dependent on the number of fields it has and the size of each field. An Int8 field only consumes one byte, but an Int64 field would consume eight bytes. Each FlexiTank object consumes three times as much space in memory as the fixed tank objects.

However, in the code you are writing, this is of no concern. You don't have very many tanks, and even if you had thousands of tanks, it would not matter. The Flexi-Tank would be a better option, as it offers more flexibility in usage. So why does the book contain definitions of fixed tanks?

By contrasting these different approaches to modeling a tank, you get a better sense of what is possible with Julia's type system. There will be cases where this kind of tradeoff is worth it. For example, imagine simulating a city of millions of people. Each person might have attributes such as position, hunger, tiredness, money in pocket, clothes, shoes, and so on. When dealing with that many objects, you might want to think harder about reducing the size of your objects.

8.2   *Maintaining invariants in your code*

An important concept to know when writing code is *invariants*. Invariants are things that must always be true during execution of your whole program or during some portion of it. This will probably sound very abstract, so let me motivate the need to express invariants by implementing a function, propellant!, which sets the quantity of propellant in a tank.

```julia
julia> tank = FlexiTank(5, 50, 10)          Dry mass 5 kg, total
FlexiTank(5.0, 50.0, 10.0)                  mass 50 kg, and 10 kg
                                            of propellant
julia> propellant!(tank, 100)
100
                                            Set propellant
                                            mass to 100 kg.
julia> totalmass(tank)
50.0

julia> mass(tank)
105.0
```

What is wrong here? You set the mass of the propellant to be larger than the max total mass of the tank. That should not be possible. At any time, the following tank invariant should be true:

```
0 <= propellant(t) + drymass(t) <= totalmass(t)
```

One way to make sure this remains true is modifying the propellant! setter method to throw an exception if the inputs are wrong.

Listing 8.7   Propellant setter maintaining the tank invariant

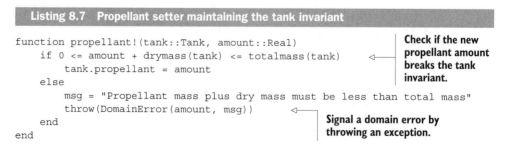

```julia
function propellant!(tank::Tank, amount::Real)          Check if the new
    if 0 <= amount + drymass(tank) <= totalmass(tank)   propellant amount
        tank.propellant = amount                        breaks the tank
    else                                                invariant.
        msg = "Propellant mass plus dry mass must be less than total mass"
        throw(DomainError(amount, msg))
    end                                                 Signal a domain error by
end                                                     throwing an exception.
```

`DomainError` is an exception type defined in Julia's standard library. Domain refers to the set of legal input values for a function argument. Thus, providing an amount larger than the `totalmass` is a domain error.

However, this is not the only way you can end up breaking your tank invariant. Here you are making a tank with 90 kg of propellant, while the total mass can only be 50 kg:

```
julia> t = FlexiTank(5, 50, 90)
FlexiTank(5.0, 50.0, 90.0)

julia> mass(t), totalmass(t)
(95.0, 50.0)
```

Dealing with these problems forces you to learn about how composite objects are created in Julia.

8.3   Making objects with constructor functions

When you define a composite type, Julia creates a special function called a *constructor* with the same name as your type. A constructor is responsible for making an instance (object) of the type it is associated with. Julia adds two methods to the constructor function, which takes the same number of arguments as you have fields. One method uses type annotations for its arguments, as specified for each field in the `struct`. The other takes arguments of `Any` type.

However, you can add methods to this constructor function in the same manner as any other function. You can add methods that create a full tank if the amount of propellant is not specified.

> **Listing 8.8   Creating full tanks when the amount of propellant is not specified**

```
function FlexiTank(drymass::Number, totalmass::Number)
    FlexiTank(drymass, totalmass, totalmass - drymass)
end

MediumTank() = refill!(MediumTank(0))
LargeTank() = refill!(LargeTank(0))
```

If you use `methods`, you can see that a third method has been added to the `FlexiTank` function:

```
julia> methods(FlexiTank)
# 3 methods for type constructor:
 [1] FlexiTank(drymass::Float64, totalmass::Float64, propellant::Float64)   ⊲──┐
 [2] FlexiTank(drymass::Number, totalmass::Number)                             │
 [3] FlexiTank(drymass, totalmass, propellant)                             ⊲───┘
```

New method you've added   **Existing methods defined by Julia**

The following is an example of using these new methods to create full tanks:

```
julia> FlexiTank(5, 50)
FlexiTank(5.0, 50.0, 45.0)        ◁─┤ Automatically filled up
                                       with 45 kg of propellant

julia> MediumTank()
MediumTank(2050.0)        ◁─┐ Filled up with
                             2,050 kg of
julia> LargeTank()           propellant
LargeTank(9250.0)
```

But what do you do if you don't want users of your types to set propellant mass independently? Perhaps you want to reduce the chance of breaking the important tank invariant discussed earlier. Is there, perhaps, a way of preventing Julia from making its own constructor methods?

8.4   Differences between outer and inner constructors

What you have just covered is called *outer constructors*, when using Julia terminology. The constructors are defined *outside* of the composite type definition. Outer constructors add methods to the built-in ones. If, instead, you want to replace Julia's constructor methods with your own, you need to define the constructor functions inside the struct definition, as follows.

Listing 8.9   Defining an inner constructor for FlexiTank

```
mutable struct FlexiTank <: Tank
    drymass::Float64
    totalmass::Float64
    propellant::Float64

    function FlexiTank(drymass::Number, totalmass::Number)        ◁─┐ Notice new
        new(drymass, totalmass, totalmass - drymass)                  replaces
    end                                                               FlexiTank
end
```

Inner constructors introduce you to a special function called new. It is only available inside an inner constructor—nowhere else. You need it because creating an inner constructor removes all constructor methods created by Julia. In other words, you can no longer call any of them.

new is very similar to the default constructor methods provided by Julia, with some important differences: you can supply new with zero or more arguments but never more arguments than the number of fields in your composite type. What happens to the fields you don't provide a value for? They get a random value.

How do you know that your inner constructor replaces all Julia-provided constructor methods? You can reload your REPL environment and test:

```
julia> t = FlexiTank(5, 50)
FlexiTank(5.0, 50.0, 45.0)
```

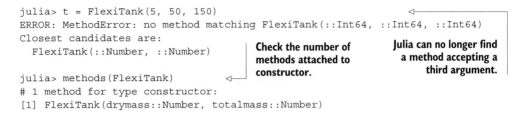

```
julia> t = FlexiTank(5, 50, 150)
ERROR: MethodError: no method matching FlexiTank(::Int64, ::Int64, ::Int64)
Closest candidates are:
  FlexiTank(::Number, ::Number)

julia> methods(FlexiTank)
# 1 method for type constructor:
[1] FlexiTank(drymass::Number, totalmass::Number)
```

Check the number of methods attached to constructor.

Julia can no longer find a method accepting a third argument.

You can now see that methods only reports a single method for the FlexiTank constructor.

8.5 *Modeling rocket engines and payloads*

Let's switch gears and talk about the payload you want to send into space and the rocket engines that will provide the rocket's propulsion. The payload could be a probe; satellite; crew capsule; or, I suppose, a Tesla Roadster if you are Elon Musk.

Listing 8.10 Defining rocket payload

```
struct Payload
    mass::Float64
end
```

This may seem simplistic, but remember you are creating models. Models only contain properties required to answer questions of interest. For example, an initial model of smartphone may just be a block of wood, with no buttons, screen, or color scheme. Why? Because, initially, the questions you want answered are, "Is this shape and size comfortable to carry in my pocket? How much space do you have available to create a screen and electronics inside?"

The same applies to designing and building a rocket. Initially, you are only interested in mass budgets. You want to know things such as the following:

1 How much propellant do I need?
2 How big of a payload can I launch into orbit?
3 How far can a given rocket go?

To answer such questions you *don't* need to include what sort of instruments exist on the space probe or what kind of batteries or solar cells it has in your model. Important attributes of a rocket engine are mass, thrust, and Isp (specific impulse). You can think of thrust as how powerful the engine is and Isp as how fuel efficient it is.

Listing 8.11 Defining a custom rocket engine

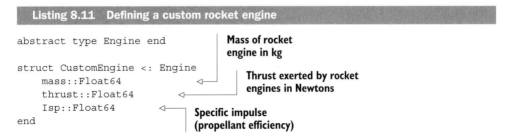

```
abstract type Engine end

struct CustomEngine <: Engine
    mass::Float64
    thrust::Float64
    Isp::Float64
end
```

Mass of rocket engine in kg

Thrust exerted by rocket engines in Newtons

Specific impulse (propellant efficiency)

```
mass(engine::CustomEngine) = engine.mass
thrust(engine::CustomEngine) = engine.thrust
Isp(engine::CustomEngine) = engine.Isp
```

You can also define types for specific engines with known properties, such as the Rutherford engine used in the Electron rocket and the Merlin engine used in the Falcon 9 rocket.

Listing 8.12   Defining the Rutherford and Merlin rocket engines

```
struct Rutherford <: Engine end          Engines are
struct Merlin <: Engine end              empty structs.

mass(::Rutherford) = 35.0                Use accessor
thrust(::Rutherford) = 25000.0           functions to get
Isp(::Rutherford) = 311.0                engine properties.

mass(::Merlin) = 470.0
thrust(::Merlin) = 845e3
Isp(::Merlin) = 282.0
```

thrust is the force produced by the rocket engine. If you know the total mass of the rocket you can calculate how much the whole rocket accelerates once the rocket engines are fired up. You get this from Newton's second law, which states that force F is proportional to mass m times acceleration a.

$$F = ma \iff a = \frac{F}{m}$$

However, to know how much mass you are pushing at any given time, you need to know how much propellant the engine consumes each second. Thrust alone cannot tell you that; you need specific impulse (Isp). A high-Isp engine is more propellant efficient, meaning it will consume less propellant for the same amount of thrust.

NOTE   In physics, you usually denote impulse with an *I*. Thus *Isp* clarifies you are referring to *specific impulse.*

Isp is analogous to gas mileage for a car. However, unlike a car on the road, a rocket in outer space continues moving even without thrust, so you cannot measure fuel efficiency (or propellant efficiency) by how far one kg of propellant gets you. Instead, you measure it in terms of how many seconds a unit of propellant can sustain a force of 1 G (the force of gravity on Earth). This allows you to calculate mass flow (consumption of propellant per second):

```
                              m/s² acceleration of              The amount of mass
                              gravity on Earth                  exiting the engine is
g = 9.80665                                                     measured in kg/s.
function mass_flow(thrust::Number, Isp::Number)
    thrust / (Isp * g)
end
```

You can, for example, use this to calculate the propellant consumed per second in a Falcon 9 rocket. It has nine Merlin 1D engines, each with a specific impulse of 282 s and thrust of 845 kN:

```
julia> engine_thrust = 845e3
845000.0

julia> isp = 282
282

julia> thrust = engine_thrust * 9
7.605e6

julia> flow = mass_flow(thrust, isp)
2749.979361594732
```

So you get that a Falcon 9 rocket consumes an estimated 2.7 tons of propellant each second.

8.6 Assembling a simple rocket

Now you have all the pieces to assemble your rocket. So let the rocket building start!

Listing 8.13 Rocket with payload, tank, and engine

```
struct Rocket
    payload::Payload
    tank::Tank
    engine::Engine
end
```

You will make a rocket resembling the Electron rocket manufactured by Rocket Lab.[1] It can put a payload into low Earth orbit weighing 300 kg. You will make one stage of this rocket with a small tank and a Rutherford engine. The Rutherford engine, a small rocket engine, is used in the first and second stage of the Electron rocket.

For compactness I have instructed the REPL not to print the value of the first three assignments by tacking on a semicolon ; . You can remove the semicolon to see the difference:

```
julia> payload = Payload(300);

julia> tank = SmallTank();

julia> engine = Rutherford();

julia> rocket = Rocket(payload, tank, engine)
Rocket(Payload(300.0), SmallTank(370.0), Rutherford())
```

---

[1] Rocket Lab is a space company originating in New Zealand, which launches small satellites of a few hundred kg into orbit.

If you know a bit about rocketry, you may realize there are multiple problems with the previous rocket configuration:

1 The real-world Electron rocket has nine Rutherford engines, not just one.

2 Space rockets have multiple stages, which separate as the rocket goes higher; your rocket only has a single stage.

8.7   Creating a rocket with multiple stages and engines

Let's fix these problems. An important insight is realizing that a multistage rocket is a bit like a Russian Matryoshka doll.[2] You could make the payload of rocket another rocket. The payload of this next rocket could be another rocket and so on. Figure 8.2 illustrates how a staged rocket is composed of multiple nested rockets.

It shows a multistage rocket, where you keep popping off the top to expose the rocket's payload. Let me cover each numbered stage:

1 The whole multistage rocket with all parts is called a *space vehicle*. The first stage is called the *booster*.

2 Pop open the space vehicle, and the *second stage* rocket is exposed.

3 The payload of the second stage is the *third stage*.

4 The third stage is protected by a *fairing*, a protective shell for the payload (your model will ignore the fairing).

5 When the launch is finished, the final payload is delivered into space. This payload will be a *spacecraft*, such as a satellite, moon lander, or capsule.

To make it possible to put rockets inside rockets, you will change Rocket to an abstract type and define new concrete subtypes, as follows.

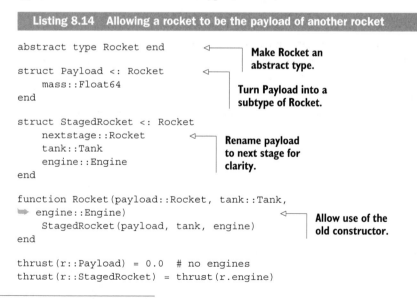

> **Listing 8.14   Allowing a rocket to be the payload of another rocket**

```
abstract type Rocket end              ◁——  Make Rocket an
                                            abstract type.
struct Payload <: Rocket              ◁——  Turn Payload into a
    mass::Float64                           subtype of Rocket.
end

struct StagedRocket <: Rocket
    nextstage::Rocket                 ◁——  Rename payload
    tank::Tank                              to next stage for
    engine::Engine                         clarity.
end

function Rocket(payload::Rocket, tank::Tank,
    engine::Engine)                   ◁——  Allow use of the
    StagedRocket(payload, tank, engine)     old constructor.
end

thrust(r::Payload) = 0.0  # no engines
thrust(r::StagedRocket) = thrust(r.engine)
```

---

[2] A *matryoshka* is a Russian nesting doll. Each doll has a smaller wooden doll inside.

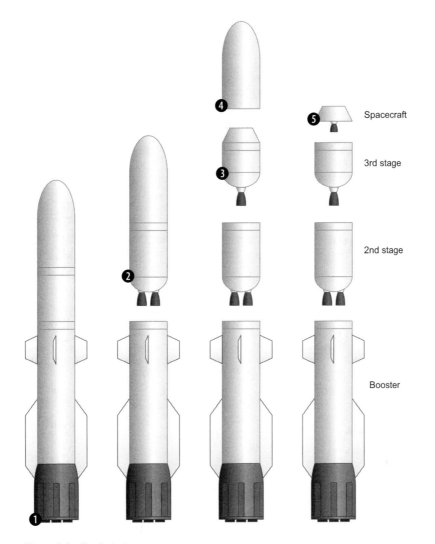

Figure 8.2   Rocket stages

But before you build a rocket, you need some more adjustments. The real-life Electron rocket has nine Rutherford engines in the first stage—what we call the booster. You currently have no way to add more than one engine. To solve this, you will define a new engine subtype called Cluster. This new type is designed to model a cluster of many identical engines.

Figure 8.3 doesn't show every type. For instance, I could only get space for the MediumTank and FlexiTank under the abstract Tank type.

Using hollow arrows, the diagram shows how StagedRocket and Payload are subtypes of the abstract type Rocket. The filled arrow shows that StagedRocket has a field, nextstage, that points to another Rocket object.

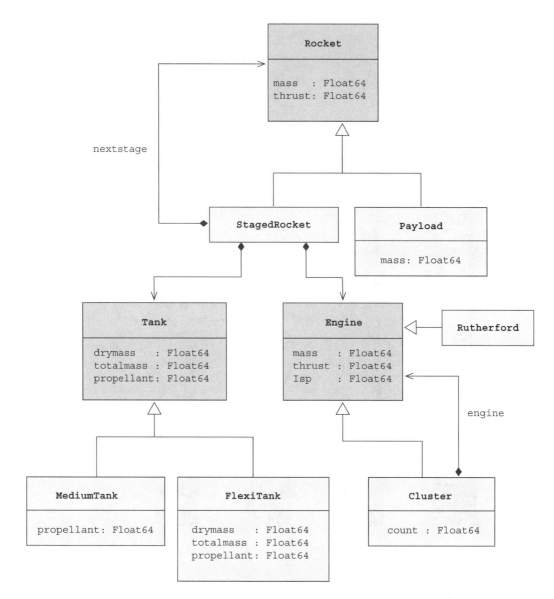

Figure 8.3   A UML diagram of relations between different parts of a rocket

Let's look at how to implement the Cluster type (listing 8.15). The UML diagram says
it is both a subtype of Engine and it points to another engine through the engine field.

Listing 8.15   Defining a cluster of rocket engines

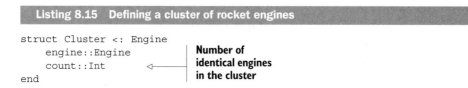

```
struct Cluster <: Engine
    engine::Engine
    count::Int          Number of
                        identical engines
end                     in the cluster
```

```
Isp(cl::Cluster) = Isp(cl.engine)
mass(cl::Cluster) = mass(cl.engine) * cl.count
thrust(cl::Cluster) = thrust(cl.engine) * cl.count
```

You will notice that the specific impulse does not change. Fuel efficiency does not change just because you add more engines. However, adding more engines will increase the mass of the cluster as well as the total thrust.

> **WHAT ABOUT A HETEROGENOUS ENGINE CLUSTER?**   Could you make a cluster of engines of different types? The challenge is deciding how to calculate the Isp of a cluster in which each engine has a different specific impulse. You will, however, make a heterogenous cluster of engines in chapter 12.

You can use these abstractions to define a function, `update!`, that takes care of depleting propellant as you simulate your rocket flying. You simulate by performing small time steps Δt.

This is a common strategy employed when writing simulations of real-time systems. When simulating something complex with many parts, it becomes too complicated to perform an analytical solution by solving a single math equation. Video games are made like this as well. Every object moving around in a game will have an `update!` function akin to the one shown in the following listing.

Listing 8.16   Updating the propellant mass after Δt time has elapsed

```
function update!(r::StagedRocket, t::Number, Δt::Number)
    mflow = mass_flow(thrust(r), Isp(r.engine))
    consume!(r.tank, mflow * Δt)
end

# Payload has no tanks with propellant to consume
update!(r::Payload, t::Number, Δt::Number) = nothing
```

Say you want to make a three-stage Electron rocket. The third stage is tiny and, thus, only needs a very tiny engine. The company developing the Electron rocket is making a tiny engine, named Curie, for this purpose. The full specifications for this engine are not yet known, so you will define this engine based on some guesswork.

Listing 8.17   Defining a tiny engine for the third stage

```
struct Curie <: Engine end

mass(::Curie) = 8.0          ⟵┐   Mass and
thrust(::Curie) = 120.0      │    Isp had to
Isp(::Curie) = 317.0         ⟵┘   be guessed.
```

The only known specification

You now have enough functionality to define an Electron rocket composed of multiple stages:

```julia
julia> payload = Payload(300)
Payload(300.0)

julia> thirdstage = Rocket(payload, SmallTank(), Curie())
StagedRocket(Payload(300.0), SmallTank(370.0), Curie())

julia> secondstage = Rocket(thirdstage, MediumTank(), Rutherford())
StagedRocket(StagedRocket(Payload(300.0),
                   SmallTank(370.0),
                   Curie()),
         MediumTank(2050.0),
         Rutherford())

julia> booster = Rocket(secondstage, LargeTank(), Cluster(Rutherford(), 9))
StagedRocket(StagedRocket(StagedRocket(
                   Payload(300.0),
                   SmallTank(370.0),
                   Curie()),
               MediumTank(2050.0),
               Rutherford()),
         LargeTank(9250.0),
         Cluster(Rutherford(), 9))
```

Later, when performing physics calculations, it is helpful to abstract away how a property, such as mass, is determined for a rocket or part of a rocket.

Listing 8.18   Calculating the total mass of a staged rocket

```julia
mass(payload::Payload) = payload.mass

function mass(r::StagedRocket)
    mass(r.nextstage) + mass(r.tank) + mass(r.engine)
end
```

You can see the benefits of abstraction of mass in how `mass(r::StagedRocket)` is defined. After implementing this function you don't have to concern yourself with details about the payload (`nextstage`). It could be a payload or another staged rocket with 20 stages. You don't have to know; the differences are abstracted away.

Likewise, you don't have to concern yourself with whether you are getting the mass of a single engine or an engine cluster. Imagine you had implemented this function *before* creating the `Cluster` type. You would not need to change this implementation because as long as `Cluster` is of type `Engine` and has implemented `mass`, everything works.

8.8 *Launching a rocket into space*

The `update!` function allows you to keep track of propellant consumption. When called, it gives you the remaining propellant. When this quantity has reached zero, you know your rocket cannot fly much higher, as the velocity will steadily decline until it becomes negative. You will implement a new function, launch!, which figures out the altitude your rocket reaches before it runs out of propellant, as well as how much time has passed when that occurs.

The rocket is pushed up with a certain force determined by the thrust of the engines T. However, this force has to work against the forces of gravity. Gravity exerts force on a rocket proportional to the mass m of the rocket and the acceleration g of gravity on Earth:

$$F = T - mg$$

From this you can determine the acceleration of the rocket when it is launched:

$$a = \frac{F}{m} \iff a = \frac{T - mg}{m}$$

During the discussion on update! I noted you are simulating the launch as a set of small time increments Δt. For one small time increment you can find how much the velocity changes in that increment (figure 8.4).

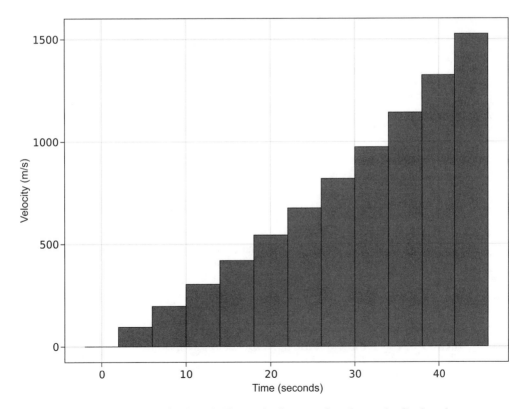

Figure 8.4 **Velocity of rocket after launch. The x-axis shows number of seconds after launch.**

These observations are the basis for implementing the `launch!` function. You add up changes in velocity, Δv, over many small time increments. For every increment, you assume velocity is constant and use that to calculate distance traveled $\Delta h = v \times \Delta t$. Adding up all the distances traveled across every little increment you get the total distance traveled, h.

This calculation can be visualized with a plot. Every bar is equal to Δh because each bar is Δt wide and v tall. Thus, adding up the area of all the bars is equal to the distance traveled. The smaller you make the increments Δt, the more accurate the calculation will become:

$$\Delta v = a\Delta t$$

In mathematical terms you are performing an approximation of the integral of the velocity. The code in listing 8.19 is an implementation of these ideas.

NOTE The code uses a cutoff point of 1,000 seconds. The rocket may not have consumed all fuel within that time if you use large tanks. You could use a while loop instead, but you would risk an infinite loop.

Listing 8.19   Simulating a rocket launch and determining the maximum altitude of the rocket

```julia
function launch!(rocket::Rocket, Δt::Real)
    g = 9.80665   # acceleration caused by gravity
    v = 0.0       # velocity
    h = 0.0       # altitude (height)

    for t in 0:Δt:1000                    ← Stop the simulation at 1,000 seconds.
        m = mass(rocket)                  ← Mass changes because
        F = thrust(rocket) - m*g            propellant is consumed.

        remaining = update!(rocket, t, Δt)

        # Any propellant and thrust left?
        if remaining == 0 || F <= 0
            return (t, h)                 ← Return time spent
        end                                 and distance traveled

        h += v*Δt                         ← Use velocity from
        a = F/m                             the previous time
        v += a*Δt                           increment.
    end
end
```

I put the `launch!` function into a file called simulate.jl, but you can just paste it into the REPL. You can then construct a rocket and launch it:

```julia
julia> engine = Rutherford();
julia> tank = SmallTank();
julia> payload = Payload(300);
julia> rocket = Rocket(payload, tank, engine)
```

```
julia> launch!(rocket, 0.5)
(45.0, 31117.8036364191)
```

From the output, you can see that your rocket spent 45 seconds getting to an altitude of about 31 kilometers. For real rockets this will be different because they have to deal with air resistance. You basically launched this rocket on an Earth without atmosphere. You can see that all the fuel in the tank has been spent:

```
julia> tank
SmallTank(0.0)
```

As an exercise, you can try launching the rocket with different payload and tank sizes. Do you notice that larger tanks don't always get you further? This is because they cause the gravitational pull on your rocket to increase. Thus the force of gravity may end up being stronger than the force of thrust from your rocket engine.

This simulated launch has a number of limitations beyond not considering air resistance. The simulation is also unable to deal with staged rockets.

Summary

- You can define your own custom constructors to make sure objects are initialized with valid values.
- An inner constructor replaces the default constructor provided by Julia. Outer constructors are just convenient constructors defined outside the composite type definition.
- An abstract type is defined with, for example, `abstract type Payload end`. Abstract types cannot have fields, and you cannot make objects of them (you cannot instantiate an abstract type).
- Both abstract and concrete types can be a subtype of another abstract type. However, no concrete type can be a subtype of another concrete type. `<:` is the subtype operator.
- Combining abstract types with multiple dispatch allows you to abstract away differences between related types, so they can be used interchangeably.

Conversion and promotion

9

This chapter covers

- Conversion of one related type to another
- How promotion finds the least common denominator among related types in an expression
- Exploring the Julia standard library using the `@edit` macro

Julia and other mainstream programming languages handle arithmetic involving different number types so effortlessly that most of us likely don't pay much attention to this fact:

```julia
julia> 3 + 4.2          ⟵┐  Numbers in the expression
7.2                        │  converted to floating-point numbers
```

```julia
julia> UInt8(5) + Int128(3e6)    ⟵┐  All integers
3000005                             │  converted to Int128
```

```julia
julia> 1//4 + 0.25
0.5
```

In reality, doing this involves quite a lot of complexity. Under the hood, most programming languages have defined a set of *promotion rules*, which say what should be done if you combine numbers of different types. Promotion rules make sure all the numbers are converted to a sensible common number type that can be used in the final calculation. Don't confuse number conversion with parsing text strings to produce numbers.

You might wonder why you should care about these concepts. Mastering Julia's promotion and conversion system opens the door to a deeper insight into how numbers work in Julia. That will make you capable of doing a wide variety of tasks, such as the following:

- Defining custom number types
- Defining a physical units system and performing conversions between different units

The main programming example in this chapter will do just that: define a unit system for different types of angles, such as degrees and radians. I will then demonstrate how the Julia promotion and conversion system can combine different angle types in the same expression.

But why create numbers with units? Why not let numbers be numbers? Because a lot of mistakes happen in software development because feet, meters, and other units get mixed up. By using numbers with units you can reduce the number of bugs in your software.

In many cases in Julia it doesn't matter what order the arguments are. For instance, if you want to check if two geometric objects overlap, then `overlap(circle, triangle)` should give the same result as `overlap(triangle, circle)`. You could imagine a similar situation when simulating battle between different types of warriors in a video game. The Julia promotion system provides an elegant technique for handling such cases without implementing the same algorithms twice.

9.1 Exploring Julia's number promotion system

Inside a microprocessor, mathematical operations are always performed between identical types of numbers. A microprocessor does not have an instruction to add an integer to a floating-point number. Microprocessors always perform arithmetic operations between identical number types.

Thus, when dealing with expressions composed of different number types, all higher-level programming languages have to convert all arguments in the expression to the same number type. But what should this common number type be? Figuring out this common type is what promotion is all about.

We express this as promoting arguments of mathematical operators to a common type. In most mainstream languages, the mechanisms and rules governing number promotion are hardwired into the language and detailed in the specifications of the language.

NOTE You will see the term *type coercion* used in other programming languages. Coercion is implicit conversion carried out by the compiler. Julia's compiler does not do that, and thus *coercion* does not occur in Julia.

Julia takes a radically different approach. In Julia, numbers are first-class objects. They are not special types with unique hardwired rules. Julia promotion rules are defined in the standard library, not in the internals of the Julia JIT compiler. That provides the benefit of you, as a developer, being able to extend the conversion and promotion system yourself. You can add new number types as well as new rules.

But doesn't that increase the risk of developers messing up the number type system? No, because you *extend* the existing system; you don't *modify* it.

Promotion rules are handled by plain-old Julia functions. Hooking into the existing system is simply a matter of adding your own methods to existing functions. You can explore the Julia source code for promotion using the `@edit` macro.

Julia environment variable setup

For the `@edit` macro to work, you need to have set the `JULIA_EDITOR` environment variable. This will depend on your operating system. For example, I use the fish shell. It requires modifying the startup configuration, `$HOME/.config/fish/config.fish`, by adding the following line:

```
set -x JULIA_EDITOR mate
```

If you use the bash shell you would modify the `$HOME/.profile` file instead:

```
export JULIA_EDITOR=mate
```

Both examples work on macOS and Linux. Windows users would use a GUI dialog to modify the `JULIA_EDITOR` environment variable. Alternatively, Windows users can install a Unix shell.

In the following snippet you are adding an integer and floating-point number. By prefixing with the `@edit` macro, Julia jumps to the definition of the function being called to handle this expression, allowing you to have a look at the source code.

```
julia> @edit 2 + 3.5
```

Everything is a function!

It is worth being aware that almost everything in Julia is a function call. When you write `3 + 5`, that is syntactic sugar for calling a function named + like this: `+(3, 5)`. Every function using a symbol such as +, -, *, and so on supports being used in prefix form.

The following code shows how every arithmetic operation on some `Number` in Julia first calls `promote` before performing the actual arithmetic operation.

Listing 9.1   Definition of arithmetic operations on numbers in Julia's standard library

```
+(x::Number, y::Number) = +(promote(x,y)...)
*(x::Number, y::Number) = *(promote(x,y)...)
-(x::Number, y::Number) = -(promote(x,y)...)
/(x::Number, y::Number) = /(promote(x,y)...)
```

The ... is called the *splat* operator, which you can use to turn arrays or tuples into function arguments. This means foo([4, 5, 8]...) is the same as foo(4, 5, 8). You can also use it to turn the tuple returned by promote into arguments to the various arithmetic functions, including +, -, *, and so on. You can perform some experiments in the Julia REPL to better understand how the promote function works:

```
julia> promote(2, 3.5)
(2.0, 3.5)

julia> typeof(1//2), typeof(42.5), typeof(false), typeof(0x5)
(Rational{Int64}, Float64, Bool, UInt8)

julia> values = promote(1//2, 42.5, false, 0x5)
(0.5, 42.5, 0.0, 5.0)

julia> map(typeof, values)
(Float64, Float64, Float64, Float64)
```

This shows that promote returns a tuple of numbers converted to the most appropriate common type. However, for everyday programming you can use typeof instead to figure out what an expression will get promoted to.

9.2   *Understanding number conversion*

Number conversion means converting from one type of number to another. This should not be confused with parsing. For instance, a text string can be parsed to produce a number, but a string and a number are not related types; hence you should not call it a conversion.

The recommended and simplest way of doing number conversion in Julia is to use the constructor of the type you want to convert to. So if you have a value x and you want to convert to some type T, then just write T(x). I'll provide some examples:

```
julia> x = Int8(32)
32

julia> typeof(x)
Int8

julia> Int8(4.0)
4

julia> Float64(1//2)
0.5
```

```
julia> Float32(24)
24.0f0
```

Keep in mind that a conversion is not always possible to perform:

```
julia> Int8(1000)
ERROR: InexactError: trunc(Int8, 1000)

julia> Int64(4.5)
ERROR: InexactError: Int64(4.5)
```

An 8-bit number cannot hold values larger than 255 ($2^8 - 1$), and integers cannot represent decimals.

In many cases, conversions are done implicitly by Julia. Julia uses the `convert` function to achieve this, not the constructor. However you are free to call `convert` explicitly yourself. Here is a demonstration:

```
julia> convert(Int64, 5.0)          ◁─┐  Convert floating-point
5                                      │  number 5.0 to integer 5.

julia> convert(Float64, 5)           ◁─┐  Convert integer 5 to
5.0                                    │  floating-point number 5.0.

julia> convert(UInt8, 4.0)
0x04

julia> 1//4 + 1//4
1//2

julia> convert(Float32, 1//4 + 1//4)
0.5f0
```

Notice the first argument in these function calls `Int64`, `Float64`, and so on. These are type objects. Types are first-class objects in Julia, meaning they can be handled like any other object. You can pass them around, store them, and define methods that operate on them. Type objects even have a type. The type of `Int64` is `Type{Int64}`, and for `Float64` it is `Type{Float64}`:

```
julia> 3 isa Int64              ◁─┐  Number 3 is of type Int64.
true

julia> Int64 isa Type{Int64}    ◁─┐  Type Int64 is of
true                               │  type Type{Int64}.

julia> "hi" isa String
true

julia> String isa Type{String}
true
                                   ┐  Type Int64 is not of
julia> Int64 isa Type{String}    ◁─┘  type Type{String}.
 false
```

You can almost think about Type as a special kind of function. Feeding this "function" an argument T returns the type of T. Formally, Type is a paramatric type, which can be parameterized with a type argument T to produce a concrete type. Don't worry if this does not make sense; it is a complex topic, and I explain this topic more thoroughly in the next chapter.

The convert function is called implicitly when performing various types of assignments, including the following:

- Assigning to an array element
- Setting the value of the field of a composite type
- Assigning to local variables with a type annotation
- Returning from a function with a type annotation

Let's look at some examples demonstrating implicit conversion:

```julia
julia> values = Int8[3, 5]
2-element Vector{Int8}:
 3
 5

julia> typeof(values[2])
Int8

julia> x = 42
42

julia> typeof(x)
Int64

julia> values[2] = x
 42
```

Assigning an Int64 value to an array element defined to be Int8, which causes convert(Int8, x) to be called

In the next example, you create a composite type Point with the fields x and y. Next, you create an instance p of Point and assign an 8-bit integer value to its x field. Since the field is of type Float64, an implicit number conversion happens.

```julia
julia> mutable struct Point
           x::Float64
           y::Float64
       end

julia> p = Point(3.5, 6.8)
Point(3.5, 6.8)

julia> p.x = Int8(10)
 10
```

Causes convert(Float64, Int8(10)) to be called

Here a type annotation is added to a function to make sure the return value is of a certain type. If it is not, a conversion is attempted with convert:

```
julia> foo(x::Int64) :: UInt8 = 2x
foo (generic function with 1 method)

julia> y = foo(42)
0x54

julia> typeof(y)
UInt8
```

Next, we will get into the details of how conversion and promotion is done using a larger code example.

9.3   *Defining custom units for angles*

In general, calculations within science can easily go wrong if you mix up units. For instance, in the petroleum industry, mixing feet and meters is easy because the coordinates of an oil well are usually given in meters, while the depth of the well is given in feet.

A famous example is the Mars Climate Orbiter (http://mng.bz/m2l8), a robotic space probe launched by NASA, which was lost due to NASA and Lockheed using different units of measure. NASA was using metric units, and Lockheed used US customary units, such as feet and pounds. Thus, there is an advantage in designing code where one does not accidentally mix up units.

In this example we will demonstrate working with different units for angles. In mathematics, angles are usually given as radians, while people navigating using maps will tend to use degrees. When using degrees, you split up the circle in 360 degrees. One degree is, thus, 1/360th of the circumference of that circle.

With radians, in contrast, we deal with how many times the radius of a circle is duplicated along the circumference to get that angle (figure 9.1). So 1 radian is the angle you get when you mark off a distance along the circumference equal to the radius of the circle.

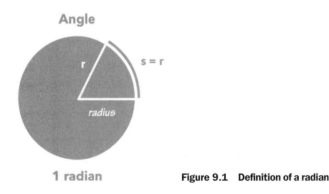

Figure 9.1   Definition of a radian

Degrees, in contrast, are more strongly tied to navigation—celestial navigation in particular. Each day the earth moves about 1 degree around the sun, since the year is made up of 365 days. An angle is further divided into 60 arcminutes, and an arcminute is divided into 60 arcseconds.

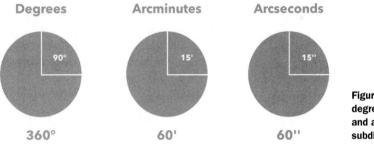

Figure 9.2 **How degrees, arcminutes, and arcseconds are subdivided**

Actually, you can work with both metric degrees and degrees, minutes, seconds (DMS), but you are working with DMS here to keep things interesting.

In this code example you will implement the following functionality:

- `Radian` and `DMS` types to represent different types of angle units
- Constructors to make it easier to construct angle objects, given degrees, arcminutes, and arcseconds
- Operations on angle types, such as addition and subtraction
- Accessors to extract degrees, minutes, and seconds
- Extending the `show` function to create a pretty display of different angle units
- Extending the `convert` function to support conversion from one angle unit to another
- Overriding the `sin` and `cos` functions to only work with angle units
- Coupling together some clever tricks to make pretty number literals for angle units
- Extending the `promotion_rule` function, so different angle units can be used in the same expression

Let's start by implementing the `Radian` and `DMS` angle types.

Listing 9.2 Defining radians and degrees as subtypes of the abstract `Angle` type

```
abstract type Angle end

struct Radian <: Angle
    radians::Float64
end

# Degrees, Minutes, Seconds (DMS)
struct DMS <: Angle
    seconds::Int
end
```

As in the rocket example, you have defined an abstract type, `Angle`, which all the concrete angle units are subtypes of. The benefits of this will become clear later.

9.3.1   *Defining angle constructors*

That DMSs are stored as seconds should be regarded as an implementation detail and not exposed to the user. Hence, users should not use that constructor directly. Instead, you will define more natural constructors, as follows.

Listing 9.3   Angle constructors for degrees, minutes, and seconds

```
Degree(degrees::Integer) = Minute(degrees * 60)
Degree(deg::Integer, min::Integer) = Degree(deg) + Minute(min)

function Degree(deg::Integer, min::Integer, secs::Integer)
    Degree(deg, min) + Second(secs)
end

function Minute(minutes::Integer)
    DMS(minutes * 60)
end

function Second(seconds::Integer)
    DMS(seconds)
end
```

9.3.2   *Defining arithmetic operations on angles*

To be able to actually run these constructors you need to be able to add together DMS numbers. The code snippet `Degree(deg) + Minute(min)` basically does a `DMS(deg, 0, 0) + DMS(0, min, 0)`. However, the + operator has not been defined for DMS types. Nor have you defined them for radians, so let's do both in the following listing.

Listing 9.4   Arithmetic for DMS and radian angles

```
import Base: -, +

+(Θ::DMS, α::DMS) = DMS(Θ.seconds + α.seconds)
-(Θ::DMS, α::DMS) = DMS(Θ.seconds - α.seconds)

+(Θ::Radian, α::Radian) = Radian(Θ.radians + α.radians)
-(Θ::Radian, α::Radian) = Radian(Θ.radians - α.radians)
```

I'll clarify how this works. As discussed in section 7.3.3, defining a method in Julia will automatically create a function if no corresponding function already exists. For example, if the + function is not imported, Julia will not know that it already exists when you define +*methods*. Thus, Julia will create an entirely new +*function* and attach your angle-specific methods to it.

THE MAIN AND BASE MODULES   All Julia types and functions belong to a module. You can think of a module as a namespace or library. Most of the functionality that comes bundled with Julia is in the module called `Base`. Previously, you have used the `Statistics` module. Functions and types you have not explicitly made part of a named module become part of the `Main` module. Every function and type you create in the Julia REPL is part of the `Main` module.

If you then try to evaluate 3 + 4, Julia will attempt a lookup of matching methods on this newly defined + function. But it has no methods dealing with regular numbers, only for angles. Thus, if you had forgotten to write `import Base: +`, you would have gotten this error message:

```
julia> 3 + 4
ERROR: MethodError: no method matching +(::Int64, ::Int64)
You may have intended to import Base.+
```

Essentially, you end up shadowing the + function defined in `Base` and its attached methods. By doing import, you are essentially telling Julia you want to add methods to a function defined in an existing module, such as `Base`. If you don't do that, your newly defined + function will become part of the `Main` module. Everything defined in the REPL that has not been imported from somewhere else is made part of the `Main` module.

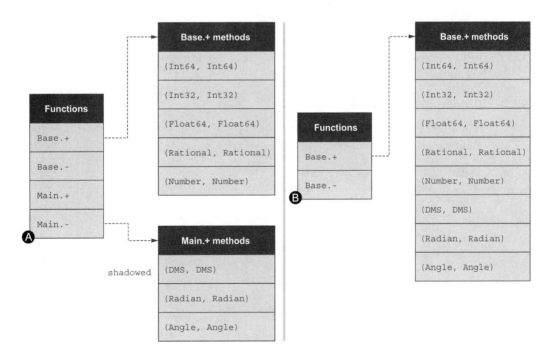

Figure 9.3 Shadowing of functions that occurs when you don't import functions before extending them

Figure 9.3 is an illustration of the shadowing problem. Function list A is what you get when you don't import + and - from `Base` before adding methods to these functions.

The result is two separate method tables for each operator: one for `Base` and another for `Main`. In the B example + and - were imported; thus, the methods are added to the method table defined by `Base`, rather than a new method table in the `Main` module being created.

9.3.3 *Defining accessors to extract degrees, minutes, and seconds*

Given an angle in DMS, let's discover the degrees, minutes, and seconds part in the following listing.

Listing 9.5 Degree and minute accessors for DMS objects

```
function degrees(dms::DMS)
    minutes = dms.seconds ÷ 60
    minutes ÷ 60
end

function minutes(dms::DMS)
    minutes = dms.seconds ÷ 60
    minutes % 60
end

seconds(dms::DMS) = dms.seconds % 60
```

You can use these functions to provide a custom display of these angles on the Julia REPL. To write that the angle is 90 degrees, 30 arcminutes, and 45 arcseconds you would use the notation 90° 30' 45''.

9.3.4 *Displaying DMS angles*

If you use the constructors now, the display you get out of the box isn't very good. It exposes the internal representation of DMS degrees as being made up of arcseconds:

```
julia> α = Degree(90, 30, 45)
DMS(325845)

julia> degrees(α)
90

julia> minutes(α)
30

julia> seconds(α)
45

julia> β = Degree(90, 30) + Degree(90, 30)
DMS(651600)

julia> degrees(β)
181

julia> minutes(β)
0
```

You can define an alternative view by adding a method to the Julia show function. The Julia REPL environment uses the show(io::IO, data) to display data of some specific type to the user. Remember in Julia you can define methods to work on generic abstract types; however, you can also add methods dealing with more concrete types, which is what you would want to do in this situation.

Listing 9.6 Defining string representation of `Radian` and `DMS` objects

```
import Base: show

function show(io::IO, dms::DMS)
    print(io, degrees(dms), "° ", minutes(dms), "' ", seconds(dms), "''")
end

function show(io::IO, rad::Radian)
    print(io, rad.radians, "rad")
end
```

You will learn more about the show and IO objects in chapter 11. But for now, this gives you a nice way of looking at DMS angles:

```
julia> α = Degree(90, 30, 45)
90° 30' 45''

julia> β = Degree(90, 30) + Degree(90, 30)
181° 0' 0''
```

9.3.5 Defining type conversions

Now that you have the basics in place, you want to be able to do something useful with these angles. You may want to use them with functions such as sin and cos, but these just take plain numbers that are radians. You need to define conversions, so DMS angles can be turned into radians.

Listing 9.7 Definining methods for direct and indirect type conversion

```
import Base: convert

Radian(dms::DMS) = Radian(deg2rad(dms.seconds/3600))
Degree(rad::Radian) = DMS(floor(Int, rad2deg(rad.radians) * 3600))

convert(::Type{Radian},  dms::DMS)   = Radian(dms)   ⟵──┐  Convert the
convert(::Type{DMS},     rad::Radian) = DMS(rad)     ⟵──  DMS value to a
                                 Convert the Radian  │    Radian value.
                                 value to a DMS value.┘
```

This contains a number of new things I'll discuss in greater detail. Notice that the convert method definitions don't specify the name of the argument, only its type. This is similar to the rocket example, where you defined the mass of a Rutherford engines as

```
mass(::Rutherford) = 35
```

You could have written engine::Rutherford, but what would the point be? The Rutherford composite type did not have any fields you could access. Likewise Type{Radian} and Type{DMS} don't have any fields you are interested in accessing in the convert definition. With these conversions in place you can implement versions of sin and cos that take numbers with units as arguments.

Listing 9.8 Overriding standard sin and cos functions to use DMS and Radian

```
sin(rad::Radian) = Base.sin(rad.radians)
cos(rad::Radian) = Base.cos(rad.radians)

sin(dms::DMS) = sin(Radian(dms))
cos(dms::DMS) = cos(Radian(dms))
```

In this case you are not importing sin and cos before creating the methods. This is because you actually want to shadow the *real* sin and cos functions, since you don't want people to accidentally call these functions using plain numbers. You want them to use radians or degrees explicitly:

```
julia> sin(?/2)
ERROR: MethodError: no method matching sin(::Float64)
You may have intended to import Base.sin

julia> sin(90)
ERROR: MethodError: no method matching sin(::Int64)
You may have intended to import Base.sin

julia> sin(Degree(90))
1.0

julia> sin(Radian(?/2))
1.0
```

Now you cannot accidentally use an angle as input to a trigonometric function without having specified whether it is given in radians or degrees.

9.3.6 *Making pretty literals*

This is nice, but it would look a lot better if you could write sin(90°) instead of sin(Degree(90)) and sin(1.5rad) instead of sin(Radian(1.5)).

In fact, you can achieve this. Observe that Julia interprets 1.5rad as 1.5*rad. Thus by defining multiplication of regular scalars with units of degrees or radians you have *magically* solved the problem.

Listing 9.9 Operations and constants to allow pretty angle literals

```
import Base: *, /

*(coeff::Number, dms::DMS) = DMS(coeff * dms.seconds)
*(dms::DMS, coeff::Number) = coeff * dms
/(dms::DMS, denom::Number) = DMS(dms.seconds/denom)
```

```
*(coeff::Number, rad::Radian) = Radian(coeff * rad.radians)
*(rad::Radian, coeff::Number) = coeff * rad
/(rad::Radian, denom::Number) = Radian(rad.radians/denom)

const ° = Degree(1)
const rad = Radian(1)
```

The last two lines show the secret sauce. They mean 90° is read by Julia as 90 *
Degree(1), which, when computed, will result in Degree(90):

```
julia> sin(90°)
1.0

julia> sin(1.5rad)
0.9974949866040544

julia> cos(30°)
0.8660254037844387

julia> cos(90°/3)
0.8660254037844387

julia> sin(3rad/2)
0.9974949866040544
```

9.3.7   *Type promotions*

The simple but labor-intensive way of adding support for doing arithmetic with different angle units would mean defining lots of functions with all possible combinations. Imagine you had another angle type: MetricDegree. It would quickly cause a combinatorial explosion, as shown in the following listing.

Listing 9.10   Combinatorial explosion of arithmetic operations

```
+(α::DMS, β::Radian)          = Radian(α) + β
+(α::MetricDegree, β::DMS)    = α + MetricDegree(β)
+(α::Radian, β::MetricDegree) = α + Radian(β)
+(α::Radian, β::DMS)          = α + Radian(β)
```

I have not even shown all the combinations. The point I am making is that you get many combinations that are hard to manage. Instead, the better solution is defining generic functions for different units, as shown in the following listing.

Listing 9.11   Simplifying arithmetic operations by utilizing promotion

```
+(Θ::Angle, α::Angle) = +(promote(Θ, α)...)
-(Θ::Angle, α::Angle) = -(promote(Θ, α)...)
```

The only remaining problem is that you have not told promote how to promote angle types. It only knows about Number types. A first guess of how to add the temperature type would be adding another promote method, but that's not how it works. Instead,

promote does its job by calling a function called promote_rule. You need to register
your types by defining promote_rule methods for *your* types.

Listing 9.12   Defining type promotion of Radian and DMS

```
import Base: promote_rule

promote_rule(::Type{Radian}, ::Type{DMS}) = Radian
```

These methods are unusual, as all the arguments are type objects. In addition, you
haven't given a name to any of the arguments because the type objects are not used for
anything but getting multiple dispatch to select the correct method of the promote_
rule function.

The promote_rule function takes two type objects as arguments and returns
another type object:

```
julia> promote_rule(Int16, UInt8)
Int16

julia> promote_rule(Float64, UInt8)
Float64

julia> promote_rule(Radian, DMS)
Radian
```

You can pose the promotion rule as the following question: given two different types,
what type should they all be promoted to? Now you have put all the pieces in place.
You have plugged into the Julia convert and promote machinery by implementing
methods for the convert and promote_rule functions:

```
julia> sin(90° + 3.14rad/2)
0.0007963267107331024

julia> cos(90° + 3.14rad/2)
-0.9999996829318346

julia> 45° + 45°
90° 0' 0''

julia> Radian(45° + 45°)
1.5707963267948966rad

julia> 45° + 3.14rad/4
1.5703981633974484rad
```

This example gives you a hint about the advantages of using a multiple-dispatch language, such as Julia. Implementing this behavior using object-oriented programming
is harder and gets increasingly difficult as you add more types into the mix. If you
defined each angle as a class, you would need several methods for every operation—
one for each type.

And there are more practical problems with the object-oriented approach. Should you ever need to add another angle unit, it will require the following:

1 Adding another class with four methods for each operator
2 Modifying every other angle class, including the base class, `Angle`, by adding a version of each operator handling the new angle unit
3 Adding another constructor in each class to handle the new angle unit (to allow conversion)

This obviously does not scale, and it breaks the open–close principle[1] in object-oriented programming. The open–close principle can be summed up in the following saying: *open for extension, closed for modification.*

If angle units were provided as a library, you could not extend it with other units without modifying the library itself. That is obviously impractical.

Julia elegantly solves this by *not* making functions a part of the types. Thus, you can add new constructor functions to a type without modifying the type definition itself. Adding `convert` and `promote_rule` functions does not require modification of the library providing the types you are attempting to define promotion rules and conversion for.

Summary

- Type promotion is handled in Julia by defining promotion rules. This is done by adding methods to the `promote_rule` function.
- Conversion of a value x to a type `T` is accomplished via two different approaches: `T(x)` and `convert(T, x)`. The latter is used when dealing with implicit conversions.
- An object x can have a type `T`. `Type{T}` is the type of a type object `T`. This knowledge helps you to add methods to the `convert` function correctly.
- By defining your own promotion rules and conversion functions, you can add new number types to Julia or add units such as degrees, meters, feet, celsius, or fahrenheit to Julia numbers. Units help make numerical code more robust. New number types can help improve accuracy in calculations, reduce memory requirements, and improve performance.
- To add methods to a function defined in another module, you need to explicitly import those functions from the module. If you don't, you will end up shadowing those functions, which will usually not provide your desired result.

---

[1] *Object Oriented Software Construction*, Bertrand Meyer, Prentice Hall, 1988, p 23.

Representing
unknown values

This chapter covers

- Understanding how undefined values are used
- Representing the absence of a value with the `Nothing` type
- Dealing with values that exist but are unknown using the `Missing` type

Something important to deal with in any programming language is representing the absence of a value. For a long time, most mainstream programming languages, such as C/C++, Java, C#, Python, and Ruby, had a value called `null` or `nil`, which is what a variable would contain if it did not have any value. More accurately phrased: `null` or `nil` indicates that a variable is not bound to a concrete object.

When would this be useful? Let's use Julia's `findfirst` function as an example. It locates the first occurrence of a substring:

```
julia> findfirst("hello", "hello world")      ⟵───┐  Substring
1:5                                                 └  hello found.

julia> findfirst("foo", "hello world")         ⟵───┐  Substring foo
                                                    └  not found.
```

But how do you indicate that a substring cannot be found? Languages such as Java, C#, and Python would use the `null` or `nil` keywords to indicate this. However, it is not without reason its inventor, British computer scientist Tony Hoare, called the null pointer his billion-dollar mistake.

It makes it difficult to write safe code because any variable could be null at any given time. In programs written using languages supporting null, you need a lot of boilerplate code performing null checks. That is because it is unsafe to perform operations on null objects.

For this reason, modern languages have tended to avoid having null objects or pointers. Julia does not have a generic null object or pointer. Instead, it has a variety of types representing unknown or absent values. This chapter will teach you more about these different types, how to use them, and when to use them.

10.1   *The nothing object*

The closest thing to `null` Julia has, is the `nothing` object of type `Nothing`. It is a simple concrete type defined in Julia, as shown in the following listing.

> **Listing 10.1   Nothing type and nothing constant as defined by Julia**

```
struct Nothing
    # look, no fields
end

const nothing = Nothing()
```

The `nothing` object is an instance of the type `Nothing`. However, every instance of `Nothing` is the same object. You can test that yourself in the REPL:

```
julia> none = Nothing()

julia> none == nothing
true

julia> Nothing() == Nothing()
true
```

However, there is *nothing* magical going on here. When you call the constructor of a composite type with zero fields, you always get the same object returned. To state this in more formal terms: for a type `T` with no fields, every instance `t` of type `T` is the same object. This example should help clarify:

```
julia> struct Empty end

julia> empty = Empty()
Empty()

julia> none = Empty()
Empty()
```

```
julia> empty == none
true

julia> Empty() == Empty()
true
```

Instances of different empty composite types are, however, considered different. Hence Empty() does not return the same object as Nothing():

```
julia> Empty() == Nothing()
false

julia> empty = Empty()
Empty()

julia> empty == nothing
false
```

Empty composite types make it easy to make special-purpose objects in Julia, which you want to assign special meaning. By convention, Julia uses nothing to indicate that something could not be found or does not exist:

```
julia> findfirst("four", "one two three four")
15:18

julia> findfirst("four", "one two three")

julia> typeof(ans)
Nothing

julia> findfirst("four", "one two three") == nothing
true
```

10.2 Using nothing in data structures

The multistage rocket is similar to a more generic data structure called a *linked-list*. Just like with the rocket example, it can often be useful to chain together multiple objects. You could, for example, use this to represent a train made up of multiple wagons holding some cargo. The following definition will not work. Can you determine why?

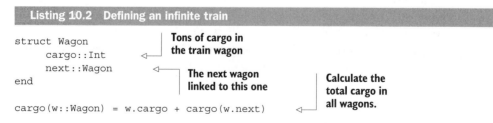

Listing 10.2   Defining an infinite train

```
struct Wagon                    Tons of cargo in
    cargo::Int                  the train wagon
    next::Wagon
end                             The next wagon
                                linked to this one        Calculate the
cargo(w::Wagon) = w.cargo + cargo(w.next)                 total cargo in
                                                          all wagons.
```

There is no way of building a train made out of these wagons with the definition we have given. I'll clarify with an example:

```
train = Wagon(3, Wagon(4, Wagon(1, Wagon(2, ....))))
```

There is no way to end this chain of wagons. Every `Wagon` constructor requires a wagon object as its second argument. To illustrate an infinite chain of wagons I inserted …. in the code example. The `next` field always has to be a `Wagon`. But what if you made `Wagon` an abstract type instead? That is one possible solution, which was already employed in the multistage rocket example.

Remember, not every `Rocket` subtype had a next stage field. However, in this chapter I will introduce a more generic solution to this problem, utilizing *parametric types*. This will just cover the basics, since chapter 18 is completely devoted to parametric types.

> **IMPORTANT**   Parametric types may look like an add-on feature only of interest to advanced Julia programmers. However, I have deliberately minimized usage of parametric types in the code examples. Real-world Julia code uses parametric types extensively. Parametric types are crucial for type correctness, performance, and reducing code duplication.

10.2.1 *What is a parametric type?*

You were exposed to parametric types when I defined ranges and pairs. If `P{T}` is a parametric type P, then `T` is the type parameter. I know this sounds very abstract, but it will become a lot clearer with some examples:

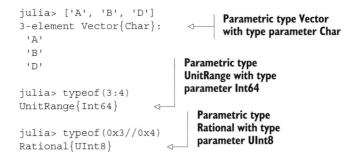

You can think of `Vector` as a template to make an actual type. To make an actual concrete vector you need to know the types of the elements in the vector. In the first example, the type parameter is `Char` because each element is a character. For `Unit-Range`, the type parameter represents the type of the start and end of the range. For `Rational`, the type parameter specifies the type of the nominator and denominator in a fraction.

Type parameters are to parametric types what values are to functions. You input a value to a function and get a value out:

```
y = f(x)
```

You input `x` to function `f` and get value `y` out. One could make the same analogy for parametric types:

```
S = P{T}
```

You input the type T to P and get the type S out. You can demonstrate this with some actual Julia types:

```
julia> IntRange = UnitRange{Int}
UnitRange{Int64}
```
◁─── **Create a range type called IntRange.**

```
julia> FloatRange = UnitRange{Float64}
UnitRange{Float64}
```
◁─── **Make a range type based on floating-point numbers.**

```
julia> IntRange(3, 5)
3:5
```

```
julia> FloatRange(3, 5)
3.0:5.0
```
◁─── **Construct a range using the custom range type.**

```
julia> NumPair = Pair{Int, Float32}
Pair{Int64, Float32}
```

```
julia> NumPair(3, 5)
3 => 5.0f0
```

```
julia> 3 => 5
3 => 5
```

In this example you can see how types can be treated much like objects. You make new type objects and bind them to variables IntRange, FloatRange, and NumPair. These custom types are then used to instantiate different types of objects.

10.2.2 *Using union types to end the wagon train*

Union is a parametric type. You can supply it with multiple type parameters to construct a new type. Union types are special in that they can serve as placeholders for any of the types listed as type parameters. Alternatively, you can think of union types as a way of combining two or more types into one type.

Say you have types named T1, T2, and T3. You can create a union of these types by writing Union{T1, T2, T3}. This creates a new type, which can be a placeholder for any of those types. This means if you wrote a method with the signature f(x::Union{T1, T2, T3}), this particular method would get called whenever x was of type T1, T2 or T3. Let's look at a concrete example:

```
julia> f(x::Union{Int, String}) = x^3
f (generic function with 1 method)
```

```
julia> f(3)
27
```

```
julia> f(" hello ")
" hello  hello  hello "
```

```
julia> f(0.42)
ERROR: MethodError: no method matching f(::Float64)
```

```
Closest candidates are:
  f(!Matched::Union{Int64, String}) at none:1
```

The last example fails because x is a floating-point number, and we have only defined a method for function f taking a union of Int and String. Float64 is not included.

Every type included in a type union will be counted as a subtype of that union. You use the <: operator to either define a subtype or test whether a type is a subtype:

```
julia> String <: Union{Int64, String}
true

julia> Int64 <: Union{Int64, String}
true

julia> Float64 <: Union{Int64, String}
false

julia> Union{Int64, String} == Union{String, Int64}
 true
```

Type parameter order does not matter.

The ordering of type parameters in a Union definition does not matter, as shown by the last evaluated expression. Armed with union types you can solve your problem with infinite trains.

Listing 10.3 Defining a finite train

```
struct Wagon
    cargo::Int
    next::Union{Wagon, Nothing}
end

cargo(w::Wagon) = w.cargo + cargo(w.next)
cargo(w) = 0
```

The next linked wagon can be nothing.

Values that are not wagons have no cargo.

Reload your Julia REPL, and paste in the new type definition. This code will allow you to create a finite chain of wagons. Notice how two cargo methods have been defined. You have two different cases to deal with, since next can be either a Wagon or nothing:

```
julia> train = Wagon(3, Wagon(4, Wagon(1, nothing)))
Wagon(3, Wagon(4, Wagon(1, nothing)))

julia> cargo(train)
8

julia> train = Wagon(3, Wagon(4, Wagon(1, 42)))
ERROR: MethodError: Cannot `convert` an object of type Int64
to an object of type Wagon
```

Attempt to use 42 as the next wagon.

The last example was included to demonstrate that due to the Union definition, next can only be a Wagon or a Nothing object. Therefore, setting next to an integer, such as 42, is not legal. It causes the Julia type system to protest loudly by throwing an exception.

10.3   *Missing values*

Missing values are represented in Julia with the `missing` object, which is of type `Missing`. This seems very similar to `nothing`, so why do you need it?

This comes about because Julia aims to be a good language for academics doing scientific computing, statistics, big data, and so on. In statistics, missing data is an important concept. It happens all the time because in almost any data collection for statistics there will be missing data. For instance, you may have a situation in which participants are filling out forms and some of them fail to fill out all the fields.

Some participants may leave a study before it is finished, leaving those who conduct the experiment with incomplete data. Missing data can also exist due to errors in data entry. So unlike the concept of `nothing`, missing data actually exists in the real world. We simply don't know what it is.

Specialized software for statisticians, such as R (see https://www.r-project.org) and SAS (see https://www.sas.com), has long established that missing data should propagate rather than throw exceptions. This means that if a missing value is introduced in any part of a larger calculation, the whole calculation evaluates to `missing`. Julia has chosen to follow this convention as well. Let's look at what that means in practice.

Listing 10.4   Comparing behavior of `missing` and `nothing` in mathematical expressions

```julia
julia> missing < 10
missing

julia> nothing < 10
ERROR: MethodError: no method matching isless(::Nothing, ::Int64)

julia> 10 + missing
missing

julia> 10 + nothing
ERROR: MethodError: no method matching +(::Int64, ::Nothing)
```

You can see in listing 10.4 that every mathematical operation involving a `missing` value evaluates to `missing`, unlike `nothing`, which causes exceptions to be thrown. The rationale for this is that a lot of serious mistakes have been made in statistical work in the past, stemming from not noticing there are missing values. Since `missing` spreads like a virus in Julia, an unhandled `missing` value will quickly get caught.

Missing can be handled explicitly. For instance, if you want to calculate the sum or averages of an array that may contain missing values, you can use the `skipmissing` function to avoid attempting to include missing values in the result:

```julia
julia> using Statistics

julia> xs = [2, missing, 4, 8];

julia> sum(xs)
missing
```

The presence of a missing value pollutes the whole calculation, causing the result to be missing.

```
julia> sum(skipmissing(xs))
14

julia> median(skipmissing(xs))
4.0

julia> mean(skipmissing(xs))
4.666666666666667
```

You skip the missing values, so you can add up the non-missing values.

10.4 Not a number

Somewhat related to missing values is the floating-point number NaN (not a number). You get NaN as a result when the result of an operation is undefined. This typically becomes an issue when dividing zero by zero:

```
julia> 0/0
NaN

julia> 1/0
Inf

julia> -1/0
-Inf
```

In this case Inf stands for *infinity* and is what you get when dividing a number other than zero by zero. This makes some sense. As the divisor approaches zero, the result tends to grow larger.

It is tempting to consider NaN as similar to missing and that they are interchangeable. After all, NaN also propagates through all calculations.

Listing 10.5 Propagation of NaN in mathematical operations

```
julia> NaN + 10
NaN

julia> NaN/4
NaN

julia> NaN < 10
false

julia> NaN > 10
false
```

However, NaN comparisons return false. The following reason is why you should *not* use NaN for missing values: if you have a mistake in your algorithm that causes a 0/0 to happen, you will get NaN. This will be indistinguishable from having missing values as input.

Listing 10.6   Cannot distinguish between calculation causing NaN or input being NaN

```
julia> calc(x) = 3x/x;

julia> calc(0)
NaN

julia> calc(NaN)
NaN
```

You may falsely believe your algorithm is working because it is removing missing values in the calculation, thus masking a defect. For example, in listing 10.6 you are not checking if the input x is zero before dividing. Thus when x is 0, you get a NaN as result. If you pass NaN as input to the calc function in order to indicate a missing value, then you are unable to make a distinction between a programmer mistake and a missing value.

10.5   Undefined data

Undefined data is something you rarely encounter in Julia, but it is worth being aware of. Undefined data occurs when a variable or field of a struct has not been set. Usually, Julia tries to be smart about this; if you define a struct with number fields, Julia will automatically initialize them to zero if you don't do anything. However, if you define a struct without telling Julia what the type of its fields are, Julia has no way of guessing what the fields should be initialized to.

Listing 10.7   Defining a composite type, instantiated with undefined values

```
julia> struct Person
           firstname
           lastname
           Person() = new()
       end

julia> friend = Person()
Person(#undef, #undef)

julia> friend.firstname
ERROR: UndefRefError: access to undefined reference
```

Julia allows the construction of composite objects with uninitialized fields. However, it will throw an exception if you try to access an uninitialized field. There are no benefits to having uninitialized values, but they help catch programmer mistakes.

10.6   Putting it all together

Distinguishing between each of these concepts of *nothing* can be a bit daunting, so I'll briefly summarize the differences: nothing is the *programmer's* type of null. It is what a programmer wants when something does not exist. missing is the *statistician's* type of null. It is what they want when a value is missing in their input data. NaN indicates that somewhere in your code there was an illegal math operation. In other words, this has to do with calculations and not with the statistical collection of data. *Undefined* is when you, the programmer, forgot to do your job and initialize all used data. Most likely, it points to a bug in your program.

As a final reminder: Julia does *not* have null in the common sense because you need to explicitly allow for a nothing value using type unions. Otherwise, a function argument cannot accidentally pass a nothing value.

Summary

- Unknown values in Julia are represented by nothing, missing, NaN, and undefined.
- nothing is of type Nothing and indicates something doesn't exist. Use as return value when a find function fails or in data structures (e.g., to terminate a linked list).
- missing is data that exists but which is missing, such as in a survey. It is of type Missing. When implementing code that reads in statistical data from a file, use missing as a placeholder for data which is missing.
- NaN is the result of illegal math operations. Should your function return NaN, you should investigate whether you have made a programming mistake. For example, are you making sure 0/0 never happens in your code?
- Undefined is when a variable was not initialized to a known value.
- Neither nothing nor missing are built-in values in the language, but they are defined as composite types without any fields.
- The Union parameterized type is practical to use with Nothing and Missing types. For instance, if a field can be either a string or nothing, define the type as Union{Nothing, String}.

Part 3

Collections

Collections are objects that store and organize other objects. In this part you look at unique features and capabilities of collections, such as arrays, sets, and strings. However, you also delve into what is common across all collections, such as iterating over all the elements in a for loop and higher-order functions, such as `map`, `filter`, and `reduce`. I briefly covered collections in the part 1, but here I go deeper on each topic.

Working with strings

11

This chapter covers

- Understanding the relationships between Unicode, code points, and UTF-8 encoding
- Comparing strings, converting them to lowercase, and performing other string operations
- When and how to use raw strings
- Learning about different kinds of string literals, including regular expressions, MIME types, and `BigInt` literals

You've already had some hands-on experience working with strings in earlier chapters; however, I'll cover many more details that will help you correctly use text strings in this chapter. In this chapter you will examine these details more closely. As long as you are working with the letters A–Z, things will be simple. However, there are a multitude of languages in the world with their own unique set of characters that Julia needs to be able to deal with.

That means the minimal required knowledge for working effectively with Julia strings includes some knowledge of *Unicode*. Unicode is the international standard for mapping numbers (code points) to characters.

Julia also has support for special string literals to aid in performing a variety of tasks. For example, there are special strings called *regular expressions* that allow you to check whether another string matches a particular pattern, such as an email address, IP address, or zip code.

11.1 UTF-8 and Unicode

Text strings in Julia are Unicode, encoded in UTF-8 format. But what does that mean, and why should you care? I'll walk you through a simple example illustrating the importance of understanding Unicode better.

Æser is the plural of *norse gods* in Norwegian. It is a four-letter word, as confirmed with the length function:

```
julia> length("Æser")
4
```

But when attempting to access individual characters in the word, you will notice something strange:

```
julia> "Æser"[1]                                        Works as
'Æ': Unicode U+00C6 (category Lu: Letter, uppercase)    expected
```

```
julia> "Æser"[2]                      You get an exception. Trying to
ERROR: StringIndexError("Æser", 2)    access the character s at index 2
                                      apparently doesn't work.
```

```
julia> "Æser"[3]
's': ASCII/Unicode U+0073 (category Ll: Letter, lowercase)
```

```
julia> "Æser"[4]
'e': ASCII/Unicode U+0065 (category Ll: Letter, lowercase)
```

Instead, the second character is at
index 3. Does this seem strange?

How about another word? *Þrúðvangr* is the name of the realm of the Norse god Thor:

```
julia> length("Þrúðvangr")
9
```

```
julia> "Þrúðvangr"[9]
'a': ASCII/Unicode U+0061 (category Ll: Letter, lowercase)
```

This is a nine-character word, but the character at index 9 is the sixth character, 'a'. What is going on here? To understand, you need to understand Unicode and how Julia strings support it through the UTF-8 encoding:

```
julia> sizeof("Æser")        Æser is encoded
5                            with 5 bytes.
```

```
julia> sizeof("Þrúðvangr")       Þrúðvangr is encoded
12                              with 12 bytes.
```

In UTF-8, every character is encoded into one to 4 bytes. Normal letters, such as A, B, and C, will take just 1 byte, while letters such as Æ, Þ, and ð, which are not used in the English language, will typically require more than 1 byte to encode. However, before I delve further into how Julia deals with this, it is useful to understand some key concepts in Unicode that are not specific to the Julia programming language.

11.1.1 Understanding the relation between code points and code units

Unicode and character encodings are complex topics many developers will struggle with at some point. Understanding the history of why Unicode and UTF-8 exist will provide important context for understanding.

Both standards evolved from the older ASCII standard, which encoded every character as 8 bit. Numbers 65 to 90 would encode letters from A–Z, and numbers 97 to 122 would encode lowercase letters a–z. You can explore the relation between ASCII codes and their corresponding characters in the Julia REPL using the constructor for the Char type:

```
julia> Char(65)
'A': ASCII/Unicode U+0041

julia> Char(90)
'Z': ASCII/Unicode U+005A
```

To deal with different languages, one would need to operate with different interpretations of these numbers from 1 to 255. However, this quickly became impractical. You could not, for example, mix text written using different alphabets on the same page. The solution was Unicode, which aimed to give a unique number to every character in the world—not just those in the Latin alphabet but also for Cyrillic, Chinese, Thai, and all the Japanese character sets.

The number given to each character is called a *code point* in Unicode terminology (https://www.unicode.org/glossary/#code_point). Originally, it was believed 16 bits would be enough to store every Unicode code point. 16 bits gives $2^{16} - 1 = 65,535$ unique numbers. Thus, one of the first Unicode encodings, UCS, used 16 bits (2 bytes) to encode every Unicode code point (https://www.unicode.org/glossary/#UCS).

Later it was determined that this would not be enough, and there would need to be 4 bytes (32 bits) to encode every possible Unicode character. At this point the UCS approach started to look flawed for the following reasons:

1 UCS was already incompatible with 8-bit ASCII code.
2 A total of 4 bytes for every character would consume a lot of space.

UTF-8 encoding solved these problems by using a variable number of bytes per character (https://www.cl.cam.ac.uk/~mgk25/ucs/utf-8-history.txt). That way, frequently used characters could be encoded with a single byte, saving space. The 1-byte characters were intentionally made backward compatible with ASCII.

With variable length character encoding a distinction between the *code point* of a character and the *code units* required to encode the character needs to be made. Every Unicode character has one number, the code point, that identifies it. Code units are used to store these code points in memory. UTF-8 requires a variable number of code units to do that (figure 11.1).

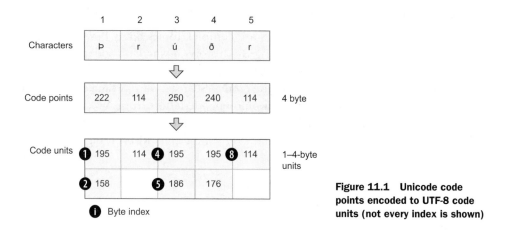

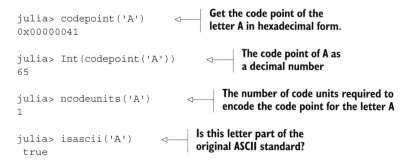

Figure 11.1 **Unicode code points encoded to UTF-8 code units (not every index is shown)**

UCS, in contrast, has fixed-sized code units. Each UCS code unit is 16 bit. Figure 11.1 illustrates the relationship between characters, code points, and code units. Every gray block for the code points represents 4 bytes. A variable number of code units are required for each character. Therefore they have been stacked to show which bytes are related to the same character. The black balls give the byte index of some of the code units making up the characters. To help clarify these concepts, you will engage in some hands-on experimentation with Unicode characters in the Julia REPL:

```
julia> codepoint('A')          ⟵  Get the code point of the
0x00000041                         letter A in hexadecimal form.

julia> Int(codepoint('A'))     ⟵  The code point of A as
65                                 a decimal number

julia> ncodeunits('A')         ⟵  The number of code units required to
1                                  encode the code point for the letter A

julia> isascii('A')            ⟵  Is this letter part of the
 true                              original ASCII standard?
```

Let's explore characters that are not part of the original ASCII standard. They should have more than one code unit and not return true when isascii() is called:

```
julia> codepoint('Æ')
0x000000c6
```

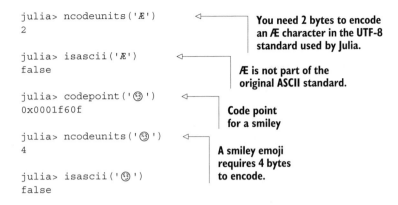

```
julia> ncodeunits('Æ')
2
```
You need 2 bytes to encode an Æ character in the UTF-8 standard used by Julia.

```
julia> isascii('Æ')
false
```
Æ is not part of the original ASCII standard.

```
julia> codepoint('😏')
0x0001f60f
```
Code point for a smiley

```
julia> ncodeunits('😏')
4
```
A smiley emoji requires 4 bytes to encode.

```
julia> isascii('😏')
false
```

There is no isUnicode function because every Julia character is a Unicode character. isascii is simply a way to test whether a given Unicode character is also part of the original ASCII standard.

Just typing letters at the REPL will also give you useful information when the character literal is evaluated:

```
julia> 'A'
'A': ASCII/Unicode U+0041 (category Lu: Letter, uppercase)

julia> 'Æ'
'Æ': Unicode U+00C6 (category Lu: Letter, uppercase)

julia> '😏'
'😏': Unicode U+1F60F (category So: Symbol, other)
```

Notice how this tells you what the Unicode code point number is.

> **TIP** You can use backslash \ and the Tab key to easily write unusual characters not present on your keyboard. For instance, to write 😏, type \:smirk: in the Julia REPL, and press Tab, to get a completion.
>
> You can even press Tab after writing just \: to get a full list of possible emojis. Norwegian letters such as ÆØÅ, which I occasionally use in my examples, can easily be written on a Mac by simply holding down the option key and entering character O, A, or ' (English keyboard layout). For other operating systems, switch to Norwegian keyboard layout or copy the letters.

Unicode code points can be written explicitly in Julia in various ways:

```
julia> '\U41'
'A': ASCII/Unicode U+0041 (category Lu: Letter, uppercase)

julia> Char(0x41)
'A': ASCII/Unicode U+0041 (category Lu: Letter, uppercase)

julia> '\U00c6'
'Æ': Unicode U+00C6 (category Lu: Letter, uppercase)
```

```
julia> Char(0xc6)
'Æ': Unicode U+00C6 (category Lu: Letter, uppercase)

julia> '\U01f60f'
'😏': Unicode U+1F60F (category So: Symbol, other)

julia> Char(0x01f60f)
'😏': Unicode U+1F60F (category So: Symbol, other)
```

You can combine these with map to create various ranges. For instance a range does not need to be merely written as numbers. 'A':'F', for example, is a perfectly valid range:

```
julia> map(lowercase, 'A':'F')
6-element Vector{Char}:
 'a'
 'b'
 'c'
 'd'
 'e'
 'f'

julia> map(codepoint, 'A':'F')
6-element Vector{UInt32}:
 0x00000041
 0x00000042
 0x00000043
 0x00000044
 0x00000045
 0x00000046
```

And you can, of course, go the opposite direction as well:

```
julia> map(Char, 65:70)
6-element Vector{Char}:
 'A'
 'B'
 'C'
 'D'
 'E'
 'F'
```

Given that the number of a character and its index is not entirely correlated, you must take care when working with strings and indices. You should use the lastindex and nextind functions, which also work for non-strings, as demonstrated with the following example:

```
julia> xs = [4, 5, 3]

julia> i = firstindex(xs)
1
```

◁— **Get the index of the first element. Thus, you don't have to assume the first element is at index 1. You can make Julia arrays with different start indices.**

```
julia> while i <= lastindex(xs)
          println((i,xs[i]))
          i = nextind(xs, i)
       end
(1, 4)
(2, 5)
(3, 3)
```

Check if you have
reached the last index.

Finds the index of the
element following index
i in array xs

In the following listing you can see if you do this with a string, the logic is entirely
the same.

Listing 11.1   Iterating over characters in a string using a while loop

```
julia> s = "Þrúðvangar"

julia> i = firstindex(s)
1

julia> while i <= lastindex(s)
          println((i, s[i]))
          i = nextind(s, i)
       end
(1, 'Þ')
(3, 'r')
(4, 'ú')
(6, 'ð')
(8, 'v')
(9, 'a')
(10, 'n')
(11, 'g')
(12, 'a')
(13, 'r')
```

Notice you skip from
index 1 to 3, going
from Þ to r.

Going from ð to v
requires skipping
index 7.

By using these functions, you abstract away the difference between strings and regular
arrays. You can see this in how, for example, nextind is implemented in the standard
library. For arrays it is just a simple increment:

```
nextind(::AbstractArray, i::Integer) = Int(i)+1
```

For strings this is a much more complex operation. I will only show parts of the implementation, edited for clarity.

Listing 11.2   Excerpt of the base implementation of nextind for strings

```
function nextind(s::String, i::Int)
    i == 0 && return 1
    n = ncodeunits(s)
    between(i, 1, n) || throw(BoundsError(s, i))
    l = codeunit(s, i)
    (l < 0x80) | (0xf8 =< l) && return i+1
```

```
    if l < 0xc0
        i' = thisind(s, i)
        return i' < i ? nextind(s, i') : i+1
    end
    …
end
```

For normal code, you don't need to deal with `nextind` and `lastindex`. Instead, you use for loops, since they will automatically fetch a whole character on each iteration:

```
julia> for ch in "Þrúðvangar"
           print(ch, " ")
       end
Þ r ú ð v a n g a r
```

If you need the indices of each character, use the `eachindex` function:

```
julia> for i in eachindex(s)
           print(i, s[i], " ")
       end
1Þ 3r 4ú 6ð 8v 9a 10n 11g 12a 13r
```

11.2 *String operations*

Working with text is such a common thing to do that it pays to be aware of the possibilities that exist in the language. My intention is not to show every single string operation that exists but to give an idea of what is possible.

I tend to frequently use Julia as an assistant when working with other programming languages. I use Julia for transforming code in different ways. I'll walk you through an example. In many programming languages it is common to see these sorts of variations in text formatting of identifiers:

- `FooBar`—Pascal case (upper camel case); it is a frequently used style for types or classes. It is sometimes used for constants.
- `foo_bar`—Snake case; it is often used for the name of variables, methods and functions.
- `fooBar`—Camel case (lower camel case); it is frequently used for methods and variable names.
- `FOO_BAR`—Upper snake case; it is often used for constants and enum values.
- `foo-bar`—Kebab case; you will find this in LISP programs and configuration files.

I will demonstrate several ways of converting between these styles and how you can turn them into handy utility functions for aiding your programming.

The following is my typical process for developing a simple function to do something: Since I am not certain about how an unfamiliar function works, I first try it out. Then I gradually combine it with more function calls to get what I want. Eventually, I have enough to implement my function.

Listing 11.3   Iterative development of a camel case function

```julia
julia> s = "foo_bar"
"foo_bar"

julia> split(s, '_')
2-element Vector{SubString{String}}:
 "foo"
 "bar"

julia> uppercasefirst("foo")
"Foo"

julia> map(uppercasefirst, split(s, '_'))
2-element Vector{String}:
 "Foo"
 "Bar"

julia> join(["Foo", "Bar"])
"FooBar"

julia> join(map(uppercasefirst, split(s, '_')))
"FooBar"

julia> camel_case(s::AbstractString) = join(map(uppercasefirst,
                                            split(s, '_')))
camel_case (generic function with 1 method)
```

Now you have a function that will do the conversion, but often you want to be able to do this quickly. Select some text in your code editor that is in snake case and which you want to turn into camel case and paste back in.

  This is where Julia's `clipboard()` function comes in handy. It can both read from and write to the clipboard. The clipboard is the place where everything you copy resides.

> **WARNING**   On Linux the `clipboard` function will not work unless you have the `xsel` or `xclip` commands installed. On Debian or Ubuntu you can install these with the following:
>
> ```
> $ sudo apt-get install xsel
> ```
>
> On Red Hat or Fedora Linux you can them install with the following:
>
> ```
> $ sudo yum install xsel
> ```

In listing 11.4, a method is added to the `camel_case` function, which does not take any string arguments but, instead, reads the clipboard. Just mark some text and copy it before running `clipboard()`. I marked the first part of this paragraph.

Listing 11.4   Turn text in the clipboard into camel case

```julia
julia> s = clipboard()
"HiHowAreYou"

julia> function camel_case()
           s = camel_case(clipboard())
           clipboard(s)
           s
       end
```

`clipboard()` gets the contents of the clipboard, while `clipboard(s)` stores the content of s on the clipboard. Whenever you are coding and want to change a snake case text to camel case, you can follow these steps:

1 Copy the text.
2 Switch to your open Julia REPL.
3 Start typing came…, and press the up-arrow key. This should complete to `camel_case()` if you called it before. Alternatively, press Tab.
4 Go back to the editor, and paste the result.

Using the Julia REPL more efficiently

To work quickly with Julia it is important to become accustomed to all the hotkeys. The up-arrow key is used to quickly search through your history. If you start writing a few letters it will filter that history to only match history beginning with those first letters.

The Tab key is used to complete a word matching a function Julia knows about. That could be a built-in one or one you have defined yourself.

Ctrl-A and Ctrl-E are used to jump to the beginning and end of a line in the Julia REPL. Say you just wrote

```julia
map(uppercasefirst, split(s, '_'))
```

You may want to alter this to

```julia
join(map(uppercasefirst, split(s, '_')))
```

Press up arrow to get back the line you just wrote. Press Ctrl-A, to jump to the beginning of the line. Write `join(`. Finally, press Ctrl-E to jump to the end, and write `)`.

11.2.1 Converting from camel case to snake case

Let's look at code for going the other direction. In this case using the `split` function will not work, but why? In this case you cannot split on a specific character; however, `split` can take functions instead of characters to decide where to split. To split on whitespace, use `split(s, isspace)`, so you could try to use the `isuppercase` function. It checks whether a character is uppercase. That is useful, since you split where characters are uppercase:

```julia
julia> isuppercase('a')
false

julia> isuppercase('A')
true

julia> s = "oneTwoThreeFour"
"oneTwoThreeFour"

julia> split(s, isuppercase)
4-element Vector{SubString{String}}:
 "one"
 "wo"
 "hree"
 "our"
```

As you can see, this approach does not work because `split` strips away the character you use for splitting. Instead, you will use one of Julia's many `find` functions. If you write `find` in the REPL and press Tab, you will see a number of possible choices:

```julia
julia> find
findall    findfirst   findlast
findmax    findmax!    findmin
findmin!   findnext    findprev
```

`findfirst` finds the first occurrence of a match, while `findall` finds all occurrences. Let's look at an example to clarify:

```julia
julia> s = "The quick brown fox";

julia> findfirst(isspace, s)
4

julia> indices = findall(isspace, s)
3-element Vector{Int64}:
  4
 10
 16

julia> s[indices]
"   "
```

You can loop over all the indices of the uppercase letters and capture the substrings using ranges.

Listing 11.5   Print out each capitalized word

```
function snake_case(s::AbstractString)
    i = 1
    for j in findall(isuppercase, s)
        println(s[i:j-1])
        i = j
    end
    println(s[i:end])
end
```

Listing 11.5 is just a demonstration of how to gradually develop the function. In this case `println` will ensure the correct output. Here, the ranges `i:j-1` will extract a substring:

```
julia> snake_case("oneTwoThreeFour")
one
Two
Three
Four
```

The following listing shows a complete example. You have removed the `println` and added an array of strings called `words` to store each individual capitalized word.

Listing 11.6   Turning a camel-case string into a snake-case string

```
function snake_case(s::AbstractString)
    words = String[]
    i = 1
    for j in findall(isuppercase, s)
        push!(words, lowercase(s[i:j-1]))
        i = j
    end
    push!(words, lowercase(s[i:end]))
    join(words, '_')
end
```

Once you have collected the words in the array, join them into one string using `join(words, '_')`. The second argument, `'_'`, causes each word to be joined, with `_` as a separator.

11.2.2   *Converting between numbers and strings*

Chapter 5 covered reading input from the user. Whether input comes from the keyboard or a file, it usually comes in the form of text strings; however you may need the input numbers. In that chapter you looked at the `parse` function to deal with this; let's look at it again in greater detail. Provide a type object as first argument to specify what type of number type you want to parse to. This could be anything from different types of integers to floating-point numbers:

```
julia> parse(UInt8, "42")
0x2a
```
42 in hexadecimal form (see chapter 2)

```
julia> parse(Int16, "42")
42

julia> parse(Float64, "0.42")
0.42
```

You can even specify the base. Julia assumes base 10 by default when parsing numbers, which refers to digits running from 0 to 9. However, you could parse the numbers as if they were binary, base 2, if you wanted. That assumes you only have the digits 0 and 1 to form numbers:

```
julia> parse(Int, "101")
101
```
Interpret the string 101 as a decimal number.

```
julia> parse(Int, "101", base=2)
5
```
As a binary number (base 2)

```
julia> parse(Int, "101", base=16)
 257
```
Parse 101 as if it represents a hexadecimal number.

These conversions can also be done in reverse. You can take a number and decide what base you want to use when converting to a text string:

```
julia> string(5, base=2)
"101"
```
Create a text string with binary number digits from decimal number 5.

```
julia> string(17, base=16)
"11"
```
Turn decimal number 17 into a string in hexadecimal form.

```
julia> string(17, base=10)
 "17"
```
Convert to a string using the decimal number system.

From the previous string chapter you may remember the named argument `color=:green`. Here you have another named argument `base=2`. This is a typical case of named argument usage because you are specifying something that only occasionally needs to be specified. Sticking with the rocket theme, I will now cover some string manipulations involving the RD-180 rocket engine made by Energomash (figure 11.2).

Figure 11.2   Energomash RD-180 rocket engine

11.2.3 *String interpolation and concatenation*

Strings can be combined in myriad ways in Julia; I will compare some different ways of doing it. Often you have objects, such as numbers, you want to turn into text strings. The following code defines some variables of different types to use in the string examples:

```
julia> engine = "RD-180"
"RD-180"

julia> company = "Energomash"
"Energomash"

julia> thrust = 3830
3830

julia> string("The ", engine,
  " rocket engine, produced by ",
  company,
```

```
" produces ", thrust,
" kN of thrust")
```

```
"The RD-180 rocket engine, produced
 by Energomash produces 3830 kN of thrust"
```

The preceding code used the `string()` function to perform concatenation of strings and to convert non-strings to strings. Alternatively, one could use the string concatenation operator `*`. If you come from other languages you may be more familiar with `+` operator being used for string concatenation. Julia has instead opted for the operator commonly used to denote concatenation in mathematical notation:

```
julia> "The " * engine *
  " rocket engine, produced by " *
  company *
  " produces " *
  string(thrust) *
  " kN of thrust"
```

```
"The RD-180 rocket engine, produced by Energomash
produces 3830 kN of thrust"
```

When dealing with lots of variables it is usually better to use string interpolation. String interpolation is done with the `$` sign:

```
julia> "The $engine rocket engine, produced by $company produces
$thrust kN of thrust"
"The RD-180 rocket engine, produced by Energomash produces 3830 kN
of thrust"
```

Observe that you often need to use `$(variable)` instead of `$variable` when there is no whitespace that can clearly distinguish the variable name from the surrounding text. The same applies if you are trying to interpolate an expression rather than a variable. For instance, consider a case when you want to write `3830kN` without the space:

```
julia> "produces $thrustkN of thrust"
ERROR: UndefVarError: thrustkN not defined
```

You cannot interpolate the thrust variable this way.

```
julia> "produces $(thrust)kN of thrust"
"produces 3830kN of thrust"
```

Correct way to do string interpolation when there is no surrounding whitespace

```
julia> "two engines produces $(2 * thrust) kN of thrust"
 "two engines produces 7660 kN of thrust"
```

String interpolation of an expression

11.2.4 *sprintf formatting*

If you are familiar with C programming you may be familiar with the `printf` and `sprintf` functions. Julia has macros called `@printf` and `@sprintf`, which mimic these functions. Unlike string interpolation, these macros allow you to specify how a variable should be displayed in greater detail.

> **NOTE** Macros are distinguished from Julia functions with the @ prefix. A macro is akin to a code generator; the call site of a macro gets replaced with other code. Macros allow advanced metaprogramming this book will not cover.

For instance you can specify the number of digits that should be used when printing a decimal number. `@printf` outputs the result to the console, but `@sprintf` and `@printf` are not in the Julia base module that is always loaded. Thus to use these macros you need to include the `Printf` module, which explains the first line:

```
julia> using Printf

julia> @printf("π = %0.1f", pi)
π = 3.1
julia> @printf("π = %0.2f", pi)
π = 3.14
julia> @printf("π = %0.5f", pi)
π = 3.14159
```

The following is a short overview of some common formatting options:

- `%d`—integer numbers
- `%f`—floating point numbers
- `%x`—integers shown in hexadecimal notation
- `%s`—shows arguments as a string

With each of these formatting options you can specify things like number of digits, decimals, or padding. First let's go over some examples of the base formatting options:

```
julia> @sprintf("|%d|", 29)
"|29|"

julia> @sprintf("|%f|", 29)
"|29.000000|"

julia> @sprintf("|%x|", 29)
"|1d|"
```

I've included bars in front of and behind the numbers, so the following padding examples are easier to read:

```
julia> @sprintf("|%2d|", 42)
"|42|"
```

```
julia> @sprintf("|%4d|", 42)
"|  42|"

julia> @sprintf("|%-2d|", 42)
"|42|"

julia> @sprintf("|%-4d|", 42)
"|42  |"
```

Notice padding can be applied to either the right or left side. Right padding is achieved by adding a hyphen. Padding is useful if you want to display columns of numbers you want aligned. You can add padding as zeros instead of space by prefixing the padding number with 0:

```
julia> @sprintf("|%02d|", 42)
"|42|"

julia> @sprintf("|%04d|", 42)
"|0042|"
```

The padding doesn't say how many spaces or zeros to add but rather how many characters the numbers should fill in total. If the padding is two and the number has two digits, then nothing will happen. However, if the padding is four, two spaces are added, resulting in a total of four characters.

11.3   *Using string interpolation to generate code*

You can create small utility functions with what you just learned. This example will cover generating C++ code. Julia may not be your primary work language; instead you could be using a more verbose language, such as C++ or Java at work, but Julia can be used as a companion to make your job easier. Next you'll review an example of how a C++ developer could simplify their work by taking advantage of the Julia programming language.

The Visualization Toolkit (VTK; https://vtk.org) is an amazing C++ library for visualizing scientific data. You can use it to create visualizations like the one in figure 11.3.

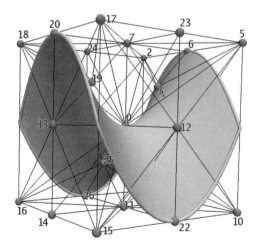

Figure 11.3   Visualization in VTK

Unfortunately, writing VTK C++ code is tedious, due to all the typical boilerplate needed in C++. The following is an example of some of the C++ code used in VTK to define a geometric line. It is not important to understand what the code in the listing does; it has been edited to remove unnecessary details from the example code.

Listing 11.7   Line class in the VTK

```
#ifndef vtkLine_h
#define vtkLine_h

class VTKCOMMONDATAMODEL_EXPORT vtkLine : public vtkCell
{
public:
  static vtkLine *New();
  vtkTypeMacro(vtkLine,vtkCell);
  void PrintSelf(ostream& os, vtkIndent indent) override;

  int GetCellType() override {return VTK_LINE;};

protected:
  vtkLine();
  ~vtkLine() override {}

private:
  vtkLine(const vtkLine&) = delete;
  void operator=(const vtkLine&) = delete;
};
```

Compare this code to the next block of code in listing 11.8 for defining a polygon; you will notice a lot of repetition. This goes for all VTK code written to define geometric primitives.

Listing 11.8   Polygon class in the VTK

```
#ifndef vtkPolygon_h
#define vtkPolygon_h

class VTKCOMMONDATAMODEL_EXPORT vtkPolygon : public vtkCell
{
public:
  static vtkPolygon *New();
  vtkTypeMacro(vtkPolygon,vtkCell);
  void PrintSelf(ostream& os, vtkIndent indent) override;

  int GetCellType() override {return VTK_POLYGON;};

protected:
  vtkPolygon();
  ~vtkPolygon() override;

private:
  vtkPolygon(const vtkPolygon&) = delete;
  void operator=(const vtkPolygon&) = delete;
};

#endif
```

Imagine you frequently write new C++ classes (types) like this for different geometric types; it would be tedious to repeat all this boilerplate. Fortunately, you can make small Julia utility functions to help (listing 11.9).

When generating text consisting of multiple lines it is practical to use triple quotation marks: `"""`. This allows you to write strings across multiple lines.

Listing 11.9 VTK C++ code generator in Julia code

```julia
function create_class(class::AbstractString)
    s = """
        #ifndef vtk$(class)_h
        #define vtk$(class)_h

        class VTKCOMMONDATAMODEL_EXPORT vtk$class : public vtkCell
        {
        public:
          static vtk$class *New();
          vtkTypeMacro(vtk$class,vtkCell);
          void PrintSelf(ostream& os, vtkIndent indent) override;

          int GetCellType() override {return VTK_$(uppercase(class));};

        protected:
          vtk$class();
          ~vtk$class() override;

        private:
          vtk$class(const vtk$class&) = delete;
          void operator=(const vtk$class&) = delete;
        };

        #endif
        """
    clipboard(s)      ⟵——  Make it easy to paste
    println(s)              generated source code for
end                         the class into a code editor.
```

The following is an example of using this utility function to create a `Hexagon` class. Notice in the two preceding lines that the generated code is also stored on the clipboard.

Listing 11.10 Use Julia to generate a C++ `Hexagon` class

```
julia> create_class("Hexagon")
#ifndef vtkHexagon_h
#define vtkHexagon_h

class VTKCOMMONDATAMODEL_EXPORT vtkHexagon : public vtkCell
{
public:
  static vtkHexagon *New();
  vtkTypeMacro(vtkHexagon,vtkCell);
  void PrintSelf(ostream& os, vtkIndent indent) override;
```

```
    int GetCellType() override {return VTK_HEXAGON;};

protected:
  vtkHexagon();
  ~vtkHexagon() override;

private:
  vtkHexagon(const vtkHexagon&) = delete;
  void operator=(const vtkHexagon&) = delete;
};


#endif
```

11.4 *Working with nonstandard string literals*

In many programming languages there are useful objects, such as dates, regular expressions, MIME types, and numbers, that start their life as strings. For instance, you cannot express very large numbers as number literals in Julia, so you have to express them as a string that gets parsed. For example, floating-point number literals are 64 bit in Julia, and that is not enough to hold a number such as 1.4e600. There are types in Julia, such as BigInt and BigFloat, which can hold arbitrarily large numbers. But how do you create such a number when number literals are limited to 64-bit floating-point values? The solution is parsing a string containing the number definition:

```
julia> 1.4e600
ERROR: syntax: overflow in numeric constant "1.4e600"

julia> x = parse(BigFloat, "1.4e600")
1.3999…9994e+600

julia> typeof(x)
BigFloat
```

Another example can be shown when working with dates. Take a scenario in which you are reading a number of dates from a file and you want to parse them. To do that, specify a date format, such as yyyy-mm-dd. This date format indicates that years come first and days last and that each component is separated by a hyphen: -. The following is an example of converting from one date format to another (date formatting options will be covered later).

Listing 11.11 Converting from one data format to another

```
using Dates

dates = ["21/7", "8/12", "28/2"];
for s in dates
    date = Date(s, DateFormat("dd/mm"))
    dstr = Dates.format(date, DateFormat("E-u"))
    println(dstr)
end
```

If you run this code you will get the following output:

```
Saturday-Jul
Saturday-Dec
Wednesday-Feb
```

This date formatting code illustrates a problem with all objects derived from strings. If you write the code in a natural fashion you end up parsing the same string over and over again. On every loop iteration you parse the strings "dd/mm" and "E-u", but this should not be necessary. Those strings are the same on every iteration; only the date strings themselves change. To avoid having to parse strings to create objects such as BigFloat and DateFormat, Julia provides special string literals such as big"1.4e600" and dateformat"dd/mm".

When the Julia parses your program code and encounters these strings it does not create String objects but rather BigInt, BigFloat, or DateFormat objects. The benefit of this approach is that objects are created when the code is parsed and not when it is run.

That may sound like a geeky detail of no significance; however, this does make a significant difference. Julia will parse the code for a for loop in your program once. But it will potentially execute the code inside the loop many times. Thus, by creating objects such as DateFormat at parse time rather than runtime, you improve performance.

I will cover each nonstandard string literal in turn in separate sections. By reading through these sections it will become clearer what this strategy implies.

11.4.1   DateFormat strings

Let's revisit the DateFormat example. In other programming languages, if you want to avoid the performance overhead of parsing DateFormat strings multiple times, you might restructure the code, as in the following listing.

> **Listing 11.12   Optimized but less-readable date formatting code**

```
using Dates

informat  = DateFormat("dd/mm")
outformat = DateFormat("E-u")

dates = ["21/7", "8/12", "28/2"]
for s in dates
    date = Date(s, informat)
    dstr = Dates.format(date, outformat)
    println(dstr)
end
```

From a performance perspective, this works. The problem is that the code becomes less clear. Glancing at the lines parsing and formatting the dates, you cannot immediately see what kind of format is used. For readability it is much nicer to be able to put the date format definition right where it is used. With the dateformat string literal you can do just that, as shown in the following listing.

Listing 11.13   Optimized and readable date formatting code

```
using Dates

dates = ["21/7", "8/12", "28/2"]
for s in dates
    date = Date(s, dateformat"dd/mm")
    dstr = Dates.format(date, dateformat"E-u")
    println(dstr)
end
```

I haven't yet covered exactly how to specify a date format string. Fortunately, the Julia online help system gives a great overview; just go into helpmode (?), and write Date-Format, which will provide you with a list of all the letters you can use and what they mean. Basically, you use letters such as y, m, and d to represent year, month, and day. If you want to write years as four digits, you specify that as yyyy. A few code examples in the REPL should give you a sense of how this works:

```
julia> d = Date(2022, 8, 28)
2022-08-28

julia> Dates.format(d, dateformat"dd-mm-yyyy")
"28-08-2022"

julia> Dates.format(d, dateformat"mm-yy")
"08-22"

julia> Dates.format(d, dateformat"yy/m")
"22/8"
```

Not all formats deal with numbers. u and U give the name of the month, such as January and February. e and E give the name of the day, such as Monday and Tuesday:

```
julia> Dates.format(d, dateformat"e u yyyy")
"Sun Aug 2022"

julia> Dates.format(d, dateformat"E U yyyy")
"Sunday August 2022"
```

11.4.2   *Raw strings*

One issue with regular Julia strings is that characters such as $ and \n have special meaning. For particular kinds of text this can be cumbersome. You can solve it by using the escape character, \\; thus $ would be written as \$ and \n as \\n. However, if you don't want to do that and don't need string interpolation, you can use raw strings:

```
julia> thrust = 3830
3830
```

```
julia> raw"produces $thrust kN of thrust" # Don't work
"produces \$thrust kN of thrust"
```

In this case the nonstandard string literal doesn't create a new type of object. Instead, it interprets the contents of the string literal differently when constructing a string object.

11.4.3 Using regular expressions to match text

Regular expressions are a kind of miniature language you can use to specify text to match. Regular expressions are widely used in Unix text processing tools and in many coding editors. For example, you can use regular expressions to search for a particular text string in your code.

In this example, you have some Julia source code stored in the variable s. You have decided you want to change the name of the Rocket type to SpaceCraft. You can use the function replace to locate some text to replace:

```
julia> s = """
       struct RocketEngine
            thrust::Float64
            Isp::Float64
       end

       mutable struct Rocket
            tank::Tank
            engine::RocketEngine          Some source code text in
       end                                which you imagine a string
       """;          ◄────────────┐      substitution is needed

julia> result = replace(s, "Rocket"=>"SpaceCraft");    ◄──┐ Replace the
                                                           │ occurrence of
julia> println(result)                                     │ Rocket with
struct SpaceCraftEngine                                    │ SpaceCraft.
    thrust::Float64
    Isp::Float64
end

mutable struct SpaceCraft
    tank::Tank
    engine::SpaceCraftEngine
end
```

As you remember from chapter 6, you use the => operator to create a pair; this was used to create key–value pairs to store in the dictionary. In this case the pair represents text to find and substitution text. So "Rocket"=>"SpaceCraft" means locate "Rocket", and replace it with "SpaceCraft".

However, as you can see from the example, this does not do exactly what you would have expected. "RocketEngine" also gets replaced with "SpaceCraftEngine". However, in this case, you only want the Rocket type to be changed. With regular expressions it is easier to be more specific about what you are looking for.

In regular expressions "." means any character; [A-D] means any character from A to D; and writing [^A-D] means any character *not* in the range A to D. So "Rocket[^A-Za-z]" would mean finding the word *Rocket* and where the first succeeding character is *not* a letter, as follows.

Listing 11.14 Text substitution using regular expressions

```
julia> result = replace(s, r"Rocket[^A-Za-z]"=>"SpaceCraft");

julia> println(result)
struct RocketEngine
    thrust::Float64
    Isp::Float64
end

mutable struct SpaceCraft
    tank::Tank
    engine::RocketEngine
end
```

In this example, you turn the string you are searching for into a regular expression by prefixing it with a r. That means it will not be a string object. This can be demonstrated in the REPL:

```
julia> rx = r"Rocket[^A-Za-z]"
r"Rocket[^A-Za-z]"

julia> typeof(rx)
Regex
```

This regular expression object is created during parsing, not at runtime. Thus, just like with DateFormat, you avoid parsing the same regular expression multiple times during runtime.

There is a lot of good documentation on regular expression syntax, so I will only provide an overview of the most basic characters used in regular expressions. The following is a list of what are called *character classes*:

Character	Meaning	Example
\d	Match any digit	"387543"
\w	Match any alphanumeric word with underscore	"foo_bar_42"
\s	Match any whitespace, tabs, linefeed, space	" "
.	Match any character	"aA ;%4t"

You also have special characters, which influence how the matching of character classes is done; these are called *quantifiers*. They can show how many times a character class should be repeated:

Character	Meaning
*	Repeat character 0 or more times
+	Repeat one or more times
?	Zero or one time

More complex interaction with the Julia regular expression system would involve working with RegexMatch objects. In this example, you want to pick out a number with multiple digits, \d+, and a word composed of multiple letters, \w+. You can do this with the match function, which will return a RegexMatch object containing all the matches:

```julia
julia> rx = r"\w+ (\d+) (\w+) \d+"        ⊲─┤ Define a regular
                                              expression.

julia> m = match(rx, "foo 123 bar 42")    ⊲─┐ Match regex
RegexMatch("foo 123 bar 42", 1="123", 2="bar")  │ against a string.

julia> m[1]        ⊲─┐
"123"                │ Access the first
                     │ and second
julia> m[2]        ⊲─┘ match.
"bar"
```

Notice how some parts of the regular expression contain parentheses; these capture that part of the string. You have set up your regular expression object rx to capture a number and a word. You can access these captures through integer indices, such as m[1] and m[2].

For more complex regular expressions it can be difficult to keep track of the position of each capture. Fortunately, regular expressions allow you to name your captures. Say you want to capture hours and minutes from the string 11:30. You could use the regular expression r"(\d+):(\d+)", but instead you will name each match using ?<s>, where s is the name of the capture:

```julia
julia> rx = r"(?<hour>\d+):(?<minute>\d+)"
r"(?<hour>\d+):(?<minute>\d+)"

julia> m = match(rx, "11:30 in the morning")
RegexMatch("11:30", hour="11", minute="30")

julia> m["minute"]
"30"

julia> m["hour"]
"11"
```

RegexMatch objects act a lot like Julia collections, so you can iterate over a RegexMatch object with a for loop. When naming your regular expression captures, the RegexMatch object works with many of the same functions applicable to dictionaries:

```
julia> keys(m)
2-element Vector{String}:
 "hour"
 "minute"

julia> haskey(m, "hour")
true

julia> haskey(m, "foo")
false
```

While regular expressions are extremely powerful and versatile, it is easy to end up overusing them. Rob Pike, one of the creators of the Go, Plan 9, UTF-8, and many other popular technologies in systems programming, has repeatedly warned against the overuse of regular expressions. They can get complex and difficult to modify as new requirements arise.

Personally, I rarely use them. In Julia you get very far with basic string and character functions, such as split, endswith, startswith, isdigit, isletter, and isuppercase.

11.4.4   *Making large integers with BigInt*

A literal syntax exists for most number types, as shown in these examples:

```
julia> typeof(42)
Int64

julia> typeof(0x42)
UInt8

julia> typeof(0x42000000)
UInt32

julia> typeof(0.42)
Float64

julia> typeof(0.42f0)
Float32

julia> typeof(3//4)
Rational{Int64}
```

In the cases it does not exist, you can do a conversion like this Int8(42), which takes a 64-bit signed integer and turns it into an 8-bit signed integer. When writing integers of arbitrary precision (any number of digits) you can do this as well by writing BigInt(42); however, this may cause some inefficiency. Everywhere this is encountered an integer has to be converted to a big int. Instead, if you write big"42", the big integer is created when the program is parsed—not each time it is run.

This isn't built into the language. Anyone can define a number literal. The following is an example of adding support for writing int8"42" to create 42 at parse time as a signed 8-bit integer. You can use this as an example to also demonstrate that macros, unlike functions, only get called once.

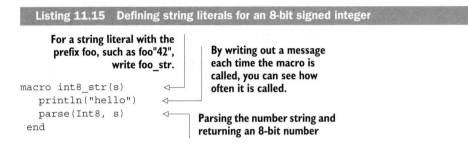

Listing 11.15   Defining string literals for an 8-bit signed integer

For a string literal with the prefix foo, such as foo"42", write foo_str.

By writing out a message each time the macro is called, you can see how often it is called.

```
macro int8_str(s)
    println("hello")
    parse(Int8, s)
end
```

Parsing the number string and returning an 8-bit number

Now you can try it out in a loop. If macros work like functions you should get a function call each time you add to the `total` in the loop:

```
julia> total = 0
0

julia> for _ in 1:4
          total += int8"10"
       end
hello

julia> total
40
```

However, you only see `hello` written once, instead of four times. That is all I will say about macros, as it is a too big topic to cover in a beginner-level textbook. However, it is useful to be aware of some of the more powerful features that exist in Julia, even if you will be unlikely to need them for your first Julia programs.

11.4.5   MIME types

Various operating systems have different systems for keeping track of the type of its files. For example, Windows famously uses a three-letter filename extension to indicate the type of a file. The original macOS stored the file type in special attributes.

However, to send files of different types between computers on the internet, one needs a common standard to identify the file types; this is what MIME types are. They are typically described as a type and subtype separated by a slash. HTML pages are denoted as `text/html`, while JPEG images are denoted as `image/jpeg`. A PNG file type would be written as `image/png` and so on. You can create a MIME type object in Julia with the following:

```
julia> MIME("text/html")
MIME type text/html

julia> typeof(ans)
MIME{Symbol("text/html")}
```

So a MIME type object `MIME("foo/bar")` would have the type `MIME{Symbol{"foo/bar"}}`. This will look somewhat cryptic until I cover parametric types in chapter 18. `MIME{Symbol{"foo/bar"}}` is long and cumbersome to write, which is why Julia offers the shortcut `MIME"foo/bar"`.

This is easy to mix up. `MIME("foo/bar")` and `MIME"foo/bar"` are *not* the same thing. The first case is an object, while the latter is the object type. The following is a simple example of how you could use this to create methods giving different outputs for different MIME types:

```
say_hello(::MIME"text/plain") = "hello world"
say_hello(::MIME"text/html") = "<h1>hello world</h1>"
```

This is useful because it allows you to define functions in Julia, which can provide different formatted textual outputs for different contexts:

```
julia> say_hello(MIME("text/plain"))
"hello world"

julia> say_hello(MIME("text/html"))
"<h1>hello world</h1>"
```

Julia code executing in a graphical notebook style environment, such as Jupyter (https://jupyter.org), would get passed an HTML MIME type, so graphs and tables can be rendered as HTML.

Summary

- Julia strings are encoded in UTF-8, which means each code point is encoded as a variable number of code units.
- `parse` is used to convert strings to other types, such as numbers.
- `string` can be used to convert numbers into strings.
- Julia strings can be combined with other object types using either the string interpolation with the `$` symbol or `string` function with a variable number of arguments.
- Strings can be concatenated with the multiplication operator `*`.
- Formatted output to `stdout` is achieved using the `@printf` macro. Use `@sprintf` to get a string value returned instead. Both are in the `Printf` module.
- String literals in Julia are extendible, but it comes with several built-in ones: raw strings, big integers, and regular expressions.

12

This chapter covers

- Understanding how collections are categorized according to the type of operations they support
- Turning staged rockets into an iterable collection
- Using common operations supported by various collection types

You have already looked at collections such as arrays and dictionaries, but there are many other types of collections, including sets, linked lists, heaps, stacks, and binary trees. In this chapter, I will cover the commonalities between different types of collections. Every collection organizes and stores multiple elements, and each collection type offers unique ways of accessing these elements. For example, with a dictionary, you can access elements by providing a key, while an array requires an index.

However, collections also have core functionality that all collections must support, such as being *iterable*. If something is iterable, you can access the individual elements in a for loop or use a higher-order function, such as map or filter.

What exactly makes something a collection? What are the differences and similarities between different collection types? And how can you make your own? You will explore these questions by expanding on the multistage rocket example from chapter 8. Because the rocket is made up of many different parts, it is possible to turn it into something Julia will recognize as a collection.

In this chapter you will add code to the `Tank` abstract type to show how interfaces are defined. You will modify the engine `Cluster` type to support iterating over engines. In the final example you will modify the `StagedRocket` type to support iteration over a multistage rocket.

12.1 Defining interfaces

What exactly is an interface? It helps to contrast interfaces with implementations. When you interact with a computer, you use a mouse and a keyboard; that is the interface to your computer—you don't need to know how the particular computer you use is built (figure 12.1). You can use the same mouse and keyboard with many different computers built in very different ways. Regardless of how much memory or what microprocessor your computer has, you can interact with it by clicking the same icons and moving around the same windows. In other words, there is a shared interface between many computer models, which insulates you from the specific hardware implementation of each computer.

Figure 12.1 A computer does not need to know how an input device works.

Separating components with clearly defined interfaces allows you to build large, complex structures. The various parts making up your system do not need to know details about implementation as long as each part uses a well-defined interface. Let's relate this to programming with Julia. Arrays and ranges are both subtypes of `Abstract-Array`, as shown in figure 12.2.

Thus if you have defined a function operating on an `AbstractArray`, you don't have to deal with the difference between an array and a range. You can make a function `addup` (see listing 12.1), which works whether you pass an array or a range as an argument.

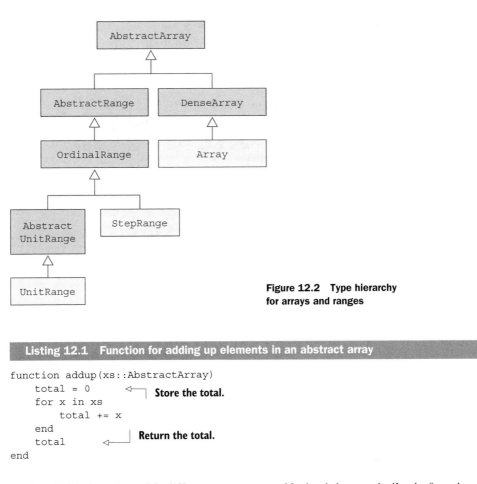

Figure 12.2   Type hierarchy for arrays and ranges

Listing 12.1   Function for adding up elements in an abstract array

```
function addup(xs::AbstractArray)
    total = 0          ◁───┐  Store the total.
    for x in xs
        total += x
    end
    total             ◁───┘  Return the total.
end
```

Let's call this function with different arguments. Notice it is very similar in function to the sum function, except it does not allow you to add up a tuple of values. Why is that?

```
julia> addup(3:5)     ◁─────── Adding a range of values
12
                              ┐  Adding an
julia> addup([3, 4, 5])   ◁──┘  array of values
12
                                   ┐  Attempting to add
                                   │  a tuple of values
julia> addup((3, 4, 5))      ◁─────┘
ERROR: MethodError: no method matching addup(::Tuple{Int64, Int64, Int64})

julia> sum((3, 4, 5))
12
```

The Tuple type is nowhere to be found in the AbstractArray type hierarchy, and thus values of type Tuple are not valid arguments to addup. Another example of a common interface can be seen in accessing elements by index both for ranges and arrays. Keep in mind that the first element of Julia arrays is at index 1:

```julia
julia> r = 3:5
3:5

julia> r[2]
4

julia> sum(r)
12

julia> a = [3, 4, 5]
3-element Vector{Int64}:
 3
 4
 5

julia> a[2]
4

julia> sum(a)
12
```

Accessing the second element looks the same.

Summing a range and an array works the same.

Define a similar-looking range and array.

Accessing the second element looks the same.

Summing a range and an array works the same.

A range doesn't have elements; elements exist implicitly. However, you can abstract away that difference by giving range and array a similar-looking interface. That allows us to define functions such as sum to work for both types, without creating two different methods.

In an object-oriented language, such as Java, C++, or C#, interfaces for an Abstract-Array are defined explicitly. The type definition in these languages includes a list of methods that subtypes must implement. Failing to do so produces a compiler error.

However, in Julia, interfaces are *informally* defined. Therefore there is no compiler telling you that you implemented an interface incorrectly.

12.2   *Propellant tank interface example*

To clarify how to define and work with interfaces in Julia, we will take a look at the propellant tank example from chapter 8 (see listing 12.2). Say you are supplying a propellant tank interface other developers can use, and you want to enable them to create their own Tank subtypes they can use when assembling rockets.

Listing 12.2   Defining an abstract propellant tank

```julia
abstract type Tank end

propellant(tank::Tank) = tank.propellant

function refill!(tank::Tank)
    propellant!(tank, totalmass(tank) - drymass(tank))
    tank
end
```

Filling a propellant tank to the max

Now imagine that another developer tries to create a concrete `Tank` subtype to use in the rocket simulation. The developer writes the following code.

> **Listing 12.3 Defining a propellant tank subtype**

```
mutable struct FlexiTank <: Tank
    drymass::Float64
    totalmass::Float64
    propellant::Float64
end
```

The developer wants to try out their new tank and writes the following code in the Julia REPL:

```
julia> tank = FlexiTank(10, 100, 0)
FlexiTank(10.0, 100.0, 0.0)

julia> refill!(tank)
ERROR: UndefVarError: totalmass not defined
```

Julia has no idea what totalmass is.

This error message makes it difficult for somebody trying to implement the `Tank` interface to know what they are supposed to do. The Julia convention to solve this problem is defining the functions in the interface and documenting them.

When looking at the code in listing 12.4, you may ask the following questions: Why is this focusing on documenting the code? Where is the interface defined? And what is the syntax for defining an interface? The answer is that there is none. That is why I say interfaces in Julia are *informally* defined. Hence documentation *is* a key part of defining a Julia interface.

Remember from chapter 7 that in Julia, methods are attached to functions, not types. You cannot associate functions with any particular type. The only reason `total-mass`, `drymass`, and `propellant` belong to the `Tank` interface is that we said so in the documentation. It is all make believe.

> **Listing 12.4 Defining a well-documented interface to propellant tanks**

```
"Stores propellant for a rocket"
abstract type Tank end

"""
    totalmass(t::Tank) -> Float64
Mass of propellant tank `t` when it is full.
"""
function totalmass end

"""
    drymass(t::Tank) -> Float64
Mass of propellant tank `t` when it is empty.
"""
function drymass end
```

```
"""
    propellant(t::Tank) -> Float64
Get remaining propellant in tank. Propellant is fuel plus oxidizer
"""
propellant(tank::Tank) = tank.propellant

"""
    refill!(tank::Tank) -> Tank
Fill propellant tankt to the max. Returns full tank
"""
function refill!(tank::Tank)
    propellant!(tank, totalmass(tank) - drymass(tank))
    tank
end
```

The Julia documentation system works by prefixing a function or type definition with a regular Julia text string. Inside this text string you document your function or type using markdown[1] syntax. In markdown you indent lines you want formatted as source code. To highlight individual words as code you use backticks `` ` ``.

> **TIP** Sometimes you want to write function definitions right in the Julia REPL. However, when you press Enter after the end of the documentation string, it gets evaluated before you can write your function definition. How do you fix this? If you hold down the Alt or Option key when you press Enter, Julia will allow you to continue writing code.

To add documentation to your functions, you can use double-quoted or triple-quoted strings (" or """). Please keep in mind that this is different from adding a comment with the hash # symbol. Comments don't get stored in the Julia help system.

Triple quotation and double quotation work slightly different. For instance if you want to use double quotes inside double-quoted text you need to *escape* the quotes by using a backslash. That is not necessary for triple quotation:

```
julia> print("file \"foo.txt\" not found")
file "foo.txt" not found
julia> print("""file "foo.txt" not found""")
file "foo.txt" not found
```

Your documentation does not need to match Julia syntax. For instance, you have used an arrow in the documentation to inform readers what sort of object the functions return:

```
"drymass(t::Tank) -> Float64"
```

Put this new definition of Tank in a file together with FlexiTank, and reload your Julia REPL with it. You can organize this almost whatever way you like. I use a file called

---

[1] Markdown is a lightweight markup language for creating formatted text using a plain-text editor.

`tank-interface.jl`, which looks like the following (I've removed documentation strings for compactness):

```
abstract type Tank end

function totalmass end
function drymass end

propellant(tank::Tank) = tank.propellant

function refill!(tank::Tank)
    propellant!(tank, totalmass(tank) - drymass(tank))
    tank
end

mutable struct FlexiTank <: Tank
    drymass::Float64
    totalmass::Float64
    propellant::Float64
end
```

Let's explore what error messages appear this time while attempting to refill the flexi tank:

```
julia> t = FlexiTank(10, 100, 0)
FlexiTank(10.0, 100.0, 0.0)

julia> refill!(t)
ERROR: MethodError: no method matching totalmass(::FlexiTank)
```

In this case, you get a better error message. Julia lets us know that `totalmass` is indeed a function, but it lacks a method for the `FlexiTank` type. By checking which methods exist, you can deduce that a method dealing with the `FlexiTank` type is necessary:

```
julia> methods(totalmass)
# 0 methods for generic function "totalmass":
```

To enter the Julia help system, hit the ? key, as discussed in chapter 2:

```
help?> totalmass
search: totalmass

  totalmass(t::Tank) -> Float64


  Mass of propellant tank t when it is full.
```

Usually, you would provide a guide to your library to explain how developers should use it. This guide explains what interfaces exist and how to implement these interfaces.

In a statically typed language, such as Java, the compiler and a sophisticated IDE[2] can inform developers about the required methods to implement and their arguments. Since Julia is a dynamically typed language, you don't have this luxury. You must adequately document your functions, so other developers know what arguments are expected and what the functions should return. As the following example shows, you can press the Tab key before you have finished writing a function call to get a list of methods and their arguments that match what you have written:

```
refill!(tank::Tank)
julia> refill!(
```

Press tab, and available methods pop up.

However, this strategy is useless for `totalmass` and `drymass`, as these functions don't have any attached methods. That is why it is essential to document required arguments for these functions.

12.3   *Interfaces by convention*

Not all interfaces in Julia are connected to a specific abstract type, as demonstrated in the previous example. For instance, there is an *iteration* interface. If you implement this interface, you will be able to iterate over your collection using a for loop. This will also make it possible to use it with functions, such as `map`, `reduce`, and `filter`, which operate on iterable collections.

The iteration interface is not represented by any particular abstract type you need to implement. Rather it is informally described. You are, at a minimum, expected to extend the `iterate` function for your collection type with the following methods:

Required methods	Purpose
`iterate(iter)`	First item and initial state
`iterate(iter, state)`	Current item and next state

There are several of these methods, which are documented thoroughly in the official Julia documentation. The following are the most useful ones:

Optional methods	Purpose
`IteratorSize(IterType)`	Indicate whether a collection has a known length
`eltype(IterType)`	The type of each element
`length(iter)`	The number of items in a collection

---

[2] IDE is short for *integrated development environment*. Visual Studio and IntelliJ IDEA are some examples of IDEs.

I will cover two different rocket-related examples in which you will implement some of these methods. In the first example, you will iterate over the engines a cluster. In the second, you will iterate over the stages of a multistage rocket.

12.4 Implementing engine cluster iteration

In chapter 8, we defined a cluster of engines like the following.

Listing 12.5 Old definition of rocket engine cluster

```
struct Cluster <: Engine
    engine::Engine
    count::Int
end
```

With this definition all the engines in the cluster have to be of the same type. But what if you want a mix of different types of engines? Some rockets actually do have a mix of engines, and you cannot model such rockets with the given `Cluster` type definition. To solve this, you will turn `Cluster` into an abstract type instead. This abstract type will have two concrete subtypes:

- A `UniformCluster`, representing identical engines
- A `MixedCluster`, representing a mix of different engines

But why introduce a second level of abstraction? Why can't `UniformCluster` and `MixedCluster` be direct subtypes of `Engine`? As you develop your code the benefits of this layer of abstraction will become clear. Open the source code for your `Cluster` type from chapter 8, and modify it with the following code.

Listing 12.6 Redesigned cluster type hierarchy

```
abstract type Cluster <: Engine end

struct UniformCluster <: Cluster
    engine::Engine
    count::Int
end

struct MixedCluster <: Cluster
    engines::Vector{Engine}          ⟵┐ A vector of elements
end                                        that are subtypes of
                                           Engine

function Cluster(engine::Engine, count::Integer)
    UniformCluster(engine, count)
end

function Cluster(engine::Engine, engines::Engine...)
    sametype(e) = (typeof(engine) == typeof(e))    ⟵┐ Define function checking
                                                        if engine e is the same as
                                                        the first engine.
    if all(sametype, engines)          ⟵┐ Check if all engines
        UniformCluster(engine, length(engines) + 1)   are of the same type.
    else                                        ⟵┐ Return a UniformCluster
                                                     if all engines are of the
                                                     same type.
```

```
        MixedCluster([engine, engines...])        ◁──┐  Return a MixedCluster if
    end                                               │  engines are of different types.
end
```

You add `Cluster` methods, which look at the types of engines passed as arguments to determine whether a uniform or mixed cluster should be created. You use a couple of new tricks here.

The `sametype` function is defined inside the `Cluster` constructor. This means it has access to the `engine` argument, without having to pass it as an argument. This is beneficial because `all` is a higher-order function expecting a function taking a single argument and returning `true` or `false`. The following are some examples to give you an idea.

Listing 12.7   Demonstrating usage of the `all` function

```
julia> iseven(3)
false

julia> iseven(4)
true
                                              Every number is
                                              even in this case.
julia> all(iseven, [4, 8, 10])        ◁──┘
true
                                              The number 3
                                              is not even.
julia> all(iseven, [3, 8, 10])        ◁──┘
 false
```

By hiding the type used to represent a cluster, you can create the illusion that there is only one `Cluster` type. That you use two different types internally becomes an implementation detail. Let's demonstrate how this works in the Julia REPL:

```
julia> Cluster(Rutherford(), Rutherford())
UniformCluster(Rutherford(), 2)              ◁──┐  Since all arguments are
                                                 │  of the same type you get
julia> Cluster(Rutherford(), Merlin())           │  a UniformCluster.
→ MixedCluster(Engine[Rutherford(), Merlin()])
```

You need a mixed cluster to hold a
Merlin and Rutherford engine.

You will need to redefine your `Isp`, `mass`, and `thrust` methods with these changes. Remember that in chapter 8 these functions were defined as

```
Isp(cl::Cluster)    = Isp(cl.engine)
mass(cl::Cluster)   = mass(cl.engine) * cl.count
thrust(cl::Cluster) = thrust(cl.engine) * cl.count
```

Implement an *iterable* interface on these cluster types to allow you to write only one implementation of `mass` and `thrust`, which works for both cluster types.

12.4.1 *Making clusters iterable*

You can try to iterate over a cluster, as it is currently defined but will not work:

```julia
julia> cl = Cluster(Rutherford(), 3)
UniformCluster(Rutherford(), 3)

julia> for engine in cl
           println(mass(engine))
       end
ERROR: MethodError: no method matching iterate(UniformCluster)
```

The Julia JIT compiler will convert this for loop into a lower-level while loop, which looks like the code in the following listing.

Listing 12.8 For loop implementation in Julia

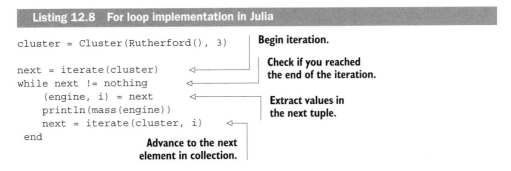

```julia
cluster = Cluster(Rutherford(), 3)        Begin iteration.

next = iterate(cluster)           ◁───    Check if you reached
while next != nothing             ◁───    the end of the iteration.
    (engine, i) = next            ◁───    Extract values in
    println(mass(engine))                 the next tuple.
    next = iterate(cluster, i)    ◁───
end
                        Advance to the next
                        element in collection.
```

So your for loop does not work because you have not yet implemented the required iterate methods. The following listing shows how to add these methods to allow iteration over the engines making up a mixed cluster.

Listing 12.9 Implementing the iteration interface for `MixedCluster`

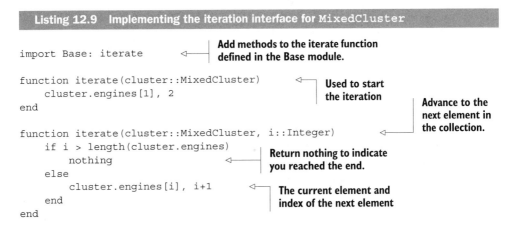

```julia
import Base: iterate             ◁──┤  Add methods to the iterate function
                                        defined in the Base module.

function iterate(cluster::MixedCluster)    ◁──   Used to start
    cluster.engines[1], 2                        the iteration
end                                                             Advance to the
                                                                next element in
function iterate(cluster::MixedCluster, i::Integer)    ◁──      the collection.
    if i > length(cluster.engines)
        nothing                  ◁──┤  Return nothing to indicate
    else                                you reached the end.
        cluster.engines[i], i+1  ◁──┐
    end                              │  The current element and
end                                     index of the next element
end
```

Importing the iterate function from Base is important, since the for loop is made to use iterate from Base and not an iterate function of the same name defined in another module. When you start iteration you need to return the very first element and the index of the next element. Thus when you start iteration you must return the index of the second element. That is why you return `cluster.engines[1]`, 2. You can call `iterate` manually to get a sense of how it works:

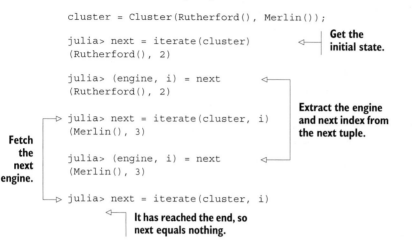

```
cluster = Cluster(Rutherford(), Merlin());

julia> next = iterate(cluster)          ⟵─┤ Get the
(Rutherford(), 2)                            initial state.

julia> (engine, i) = next          ⟵─┐
(Rutherford(), 2)
                                           Extract the engine
julia> next = iterate(cluster, i)          and next index from
(Merlin(), 3)                              the next tuple.

julia> (engine, i) = next          ⟵─┘
(Merlin(), 3)

julia> next = iterate(cluster, i)
```

Fetch the next engine.

⟵─┤ It has reached the end, so
    next equals nothing.

Now the implementation of `iteration` for `UniformCluster` in the following listing should make more sense.

Listing 12.10   Implementing iteration for `UniformCluster`

```
import Base: iterate

function iterate(cluster::UniformCluster)
    cluster.engine, 2
end

function iterate(cluster::UniformCluster, i::Integer)
    if i > cluster.count
        nothing
    else
        cluster.engine, i+1
    end
end
```

You can see that this implementation is simpler because you are always returning the same engine. The `i` index is only used to keep track of whether you have reached the end of the iteration. Because both `Cluster` types now support iteration, you can implement `mass` and `thrust` in terms of iteration, as in the following listing.

Listing 12.11   Defining `mass` and `thrust` for clusters

```
mass(cluster::Cluster)   = sum(mass, cluster)
thrust(cluster::Cluster) = sum(thrust, cluster)
```

How does this work? The `sum` function iterates over the collection supplied as the second argument. `sum` will apply the function provided as the first argument to each element it iterates over. `sum(thrust, cluster)` is equivalent to writing `sum(map(thrust, cluster))`. Neither call will work until you implement `length` for clusters (listing 12.12); otherwise Julia cannot figure out how large the result vector should be before starting iteration.

Listing 12.12 Giving Julia a way to figure out how many engines are in a cluster

```
import Base: length

length(cluster::UniformCluster) = cluster.count          Extend the length function
length(cluster::MixedCluster) = length(cluster.engines)  to support cluster types.
```

Remember, there are `sum` methods that take both one and two arguments. For `Isp` you cannot sum values; rather you would have to find an average, as follows.

Listing 12.13 Calculating the specific impulse of a cluster of engines

```
Isp(cl::Cluster) = sum(Isp, cl)/length(cl)
```

This code also lets the collection support `length`, which is sensible for most collections to support. Naturally, developers want to be able to check how many elements are contained within a collection.

With these changes, it should be more apparent why you made `Cluster` an abstract type. It allowed you to share your implementation of `mass`, `Isp`, and `thrust` across multiple cluster types. The usage of abstract types is a good way of achieving code reuse.

Next you will explore iterating across rocket stages. This will be a bit different, since you cannot access rocket stages by index.

12.5 Implementing rocket stage iteration

The following listing shows the definition of a rocket stage used in chapter 8.

Listing 12.14 Definition of a rocket stage

```
struct StagedRocket <: Rocket
    nextstage::Rocket
    tank::Tank
    engine::Engine
end
```

Notice that you don't have a vector from which you can pull individual stages. Thus, the element in the tuple you return from `iterate` will not be an integer index.

Listing 12.15 Initiate iteration of a staged rocket

```
import Base: iterate

iterate(r::StagedRocket) = (r, r.nextstage)
iterate(r::Rocket) = nothing
```

The code in listing 12.15 handles two different cases:

- A staged rocket that actually has a payload
- All other rockets that are not staged and thus have no next element

This means you don't have to add `iterate` for every possible subtype of `Rocket`. Instead, you make `Rocket` types default to not supporting iteration. You also need to support advancing through the collection of stages, which is what the `iteration` methods in the following listing will do.

Listing 12.16 Advance to the next stage of the rocket

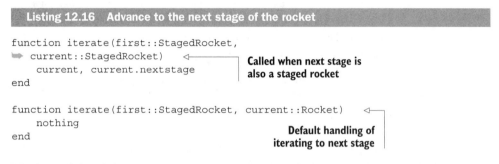

```
function iterate(first::StagedRocket,
    current::StagedRocket)
    current, current.nextstage
end
```
Called when next stage is also a staged rocket

```
function iterate(first::StagedRocket, current::Rocket)
    nothing
end
```
Default handling of iterating to next stage

You have defined these new methods such that you default to ending the iteration. That is accomplished by specifying the type of `current` as `Rocket`. Then you make an exception for when `current` is of type `StagedRocket`. In this case you know there is a `nextstage` field, which you can access to advance to the next element in the collection.

Thus, while the first example with the `Cluster` type makes it look as if `current` is an integer index, that is not really true. The second argument to `iterate` does not need to be an integer. It can be any data that helps you remember your current position in a collection you are iterating over. You can test iteration with a small program by putting the code in the following listing in the REPL or a file you load into the REPL.

Listing 12.17 Iterating over rocket stages

```
payload = Payload(300)

thirdstage = Rocket(payload, SmallTank(), Curie())
secondstage = Rocket(thirdstage, MediumTank(), Rutherford())
booster = Rocket(secondstage, LargeTank(), Cluster(Rutherford(), 9))

for rocket in booster
    println("Mass of rocket: ", mass(rocket))
    println("Thrust of rocket: ", thrust(rocket))
    println()
end
```

Make sure you have loaded your rocket code into your REPL first. When you run this program you should get the following output:

```
Mass of rocket: 13568.0
Thrust of rocket: 225000
```

```
Mass of rocket: 3053.0
Thrust of rocket: 25000

Mass of rocket: 718.0
Thrust of rocket: 120
```

This shows that iteration within a for loop works. However you cannot use it with functions such as sum, map, and collect. The following REPL session shows a failed attempt at using the map and collect functions on the booster stage.

```
julia> map(mass, booster)
ERROR: MethodError: no method matching length(::StagedRocket)

julia> collect(booster)
ERROR: MethodError: no method matching length(::StagedRocket)
```

Making this work will be the next step.

12.5.1 *Adding support for map and collect*

map and collect fail because you lack implementation for a length method for the Rocket type. To develop an understanding of this problem, I will first show a naive solution, as follows.

Listing 12.18   Calculating a number of stages in a staged rocket

```
import Base: length

length(::Rocket) = 0
length(r::StagedRocket) = 1 + length(r.nextstage)
```

While this works, it has poor performance characteristics. The time it takes to calculate the length of a stage rocket is proportional to its length. Such algorithms are referred to as *linear* or O(n) in big-O notation.

BIG-O NOTATION

In computer science, we often talk about memory requirements and processing power of data structures and algorithms in what is called *big-O notation*. If the time it takes to find an item with an algorithm is linear (e.g., it depends on the number of elements in a collection), then we write that as O(n). The n refers to n elements in your whole collection. Thus, if n doubles, then an O(n) algorithm will take twice the amount of time to finish. An algorithm that uses a for loop to look at every element is referred to as a O(n) algorithm, and an algorithm with constant time is written as O(1).

Julia gives us a way of telling its iteration machinery that there is no effective method for determining the length of the collection you iterate over. You do that by implementing an IteratorSize method, as follows.

Listing 12.19   Add the `SizeUnknown` trait to the `Rocket` subtypes

```
import Base: iterate, IteratorSize

IteratorSize(::Type{<:Rocket}) = Base.SizeUnknown()
```

This concept is not easy to grasp at first glance. It is what we call the *holy traits pattern*. Patterns in programming refer to particular ways of solving problems that get reused in many different contexts. In Julia you use the holy traits pattern to add traits to types. A *trait* is like an ability or characteristic (figure 12.3). For instance, an archer might have the `CanShoot` trait; a knight could have the `CanRide` trait; and a horse archer, such as a Mongol warrior, could have both the `CanShoot` and `CanRide` traits.

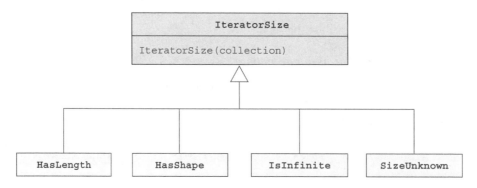

Figure 12.3   The `IteratorSize` trait and its subtypes

Iterable Julia collections can have different traits, with one of these traits being `IteratorSize`. How exactly does this work? When you call `collect(rocket)`, this gets translated to the following code.

Listing 12.20   Implementation of the `collect` function

```
_collect(rocket, IteratorEltype(rocket), IteratorSize(rocket)).
```

Attached to the `_collect` function are several different methods for dealing with collections with different traits. You can see here that the behavior of `collect` depends on two different traits: `IteratorEltype` and `IteratorSize`. You don't always have to register traits for your collections because the defaults are fine. The following listing shows how the default for `IteratorSize` is defined.

Listing 12.21   Default `IteratorSize` for Julia collections

```
IteratorSize(x) = IteratorSize(typeof(x))
IteratorSize(::Type) = HasLength()
```

When the IteratorSize trait is defined as HasLength, Julia will call length to determine the size of the result array produced from collect. When you define this trait as SizeUnknown, Julia will instead use an empty array for output that grows as needed.

In Julia, traits are defined as abstract types. The values a trait can have are determined by a concrete subtype. HasLength and SizeUnknown are both subtypes of IteratorSize. You may recognize a similar pattern from chapter 9: both the convert and promote_rule functions take types as arguments; however in this case you add the little twist of describing the argument type as Type{<:Rocket}.

The subtype operator <: is used to indicate that *all* subtypes of Rocket have the value SizeUnknown for the IteratorSize trait. I know this is a mouthful, but fortunately, it is something you can usually look up when needed. It is more important to be aware of traits than to remember exactly how they work. Having defined the IteratorSize trait for Rocket, you can now use map, sum, and other higher-order functions operating on collections:

```julia
julia> booster = Rocket(secondstage,
                LargeTank(),
                Cluster(Rutherford(), 9));
```
Remember to define the second and third state if you haven't already.

```julia
julia> map(mass, booster)
3-element Vector{Float64}:
 13568.0
  3053.0
   718.0
```
Get the mass of every stage.

Add up the thrust of all engines on the multistage rocket.

```julia
julia> sum(thrust, booster)
 250120
```

The most basic operation a collection needs to be able to support is iteration. You have looked at how that is achieved on two different types of collections. The rocket clusters behave mostly like arrays; however, your staged rocket behaves more like a data structure called a *linked list*. In the next section, you will compare linked lists and arrays to better understand how different collection types have different tradeoffs.

12.6 Comparison of linked lists and arrays

The way you link stages to each other through nextstage, is the same as how a *linked list* works: they are often contrasted with arrays. With an array, you can quickly determine the length or look up an arbitrary element, given an index. You will add support for index-based lookup to your Cluster subtypes and later contrast it with the linked list of rocket stages.

Recalling that for loops actually get turned into while loops, there is actually a similar case when accessing and replacing elements in an array. Say you have created a cluster in which you access elements.

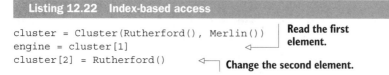

Listing 12.22   Index-based access

```
cluster = Cluster(Rutherford(), Merlin())
engine = cluster[1]                          ◁── Read the first
cluster[2] = Rutherford()                          element.
                                             ◁── Change the second element.
```

The code in listing 12.22 will be translated by the Julia compiler through several stages. One of these stages, called *lowering*, turns this code into the following.

Listing 12.23   Index-based access under the hood

```
cluster = Cluster(Rutherford(), Merlin())
engine = getindex(cluster, 1)
setindex!(cluster, Rutherford(), 2)
```

Thus to make your `Cluster` subtypes support accessing elements by index, you need to add methods to the `getindex` and `setindex!` functions found in the `Base` module. These are the functions used for implementing element access with square brackets: `[]`.

Listing 12.24   Adding index-based access to rocket clusters

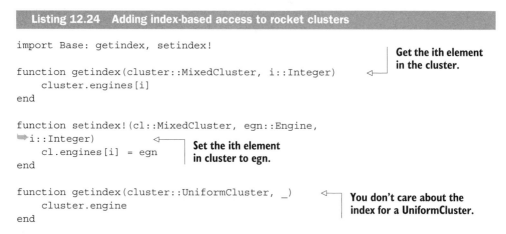

```
import Base: getindex, setindex!
                                                        ┐  Get the ith element
function getindex(cluster::MixedCluster, i::Integer)    │  in the cluster.
    cluster.engines[i]                          ◁───────┘
end

function setindex!(cl::MixedCluster, egn::Engine,
➥i::Integer)                      ◁──┐  Set the ith element
    cl.engines[i] = egn               │  in cluster to egn.
end

function getindex(cluster::UniformCluster, _)   ◁──┐  You don't care about the
    cluster.engine                                 │  index for a UniformCluster.
end
```

You can see some differences between `MixedCluster` and `UniformCluster`, and you can easily support getting elements from a `UniformCluster` because every element is the same. However, you cannot support setting an element because it would no longer be uniform. Hence, you have not added a method for `setindex!` dealing with the `UniformCluster`. While you could define index-based access for a linked list, it isn't very efficient, as shown in the following listing.

Listing 12.25   Accessing rocket stage by index

```
import Base: getindex
function getindex(r::StagedRocket, i::Integer)
    for _ in 1:i-1           ◁──┐  _ is used when you
        r = r.nextstage          │  don't care about the
    end                          │  name of a variable.
    r
end
```

Such a lookup is an O(n) operation (linear). The more stages you have, the more times the for loop has to be repeated. A lookup in an array, in contrast, is a O(1) operation. That is another way of saying it is a *constant operation*. The time to look up an element in an array with three elements is exactly the same as in an array with millions of elements.

However, you can add support for other types of operations that work faster. Let's look at some of the most common operations supported in Julia for adding elements to collections.

12.6.1 *Adding and removing elements*

Arrays allow you to add elements to the front and back of the array as well as remove elements from both ends. Notice in the examples how push! and pushfirst! allow you to add more than one element in a single function call.

```
julia> xs = Int[7]          ◁────┐     Create array xs with
1-element Vector{Int64}:          │     one element 7.
 7

julia> push!(xs, 9, 11)     ◁────┐     Add 9 and 11 to the
3-element Vector{Int64}:          │     back of the array.
 7
 9
 11
                                        Add 3 and 5 to the
                                        front of the array.
julia> pushfirst!(xs, 3, 5) ◁────┘
5-element Vector{Int64}:
 3
 5
 7
 9
 11
                           Remove the
                           last element.
julia> pop!(xs)     ◁────┘
11
                           Remove the
                           first element.
julia> popfirst!(xs)  ◁────┘
 3
```

Figure 12.4 may help clarify how these operations work.

For linked lists, removing and adding elements to the front is effective (figure 12.5). Thus, you can support operations like pushfirst! and popfirst!. However, you need to make some adjustments and preparations to make it more convenient to implement these functions.

When dealing with linked lists, it is useful to have something obvious to terminate a chain of objects. Often this will be a nothing object, but with the multistage rocket, an emptypayload would be a natural fit.

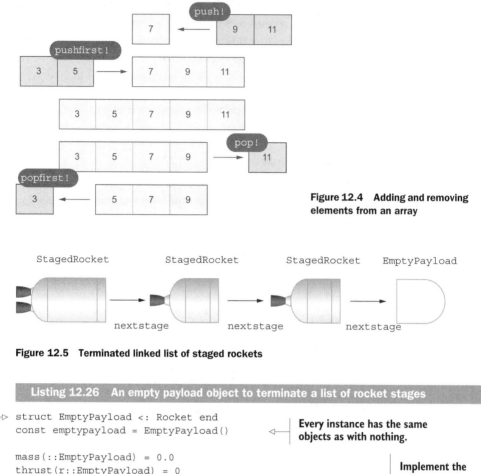

Figure 12.4   Adding and removing elements from an array

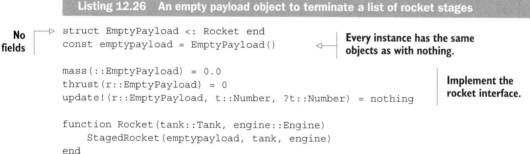

Figure 12.5   Terminated linked list of staged rockets

Listing 12.26   An empty payload object to terminate a list of rocket stages

No fields

```
struct EmptyPayload <: Rocket end
const emptypayload = EmptyPayload()

mass(::EmptyPayload) = 0.0
thrust(r::EmptyPayload) = 0
update!(r::EmptyPayload, t::Number, ?t::Number) = nothing

function Rocket(tank::Tank, engine::Engine)
    StagedRocket(emptypayload, tank, engine)
end
```

Every instance has the same objects as with nothing.

Implement the rocket interface.

Having a representation of an empty payload provides a number of advantages, such as having a sensible default constructor for a single-stage rocket, as shown in listing 12.26. The example, however, is not quite done. A new type is needed and an existing one needs to be modified. StagedRocket was initially made immutable, which will hinder, for example, popfirst! from working, as you need to modify the nextstage field. You cannot modify fields on immutable objects (objects which cannot be changed).

> **IMPORTANT**   Whenever you change a type definition, such as by making a struct mutable, you need to restart the Julia REPL. This is because Julia types are fixed; they cannot be modified at runtime like many other dynamic languages.

Next I will introduce the `SpaceVehicle` type (listing 12.27). Figure 12.6 shows how it is conceptually related to other rocket parts.

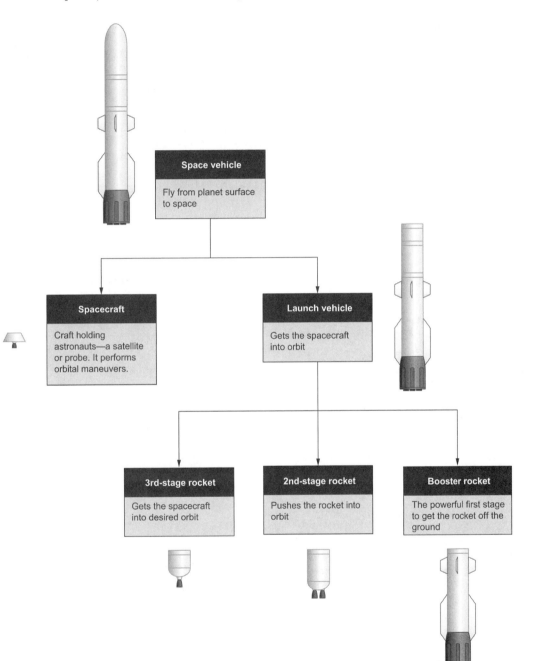

Figure 12.6   Rocket terminology overview

The `SpaceVehicle` is the whole thing with all the rocket stages. This abstraction is useful to wrap around the stages, so you can keep track of where the first rocket stage starts. This is useful when implementing `pushfirst!` and `popfirst!` because it allows you to add and remove stages relative to something else.

Listing 12.27   New and modified type definitions

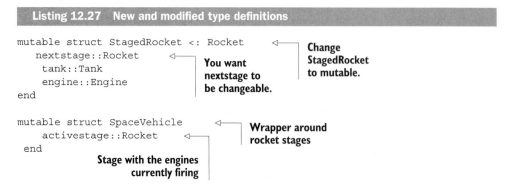

```
mutable struct StagedRocket <: Rocket                    Change
    nextstage::Rocket                                    StagedRocket
    tank::Tank                   You want                to mutable.
    engine::Engine               nextstage to
end                              be changeable.

mutable struct SpaceVehicle                  Wrapper around
    activestage::Rocket                      rocket stages
end
                     Stage with the engines
                     currently firing
```

With these type definitions in place, you have the foundation for implementing your `popfirst!` and `pushfirst!` methods (listing 12.28). Because they are standard functions for Julia collections, you import them from `Base` to extend them with methods dealing with your specific collection: `SpaceVehicle`.

Listing 12.28   Removing stages from the bottom

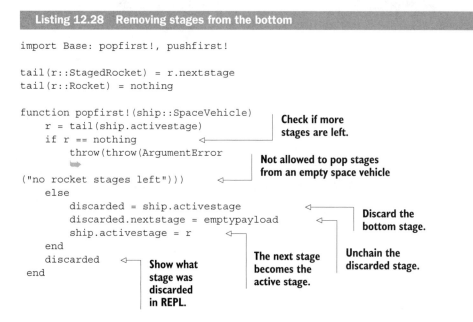

```
import Base: popfirst!, pushfirst!

tail(r::StagedRocket) = r.nextstage
tail(r::Rocket) = nothing

function popfirst!(ship::SpaceVehicle)          Check if more
    r = tail(ship.activestage)                  stages are left.
    if r == nothing
        throw(throw(ArgumentError             Not allowed to pop stages
                                              from an empty space vehicle
("no rocket stages left")))
    else
        discarded = ship.activestage                     Discard the
        discarded.nextstage = emptypayload               bottom stage.
        ship.activestage = r
    end                                                  Unchain the
    discarded          Show what       The next stage    discarded stage.
end                    stage was       becomes the
                       discarded       active stage.
                       in REPL.
```

The `tail` function requires some explanation. You add two methods: one for handling a `StagedRocket` and another for subtypes of `Rocket`. This is a simple way to check whether there are any stages left on the `SpaceVehicle`. Since the `activestage` field of `SpaceVehicle` is of type `Rocket`, you cannot be guaranteed that a `nextstage` exists. Why not make it a `StagedRocket` then? Because you want to allow stages to be detached until you have only a payload representing a satellite or crew capsule left.

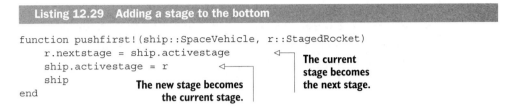

```
function pushfirst!(ship::SpaceVehicle, r::StagedRocket)
    r.nextstage = ship.activestage
    ship.activestage = r
    ship
end
```

With `pushfirst!` you put a new stage `r` in front of the existing active stage (listing 12.29). The old active stage changes its role to become the next stage of the new active stage. You can make all these edits and modifications and spin up a new REPL to get a feel for how these new functions work. To help make it more visually distinct, I will present an example of a rocket with stages named a, b, and c. Each stage has bigger tanks and a bigger engine than the previous one:

```
julia> a = Rocket(SmallTank(), Curie());

julia> b = Rocket(MediumTank(), Rutherford());

julia> c = Rocket(LargeTank(), Merlin());
```

The example begins by creating a space vehicle with a small 40-kg payload:

```
julia> ship = SpaceVehicle(Payload(40));
```

Next, `pushfirst!` is used to add stages to this space vehicle:

```
julia> pushfirst!(ship, a)
SpaceVehicle(StagedRocket(Payload(40.0), SmallTank(370.0), Curie()))

julia> pushfirst!(ship, b)
SpaceVehicle(StagedRocket(
            StagedRocket(
                Payload(40.0),
                SmallTank(370.0),
                Curie()),
            MediumTank(2050.0),
            Rutherford()))

julia> pushfirst!(ship, c)
SpaceVehicle(StagedRocket(
            StagedRocket(
                StagedRocket(
                    Payload(40.0),
                    SmallTank(370.0),
                    Curie()),
                MediumTank(2050.0),
                Rutherford()),
```

```
        LargeTank(9250.0),
        Merlin()))
```

I have edited the REPL output by adding whitespace and indentation to more clearly show the structure being created while adding more stages. You can see how the smallest stage is at the deepest indentation level. That is because it is nested deepest. The booster stage with the large engine and tank is at the bottom.

You can knock off all these stages again using the `popfirst!` function:

```
julia> popfirst!(ship)
StagedRocket(EmptyPayload(), LargeTank(9250.0), Merlin())

julia> popfirst!(ship)
StagedRocket(EmptyPayload(), MediumTank(2050.0), Rutherford())

julia> popfirst!(ship)
StagedRocket(EmptyPayload(), SmallTank(370.0), Curie())

julia> ship
SpaceVehicle(Payload(40.0))
```

On each pop, the stage that was discarded is returned. Notice how the largest stage with the `Merlin` engine comes off first. The next stage involves the medium-sized tank. The top stage with the small tank comes last. Finally, the space vehicle only containing the initial 40-kg payload remains.

12.7 *Utility of custom types*

A linked list isn't used often in actual code, as arrays are more versatile and have better performance most of the time. However, linked lists are useful to understand, as the principles applied here apply to more complex data structures. Tree structures and graphs also link elements together.

While you are unlikely to spend much time writing completely generic data structures, such as arrays, linked lists, and dictionaries, you will find it helpful to turn custom data structures (rocket stages) into collections. Once a data structure implements the interface of a well-established category of types, such as a collection, you make a host of functions applicable to them. For example, by making a staged rocket iterable, you can suddenly use `map`, `reduce`, `filter`, `sum`, `collect`, and other functions with it for free.

Summary

- For loops and index access with square brackets both translate to Julia function calls such as `iterate`, `getindex`, and `setindex!`.
- Collections must, at a minimum, support iterations. That is done by implementing two `iterate` methods for your collection type—one to start the iteration and another to get the next element.

- Julia types can be configured with different capabilities using the holy traits pattern. Julia collections can be configured with different traits, such as `Iterator-Size` and `IteratorEltype`.
- Collections for which calculating the number of elements is slow should configure `IteratorSize` to `SizeUnknown`.
- Arrays offer fast access of elements at any index but don't allow quick insertion of elements except at the end of the array.
- Linked lists have slow access of elements by index but fast insertion and removal of elements at the front.
- Implementing well established Julia interfaces can make your own data types more versatile. For example, by turning your data structure into a Julia collection, you can leverage many of the prebuilt Julia-collection-related functions.

Working with sets

This chapter covers

- Comparing differences between sets and arrays
- Creating sets in different ways
- Using union and intersect operations to locate items in different types of software
- Understanding tradeoffs between usings sets and search operations

It does not take much time to define a set and show what operations they can be used for. What does take time is developing an understanding or intuition about what sort of problems you can solve with sets.

Many problems related to organizing and locating data can be solved beautifully by utilizing sets and set operations, but that is not always apparent. In this chapter, I will go through what sets are as well as what you can do with them, and then I'll walk you through various realistic examples showing the power of storing data in sets.

13.1 What kind of problems can sets help solve?

Lots of software requires organizing large amounts of data, including the following:

- Photo albums
- Email clients
- Bug-tracking systems
- Online shopping
- Software-development projects
- Specialist software, like modeling software for geologists

For a long time the most popular way of organizing data was via tree structures. To find an item you would drill down into subcategories until you found what you were looking for. The problem with this approach is that many items can potentially exist underneath multiple subcategories instead of just one.

A webshop such as McMaster-Carr (figure 13.1), which sells a huge number of mechanical components, is a great example of this problem.

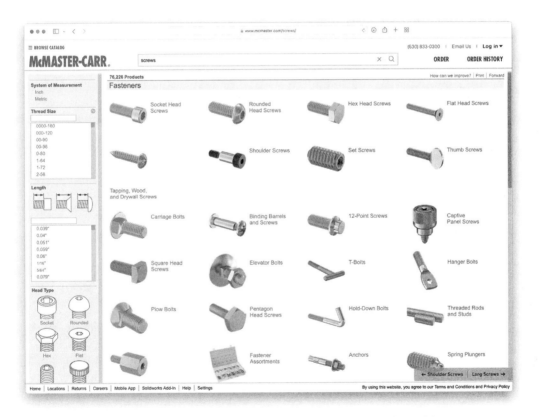

Figure 13.1 McMaster-Carr webshop showing how screws can be categorized in multiple ways

On the side of the screen you can see various categories for screws:

- *System of measurement*—Are the screw dimensions given in imperial or metric units?
- *Thread size*—What is the actual measurement of the threads and threads per inch?
- *Material*—Is the screw made of steel, plastic, or wood?
- *Length*—What is the length from under the screw head to the end of the threads?
- *Head type*—Is it flat, rounded, or hex shaped?

There are far more categories than I have shown here. The point, however, is that you cannot turn this into a tree hierarchy. Both a plastic screw and a steel screw can have a rounded head, for example.

Another case is photo albums. How do you organize them? You could organize pictures by every family member, so your wife and each child gets their own album. Or maybe organizing albums based on events, such as visiting Barcelona or Hawaii, makes more sense. Or maybe one would prefer activity-based organization such as by creating albums for particular types of attractions like technical museums or zoos. Organization is difficult, so let's look at how sets and set operations can help you achieve this task.

13.2 What is a set?

A *set* is a collection type just like arrays or dictionaries. The following is an example of creating a set:

```
julia> fruits = Set(["apple", "banana", "pear", "orange"])
Set{String} with 4 elements:
  "pear"
  "orange"
  "banana"
  "apple"

julia> fruits = Set([:apple, :banana, :pear, :orange])     ⟵— Symbols
Set{Symbol} with 4 elements:                                    instead of
  :pear                                                         strings
  :apple
  :banana
  :orange

julia> odds = Set([1, 3, 5, 7, 9])
Set{Int64} with 5 elements:
  5
  7
  9
  3
  1
```

```
julia> nodups = Set([3, 3, 3, 1, 2])
Set{Int64} with 3 elements:
  2
  3
  1
```
◁─┐ **Attempted to
    add duplicates**

In the first case, a set of fruits is created, where each fruit is represented by a string. The second case is similar, but symbols are used instead of strings to represent fruits. It is a useful example, since symbols are often used in Julia to represent keys.

Sets are like the keys of a dictionary; no element occurs twice. Notice in the last example, nodups, 3 is attempted to be added multiple times. Like a dictionary, the elements don't exist in any particular order. When you iterate over a set, elements will appear in a specific order. However, you have no control over this order. If you add or remove elements the order can change.

That behavior is different from, say, an array, where you have full control over how the addition and removal of elements affects the order of the array. If you add an element to an array using push!, then every element stays in the same position as before. Every element can be accessed with the exact same index as previously.

13.2.1 Comparing properties of sets and arrays

You can get a better sense of what a set is by comparing its properties with those of an array (table 13.1).

Table 13.1 Differences and similarities between sets and arrays

Property	Sets	Arrays
Duplicates allowed	No	Yes
Elements ordered	No	Yes
Random access	No	Yes
Quick membership test	Yes	No
Iterable	Yes	Yes

The following are two desirable properties offered by sets:

1 Sets are guaranteed not to have any duplicate elements.
2 It is very quick to check if a set contains a specific object.

Arrays, in contrast, don't offer a quick way of checking whether they contain a specific object because determining whether an array contains an element or not requires looking at every element in the array. So looking for a particular element in an array of two million elements will, on average, take twice as long as looking for it in an array of one million elements.

This is called a *linear* relationship. However, for a set, the number of operations required to locate an element does not grow with the size of the set. There is no linear relationship.

Sets can be implemented in different ways; thus, in some variants on average, *log(n)* checks are required to look up an element in a set of *n* elements. To help you better understand the benefits of using sets, let's make some comparisons of sets with arrays for different types of operations sets are optimized for.

SEARCHING A SORTED ARRAY

In a sorted array you can perform a *binary search*. Consider the following sorted array of numbers for a quick idea of how that works:

```
A = [2, 7, 9, 10, 11, 12, 15, 18, 19]
```

This sorted array has 9 numbers. Say you are looking for the number 18. The number is somewhere in the range 1:9 (index range). Normally, finding the number would require 8 comparisons, but with binary search you begin in the middle A[5] == 11 and ask if 18 > 11 or if 18 < 11.

Because the array is sorted, you can conclude 18 is somewhere in the upper half of the array or, more specifically, the index range 6:9. This search process is repeated by checking the middle of this range. Since there isn't a middle in this range one could round down the index to A[7] == 15. You find that 18 is above this value. Hence in 3 comparisons, rather than 8, you can locate the answer. Julia has several functions for doing this type of search:

```
julia> searchsorted(A, 18)
8:8

julia> searchsortedfirst(A, 18)
8

julia> searchsortedlast(A, 18)
8
```

The downside of using sorted arrays is that the programmer has to make sure the array is sorted at all times. It makes insertions slow, as you must re-sort the array each time. Sets have the benefit of allowing not only fast checks on membership (e.g., determining whether an element is in the set) but also fast insertion and removal.

PERFORMING OBJECT MEMBERSHIP TESTS

You can turn the array A into a set S. Both support membership test with `in` or its Greek equivalent ∈. You can also use ⊆ or `issubset` to check if multiple elements are members:

```
julia> S = Set(A);

julia> 18 in S
true
```

```
julia> 18 ∈ A
true

julia> [11, 15] ⊆ A
true

julia> issubset([11, 15], S)
true
```

Arrays look similar in behavior, but these operations will happen faster on a set. The exception is for small collections. With few elements, no collection is as fast as an array. Once you go above 30–40 elements a set will start outperforming an unsorted array on membership tests.

However, it is still advisable to use sets for small collections if maintaining a unique set of elements is important and order isn't. It helps *communicate* to the reader of your code how it is supposed to work. Using more sophisticated collection types, such as Dictionary or Set, really starts to pay off once you have a large number of elements.

SETS DON'T ALLOW DUPLICATES

What happens when you attempt to create a Set with duplicates? The following example explores this topic:

```
julia> apples = ["apples", "apples", "apples"]
3-element Vector{String}:
 "apples"
 "apples"
 "apples"

julia> appleset = Set(apples)
Set(["apples"])

julia> length(appleset)
1

julia> numbers = [1, 1, 1, 2, 2, 2, 3, 3];

julia> length(numbers)
8

julia> S = Set(numbers)
Set([2, 3, 1])

julia> length(S)
3
```

Duplicates are allowed in arrays but not in sets.

RANDOM ACCESS AND ORDERING OF ELEMENTS

I will create a set and an array with the same elements to demonstrate how random access and ordering is entirely different:

```
A = [3, 5, 7]
S = Set(A)
```

If you use collect or foreach they will iterate over the collections. You can see the order is different; it is not guaranteed and can change between different versions of Julia:

```
julia> collect(S)
3-element Vector{Int64}:
 7
 3
 5

julia> collect(A)
3-element Vector{Int64}:
 3
 5
 7

julia> foreach(print, S)
735

julia> foreach(print, A)
357
```

I am able to use brackets to access array elements by index:

```
julia> A[2]
2
```

But this is not possible to do with a set:

```
julia> S[2]
ERROR: MethodError: no method matching getindex(::Set{Int64}, ::Int64)
```

With an array, push! adds each element to a predictable location:

```
julia> push!(A, 9)
4-element Vector{Int64}:
 3
 5
 7
 9
```

However for sets, the element can end up anywhere:

```
julia> push!(S, 9)
Set([7, 9, 3, 5])
```

With an array, pop! will remove the last element added:

```
julia>  pop!(A)
9
```

However, with a `Set` this operation is best avoided, as you have no control over what element you actually end up removing:

```
julia> pop!(S)
7
```

In this case, it may have been more appropriate for Julia to throw an exception, rather than letting the user perform `pop!`.

13.3 *How to use set operations*

Set operations are used to combine sets to create new sets. However, set operations are not actually limited to sets. You can perform set operations between arrays as well. The difference is that sets are designed to support this, while arrays are not. Arrays only perform set operations efficiently for small collections of elements.

Set operations allow you to answer questions such as the following: *Give me the pictures of Bob when he visited Spain and Greece.* If `Bob` represents all images of your uncle Bob in your photos application, `Spain` is a set of all your pictures from Spain, and `Greece` is a set of all your pictures from Greece, then such a question can be answered with either of these two equivalent expressions:

```
S = Bob ∩ (Spain ∪ Greece)
S = intersect(Bob, union(Spain, Greece))
```

This demonstrates the use of the `union` and `intersect` operations. These can also be written using the ∪ and ∩ symbols. The best way to visualize the behavior of the different set operations is by using Venn diagrams[1] (figure 13.2).

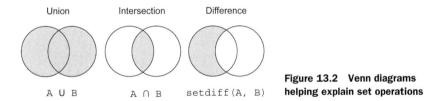

Figure 13.2   Venn diagrams helping explain set operations

The two circles in each example represent the sets A and B. These are overlapping sets, meaning some of the elements in A also exist in B.

The colored area shows which elements are included in the set resulting from the set operation. For instance, with a *set union* all the elements in A and B are included in the result. For *set intersection*, however, only elements shared between A and B are part of the result. You might recognize an analogy with the AND `&&` and OR `||` operators

---

[1] Venn diagrams are usually used to illustrate the logical relationships between two or more sets of items.

used in Boolean logic. With *union* the elements must be in set A *or* set B. With *intersection* they must be in set A *and* set B.

With *set difference* the order is important. `setdiff(A, B)` returns the elements in A remaining after you've removed elements in A that also exist in B. Let's look at a practical example of how this is used. Imagine having some sets of photo captions:

```
bob = Set(["Bob in Spain", "Bob in Greece", "Joe and Bob in Florida"])
joe = Set(["Joe in Texas", "Joe and Eve in Scotland", "Joe and Bob in Florida"])
eve = Set(["Eve in Wales", "Joe and Eve in Scotland", "Eve in Spain"])
```

So there are three people—Bob, Joe, and Eve—who have been on various vacations abroad, where they have taken pictures. In this example, those pictures are represented as their caption text.

In this scenario, you want to use set operations to find pictures containing more than one of these people. `bob` is a set of all pictures Bob has been in, `joe` is a set of all pictures Joe has been in, and `eve` is a set of all pictures Eve has been in. This code finds pictures in which Bob and Joe were together on vacation:

```
julia> bob ∩ joe
Set{String} with 1 element:
  "Joe and Bob in Florida"
```

Perhaps Eve broke up with Joe, so you don't want pictures with Joe in them. Eve can then use `setdiff` to exclude Joe pictures:

```
julia> setdiff(eve, joe)
Set{String} with 2 elements:
  "Eve in Wales"
  "Eve in Spain"
```

Perhaps Joe wants to find all vacations he spent together with somebody else:

```
julia> (bob ∪ eve) ∩ joe
Set{String} with 2 elements:
  "Joe and Eve in Scotland"
  "Joe and Bob in Florida"
```

Sets can, of course, contain any kind of object. Let's do some slightly less exciting set operations with numbers. A is a set of mostly even numbers, while B contains mostly odd numbers:

```
A = Set([1, 2, 4, 6])
B = Set([1, 3, 5, 6])
```

You can get the set intersection in two different ways:

```
julia> A ∩ B
Set{Int64} with 2 elements:
  6
  1
```

```
julia> intersect(A, B)
Set{Int64} with 2 elements:
  6
  1
```

You can also get the set union:

```
julia> A ∪ B
Set{Int64} with 6 elements:
  5
  4
  6
  2
  3
  1

julia> union(A, B)
Set{Int64} with 6 elements:
  5
  4
  6
  2
  3
  1
```

And finally, you can get the set difference of A and B:

```
julia> setdiff(A, B)
Set{Int64} with 2 elements:
  4
  2

julia> setdiff(B, A)
Set{Int64} with 2 elements:
  5
  3
```

As you can see, order matters with set difference.

13.4   *How to use sets in your code*

The basic operations of sets are not hard to learn. It takes more time to get a sense of when to use sets in your code.

Often I have been surprised by how sets can provide powerful and elegant solutions to difficult problems. It is very easy to forget that sets are lying in your toolbox.

In the following sections you will look at problems that can be solved using sets. I will also contrast using sets with other solutions.

I will first show how to create sets for different product categories using the Set constructor. Afterwards, I will demonstrate the process of finding screws matching different criteria by using the intersect and setdiff operations. The alternative solution will be based on defining a Screw composite type with different properties.

I will show how to use the `filter` function to find `Screw` objects matching desired criteria.

13.5 *Searching for products using set operations*

When dealing with products in, say, a Web shop, you would typically use an SQL[2] database. This process is conceptually similar to using set operations, which is why I will expand on the example of buying screws from an online hardware shop.

A screw can have different head types:

```
head_type = [rounded, flat, headless, tslot]
```

You may want a flat screw if you want the screw flush with the surface or a headless one for things like set screws for axle collars. The screw can have a drive style, which indicates what kind of tip you need to have on your screwdriver to turn the screw around:

```
drive_style = [hex, phillips, slotted, torx]
```

Material should be obvious:

```
material = [aluminium, brass, steel, plastic, wood]
```

This is the list of categories. Each item in the list is actually a `Set`, and the set contains a product number uniquely identifying that screw. For practical reasons I will demonstrate inventing some 3-digit product numbers. The following example uses ranges to quickly create a large number of product numbers:

```
rounded  = Set(100:4:130)
flat     = Set(101:4:130)
headless = Set(102:4:130)
tslot    = Set(103:4:130)

hex      = Set(100:108)
phillips = Set(109:115)
slotted  = Set(116:121)
torx     = Set(122:129)

aluminium = Set(100:3:120)
brass     = Set(101:3:120)
steel     = Set(102:3:120)
plastic   = Set(121:2:130)
wood      = Set(122:2:130)
```

If you look carefully at the numbers, you will see that they are overlapping. For example, some of the aluminum product numbers are the same as the hex product numbers.

---

[2] Structured Query Language (SQL) is a specialized language for formulating database queries. A query is a request for data in a database matching one or more criteria.

With these sets defined, I can ask various useful questions, such as the following: Which screws in your product catalog have a rounded head, are made of wood, and can be fastened with a torx screwdriver? Answering this requires just a simple set operation:

```
julia> intersect(rounded, torx, wood)
Set{Int64} with 2 elements:
  124
  128
```

Or how about getting all steel screws that can be fastened with a Phillips screwdriver?

```
julia> intersect(phillips, steel)
Set{Int64} with 2 elements:
  114
  111
```

Or maybe you just want to know whether T-slot screws not made of plastic exist:

```
julia> setdiff(tslot, plastic)
Set{Int64} with 5 elements:
  107
  103
  115
  111
  119
```

This is one way of using sets, but you can accomplish the same with entirely different designs, not utilizing sets at all. Instead, you could define a screw as a richer data type with properties for each attribute:

```
struct Screw
    prodnum::Int
    headtype::HeadType
    drivestyle::DriveStyle
    material::Material
end
```

Instead of dealing with screws as just numbers, there is a data type with properties, with which you could attempt to match some given search criteria. You can see the various properties are represented by the custom types HeadType, DriveStyle, and Material. In a different example, these could be with these strings or symbols, but instead they are made as particular types to catch cases in which an illegal category is assigned to any of the attributes.

13.5.1 *Defining and using enumerations*

To represent different categories, you use enumerations, or enum for short. Enumerations exist in a number of different languages. In Julia they are a bit peculiar because they are defined using macros. Now restart Julia, as these variables are already defined; otherwise there will be complaints about variables already being defined:

```
@enum HeadType rounded flat headless tslot
@enum DriveStyle hex phillips slotted torx
@enum Material aluminum brass steel plastic wood
```

The giveaway is the @ prefix. You can think of hex, slotted, and torx as instances of the DriveStyle type. In fact, you can use the DriveStyle constructor to create them:

```
julia> DriveStyle(2)
slotted::DriveStyle = 2

julia> DriveStyle(3)
torx::DriveStyle = 3

julia> DriveStyle(4)
ERROR: ArgumentError: invalid value for Enum DriveStyle: 4
```

However, you can see the added type safety in the last example. It is not possible to create other values for DriveStyle than the ones specified when the enumeration was defined.

13.5.2 *Creating test data to perform queries on*

To demonstrate using this type to locate screws with different properties, you need to create some test data to operate on:

```
function make_screw(prodnum)
    headtype = rand(instances(HeadType))
    drivestyle = rand(instances(DriveStyle))
    material = rand(instances(Material))

    Screw(prodnum, headtype, drivestyle, material)
end

screws = map(make_screw, 100:150)
```

This code creates an array of screws with product numbers in the range 100 to 150, and you pick values for each property at random. The instances function returns an array of every possible value for an enumeration:

```
julia> instances(DriveStyle)
(hex, phillips, slotted, torx)

julia> instances(Material)
(aluminium, brass, steel, plastic, wood)
```

13.5.3 *Searching for screws*

The first example showed screws matching your desired criteria using set operations. Now you will find desired screws by searching through all the screws in an array and checking whether each screw matches all desired criteria. The example will show how to do that by specifying predicate functions. A predicate function will take a screw as an argument and return `true` or `false`, depending on whether the criteria the predicate function tests for was met. `isroundwood` will test whether the given screw has rounded heads made of wood:

```
function isroundwood(screw)
    screw.headtype == rounded &&
    screw.material == wood
end
```

This predicate can then be used (function returning a Boolean value) to filter screws:

```
julia> roundedwood = filter(isroundwood, screws)
3-element Vector{Screw}:
 Screw(100, rounded, torx, wood)
 Screw(113, rounded, slotted, wood)
 Screw(129, rounded, torx, wood)
```

How about finding what nonplastic T-slot screws are offered in the store?

```
julia> function isnonplastic(screw)
           screw.headtype == tslot &&
           screw.material != plastic
       end

julia> nonplastic = filter(isnonplastic, screws)
15-element Vector{Screw}:
 Screw(105, tslot, hex, wood)
 Screw(106, tslot, hex, wood)
 Screw(107, tslot, hex, brass)
 Screw(108, tslot, phillips, steel)
 Screw(117, tslot, phillips, wood)
 Screw(118, tslot, hex, wood)
 Screw(125, tslot, phillips, wood)
 Screw(128, tslot, phillips, wood)
 Screw(130, tslot, phillips, wood)
 Screw(131, tslot, torx, brass)
 Screw(133, tslot, hex, wood)
 Screw(134, tslot, slotted, wood)
 Screw(138, tslot, hex, steel)
 Screw(141, tslot, phillips, steel)
 Screw(146, tslot, torx, brass)
```

13.5.4 *Putting screw objects into sets*

The best solution for each case is not always easy to determine, so it is worth knowing about different approaches. Sometimes it makes sense to combine solutions. You can put these screw objects into sets as well.

You can use the `filter` function to produce sets, which can be reused later:

```julia
julia> issteel(screw) = screw.material == steel;
julia> steel_screws = Set(filter(issteel, screws));

julia> ishex(screw) = screw.drivestyle == hex
julia> hex_screws = Set(filter(ishex, screws))
```

You can then use these sets in set operations:

```julia
julia> steel_screws ∩ hex_screws
Set(Screw[
    Screw(126, headless, hex, steel),
    Screw(115, headless, hex, steel),
    Screw(121, flat, hex, steel),
    Screw(107, headless, hex, steel),
    Screw(108, flat, hex, steel)
])
```

However, this solution can be further improved upon.

13.5.5 *Looking up screws using dictionaries*

Frequently, buyers know the product number of the screw they want and want to lookup the screw using this number rather than a complex search critera. By storing screws in a dictionary, where the key is the product number, you can solve this use case:

```julia
julia> screwdict = Dict(screw.prodnum => screw for screw in screws)
Dict{Int64,Screw} with 51 entries:
  148 => Screw(148, rounded, hex, brass)
  124 => Screw(124, rounded, hex, aluminium)
  134 => Screw(134, tslot, slotted, wood)
  136 => Screw(136, rounded, torx, aluminium)
  131 => Screw(131, tslot, torx, brass)
  144 => Screw(144, rounded, slotted, steel)
  142 => Screw(142, flat, slotted, steel)
  150 => Screw(150, rounded, hex, steel)
  ...

julia> screwdict[137]
Screw(137, headless, phillips, aluminium)

julia> screwdict[115]
Screw(115, flat, phillips, aluminium)
```

This code change allows you to get back to the original solution where you use product numbers in your sets. Let's first make some new sets based on product numbers:

```
prodnums = keys(screwdict)

function isbrass(prodnum)
    screw = screwdict[prodnum]
    screw.material == brass
end
brass_screws = Set(filter(isbrass, prodnums))

function istorx(prodnum)
    screw = screwdict[prodnum]
    screw.drivestyle == torx
end
torx_screws = Set(filter(istorx, prodnums))
```

Now you are back to the elegance of using set operations to pick desired products, based on product keys in sets:

```
julia> brass_screws ∩ torx_screws
Set([100, 122, 144])

julia> [screwdict[pn] for pn in brass_screws ∩ torx_screws]
3-element Vector{Screw}:
 Screw(100, rounded, torx, brass)
 Screw(122, tslot, torx, brass)
 Screw(144, flat, torx, brass)
```

13.6 Search in bug tracker using sets

When developing larger pieces of software, particularly in a team, companies will usually use some form of bug-tracking tool. Commonly, these are web applications that allow testers to submit descriptions of bugs. Managers or product specialists may then review these bugs and assign priorities and severity before the bugs finally get assigned to software developers.

Some common attributes recorded for a bug include the following:

- *Project*—What software project is it part of?
- *Priority*—How important is this bug to fix?
- *Severity*—Is it a minor annoyance or a crash in critical functionality?
- *Component*—Is this in a user interface, client, server, or so on?
- *Assignee*—Who is assigned to deal with the bug currently?

Just like with products, bugs will usually be uniquely identified by a bug number. Thus, a very similar approach to the one described previously can be used: you can use bugs in dictionaries, where the keys are the bug numbers.

I'll demonstrate defining sets composed of different bug numbers. The following are some questions you can imagine being solved using sets:

What are the most critical bugs assigned to Bob in the Lunar Lander project?

```
bob ∩ critical ∩ lunar_lander
```

It may not be practical to have names for each set like this, and sets should be organized according to the fields in the bug tracker. The following shows using dictionaries to group related sets:

```
assignees["Bob"] ∩ severity[:critical] ∩ projects["Lunar Lander"]
```

When doing the set operation on multiple objects, it may be more practical not to use the operator symbols. This is equivalent:

```
intersect(assignees["Bob"], severity[:critical], projects["Lunar Lander"])
```

A manager may ask the following:

What top priority bugs are being handled by Bob and Eve?

```
assignees["Bob"] ∪ assignees["Bob"] ∩ priorities[:top]
```

We could have looked at many more examples, but hopefully, this gives you a good idea of how you can use sets to simplify problems in your own applications.

13.7   *Relational databases and sets*

If you have worked with SQL and relational databases before, then a lot of what you have seen in this chapter might look familiar. In the SQL database query language, one can perform many operations similar to set operations. What is called an *inner join* in the database world is equivalent to a *set intersection*.

Relational databases are built upon a branch of mathematics called *relational algebra*, which covers modeling data and queries on it. In this chapter, you have explored set theory, which is more basic. With relational databases, you can create tables of data with multiple columns that have relations to other tables. The Julia data structure most similar to database tables is called a `DataFrame`[3] and exists in the `DataFrames` package.[4] For in-depth coverage of the `DataFrames` package, see Bogumił Kamiński's *Julia for Data Analysis* (Manning, 2022).

Summary

- Sets can help you organize data such as photo albums, defects in a bug-tracking tool, or items sold in a web shop.
- Sets don't have duplicates and allow very quick membership tests, unlike arrays of elements.
- Elements in sets have no well-defined order, unlike arrays. Elements cannot be inserted at specific positions in the set.

---

[3] A dataframe has multiple named columns. Each column can contain different types of data.
[4] See https://dataframes.juliadata.org/ for more information on DataFrames packages.

- Create a set by providing an array of elements such as `Set([4, 8, 10])`.
- Combine sets using set operations such as `union`, `intersect`, and `setdiff`.
- Check if an element `x` is in a set `S` with the `in` function. This can be written as `in(x, S)` or `x in S`.
- Create an enum type with the `@enum` macro. `@enum Fruit apple banana` creates an enum type `Fruit` with legal values `apple` and `banana`.
- You can achieve operations similar to set operations using `filter` on an array. However, performance will not be equally good for large datasets.
- Set theory and relational algebra (used in relational databases) allow you to do similar operations. However, sets deal with values, while relational databases deal with tables and their relations.

14

Working with vectors and matrices

This chapter covers

- Working with numbers in matrices and performing calculations
- Slicing and dicing arrays
- Concatenating arrays along different dimensions to form larger arrays

In chapter 4, you explored basic operations, such as push!, on one-dimensional arrays, called vectors. In this chapter, you will focus more on working with multidimensional arrays, such as matrices.

What can you use a matrix and vector for? They can be combined to solve a great number of problems. For example, it is popular to use vectors in a geometric interpretation; in this case they represent points in space. You can use matrices to move and rotate these points.

Matrices can even be used to solve mathematical equations, and they are very popular in machine learning. A matrix can be used to represent an image. Every element in a matrix can represent the color of a single pixel. Each of these topics deserves its own chapter or book, so in this chapter I will only cover the essentials of working with vectors and matrices.

14.1 Vectors and matrices in mathematics

A matrix or a vector is not just a dumb container of numbers. For instance, in mathematics, sets, tuples, and vectors may all look like a list of numbers and, hence, seem similar. But what you can *do* with them is different.

The study of vectors and matrices is part of the field of mathematics called *linear algebra*. In linear algebra, single values such as 1, 4, and 8 are called *scalars*. While multiple values in a row or column are *vectors*, tables are *matrices*, and if the data is arranged in a 3D array, it may be referred to as a *cube*. Vectors can further be divided into column vectors and row vectors (figure 14.1).

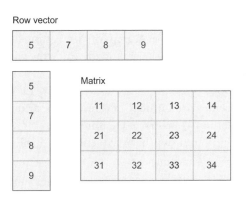

Figure 14.1 **Arrays of different dimensions**

14.2 Constructing a matrix from rows and columns

A matrix can be constructed either by specifying multiple rows stacked on top of each other or by columns lined up, one after the other. When constructing a matrix from row vectors, you separate each row with a semicolon ; ; notice how you don't separate individual elements with a comma. If you have forgotten about this, then review the discussion of row vectors and column vectors in chapter 4:

```julia
julia> table = [2   6 12;
                3   4 12;
                6   2 12;
               12   1 12]
4×3 Matrix{Int64}:
  2   6   12
  3   4   12
  6   2   12
 12   1   12
```

To create a matrix from multiple columns, you can define each column separately and then combine them into a matrix:

```julia
julia> x₁ = [2, 3, 6, 12]
julia> x₂ = [6, 4, 2, 1]
julia> x₃ = [12, 12, 12, 12]
julia> table = [x₁ x₂ x₃]
4×3 Matrix{Int64}:
  2   6   12
  3   4   12
  6   2   12
 12   1   12
```

This is identical to writing the column vectors inline like this:

```julia
table = [[2, 3, 6, 12] [6, 4, 2, 1] [12, 12, 12, 12]]
```

Notice how Julia provides a summary of what kind of `Array` you are getting as a result, with the line `4×3 Matrix{Int64}`. This tells you that Julia made an array with 4 rows and 3 columns, where each element is of type `Int64`.

You can query an arbitrary array about these properties: `eltype` provides the type of each element in the array, `ndims` provides the number of dimensions, and `size` provides the number of components (elements) along each dimension. Normally, we think of the dimensions as length, height, and depth, but in this case I will normally speak of rows and columns:

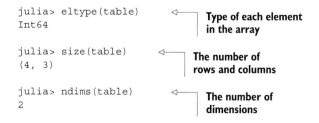

```julia
julia> eltype(table)
Int64
```
◁── **Type of each element in the array**

```julia
julia> size(table)
(4, 3)
```
◁── **The number of rows and columns**

```julia
julia> ndims(table)
2
```
◁── **The number of dimensions**

Figure 14.2 helps clarify what these different properties mean by showing vectors and matrices of different shapes. They have different numbers of rows and columns as well as different orientations and dimensions.

14.3 *The size, length, and norm of an array*

If you come from other programming languages it can be easy to confuse these array concepts:

- `size`—The dimensions of an array
- `length`—Total number of elements in array
- `norm`—Magnitude of a vector

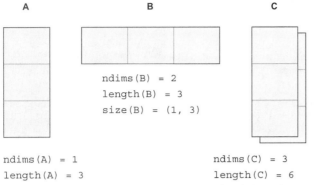

A

ndims(A) = 1
length(A) = 3
size(A) = (3,)

B

ndims(B) = 2
length(B) = 3
size(B) = (1, 3)

C

ndims(C) = 3
length(C) = 6
size(C) = (3, 1, 2)

D

ndims(D) = 2
length(D) = 4
size(D) = (2, 2)

E

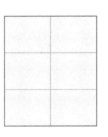

ndims(E) = 2
length(E) = 6
size(E) = (3, 2)

Figure 14.2   Properties of arrays of different shape

A table with 4 rows and 3 columns has been created, making a total of 12 elements:

```
julia> length(table)
12
```

The norm function is trickier to grasp. To explain it, I will use a small vector, with the elements 3 and 4:

```
julia> using LinearAlgebra

julia> norm([3, 4])
5.0
```

Looking at a right-angled triangle will help you visualize what norm is doing. You can think of the elements of the vector as the sides *a* and *b* in the triangle (figure 14.3). norm provides the length of the longest side, the *hypotenuse*.

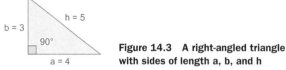

Figure 14.3 **A right-angled triangle with sides of length a, b, and h**

The *Pythagorean theorem* reveals the relationship between all the sides in a right-angled triangle. You can think of norm as applying the Pythagorean theorem to figure out the length of the *hypotenuse*:

$$5^2 = 3^2 + 4^3$$

14.4 *Slicing and dicing an array*

Julia has great support for selecting slices of arrays of different dimensions. This flexibility comes from the fact that the setindex! and getindex functions are invoked when you use square brackets [] to access elements or assign to them. I'll now explore how this slicing works (table 14.1).

Table 14.1 **Relation between element access and Julia function calls**

Syntax sugar	Translates to	Description
xs[i]	getindex(xs, i)	Get element at index i
xs[i,j]	getindex(xs, i, j)	Get element at row i and column j
xs[i] = 42	setindex!(xs, 42, i)	Set element at index i
xs[i,j] = 42	setindex!(xs, 42, i, j)	Set element at row i and column j

I'll begin simply by first looking at accessing individual elements on a one-dimensional array. Figure 14.1 illustrates how one or more elements can be selected in one-dimensional arrays. While the figure shows selections within row vectors, the same principles apply to column vectors.

You can use begin and end within square brackets to refer to the first or last element in a vector along a row or column. In Julia, the first element in an array is at index 1 by default. However, it is possible to create arrays with any start index in Julia, which makes the begin keyword very useful (figure 14.4).

Notice how there are many ways of accessing the same elements. For example, if you had an array A, then A[3] and A[begin+2] would represent the exact same element.

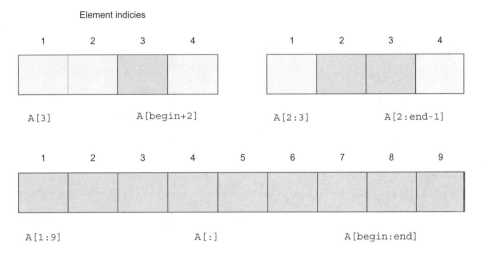

Figure 14.4   Slicing a one-dimensional array A in different ways

For an array with four elements, as in the first two examples, A[4] and A[end] refer to the same element. Likewise A[3] and A[end-1] grab the same array element. You can experiment with these concepts in the Julia REPL:

```julia
julia> A = collect('A':'F')
6-element Vector{Char}:
 'A'
 'B'
 'C'
 'D'
 'E'
 'F'

julia> A[begin+1]
'B': ASCII/Unicode U+0042

julia> A[end-1]
'E': ASCII/Unicode U+0045

julia> A[2:5]
4-element Vector{Char}:
 'B'
 'C'
 'D'
 'E'

julia> A[begin+1:end-1]
4-element Vector{Char}:
 'B'
 'C'
 'D'
 'E'
```

If you don't care about the specific index, and just want all the elements, you can write A[:]. How is that different from just writing A? All slice operations return copies of data. This example will help clarify:

```julia
julia> A = [8, 1, 2, 7];

julia> B = A[:];

julia> B[2] = 42
42

julia> B
4-element Vector{Int64}:
  8
 42
  2
  7

julia> A
4-element Vector{Int64}:
 8
 1
 2
 7
```

Do you see how the second element of B got changed but not the second element of A? Had you written B = A instead of B = A[:], the second element would have been changed in A as well, since A and B would have referred to exactly the same array object.

But what if you want to select a slice of an array without making a copy? Especially when working with very large amounts of data, it can kill performance to frequently copy thousands of elements in some tight inner loop. In these cases, you can create what is called a *view* in a subsection of the array. The slices are not copies of elements of an array but are those elements themselves. You can turn a slice into a view by using the @view macro:

```julia
julia> B = @view A[3:end]
2-element view(::Vector{Int64}, 3:4) with eltype Int64:
 2
 7

julia> B[2] = 1331
1331

julia> A
4-element Vector{Int64}:
    8
    1
    2
 1331
```

The last result shows that changing the second element of B caused the fourth element of A to be changed.

Many of these examples should be relatable, since you have worked with one-dimensional arrays in many previous chapters. It gets more interesting when you are dealing with slices for multidimensional arrays, such as matrices.

Let's create a 2D matrix A to experiment on, using Julia's reshape function. reshape takes an `AbstractArray` as input. Let me explain the next code example: The range `1:12` is used as input. All ranges are subtypes of `AbstractArray`, hence Julia sees the range as a one-dimensional array with 12 elements. The reshape function rearrange these 12 elements to a matrix with 3 rows and 4 columns, referred to as a 3×4 matrix.

```julia
julia> A = reshape(1:12, 3, 4)
3×4 reshape(::UnitRange{Int64}, 3, 4) with eltype Int64:
 1  4  7  10
 2  5  8  11
 3  6  9  12
```

I will demonstrate how to slice a matrix in different ways, but first I will give some advice on how to think about slicing, so you can make sense of the demonstrations.

IMPORTANT The shape of a matrix is how many rows and columns it has. Hence, the function for changing the number of rows and columns is called reshape in Julia. Keep in mind that the length of the matrix cannot be changed by reshape. You can reshape an array A of six elements to a 3×2 or 2×3 matrix, but you *cannot* reshape it to a 3×3 matrix, as that contains nine elements (see figure 14.5).

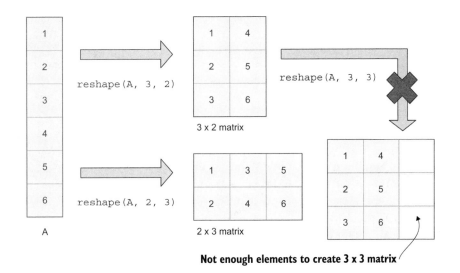

Figure 14.5 An array can be reshaped to matrices with the same number of elements. The cross indicates that you cannot reshape an array of six elements to one with nine elements.

I like to think about array slicing in terms of the set intersection operation ∩. Thus, A[2, 3] can be read as the following: *Give me the intersection of all the elements of row 2 and column 3.*

Figure 14.6 provides a visualization of this idea. The shaded squares represent the row and columns you have selected, and the squares in darker shade represent the intersection between these row and column selections.

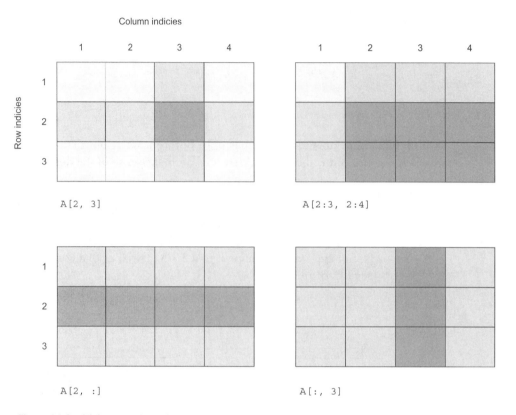

Figure 14.6   Slicing two-dimensional arrays.

This conceptualization makes it easier to understand the selection A[2:3, 2:4]. You can read this as the following: *Give me the intersection of all the elements in rows 2 to 3 and columns 2 to 4.*

Following this logic, it becomes apparent how to select an entire row or column in a matrix. You can experiment with this in the REPL:

```julia
julia> A[1, 2]
4

julia> A[3, 4]
12
```

```
julia> A[:, 4]
3-element Vector{Int64}:
 10
 11
 12

julia> A[2, :]
4-element Vector{Int64}:
  2
  5
  8
 11
```

It is also worth noting that even multidimensional arrays can be treated as one-dimensional ones:

```
julia> A[1]
1

julia> A[4]
4
```

14.5   *Combining matrices and vectors*

Data does not always come in the shape and form you'd like for performing matrix operations. You may have *n* vectors, but really have wanted a matrix with *n* columns instead.

Fortunately, Julia has a number of functions for concatenating matrices. This first example shows how to concatenate two row vectors, either horizontally using hcat or vertically using vcat (figure 14.7).

A = [1 3 5]   B = [7 9 11]

hcat(A, B)

cat(A, B, dims = 2)

vcat(A, B)

cat(A, B, dims = 1)

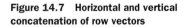

Figure 14.7   Horizontal and vertical concatenation of row vectors

The `cat` function allows you to specify along which dimension you are concatenating. This is useful if you are dealing with higher-dimension arrays. You can perform similar operations with column vectors (figure 14.8).

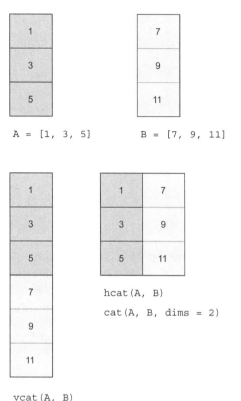

vcat(A, B)

cat(A, B, dims = 1)

Figure 14.8 Horizontal and vertical concatenation of column vectors

The same principles apply to combining matrices; you can concatenate along any dimension. Horizontal and vertical concatenation have their own functions, `hcat` and `vcat`, because they are done so frequently (figure 14.9).

These concatenation functions can take any number of argument; you are not limited to two:

```julia
julia> x = [1, 2, 3]
3-element Vector{Int64}:
 1
 2
 3

julia> y = [8, 6, 4]
3-element Vector{Int64}:
```

```
 8
 6
 4

julia> hcat(x, y, x, y)
3×4 Matrix{Int64}:
 1  8  1  8
 2  6  2  6
 3  4  3  4

julia> hcat(x, 2y, 2x, 3y)
3×4 Matrix{Int64}:
 1  16  2  24
 2  12  4  18
 3   8  6  12
```

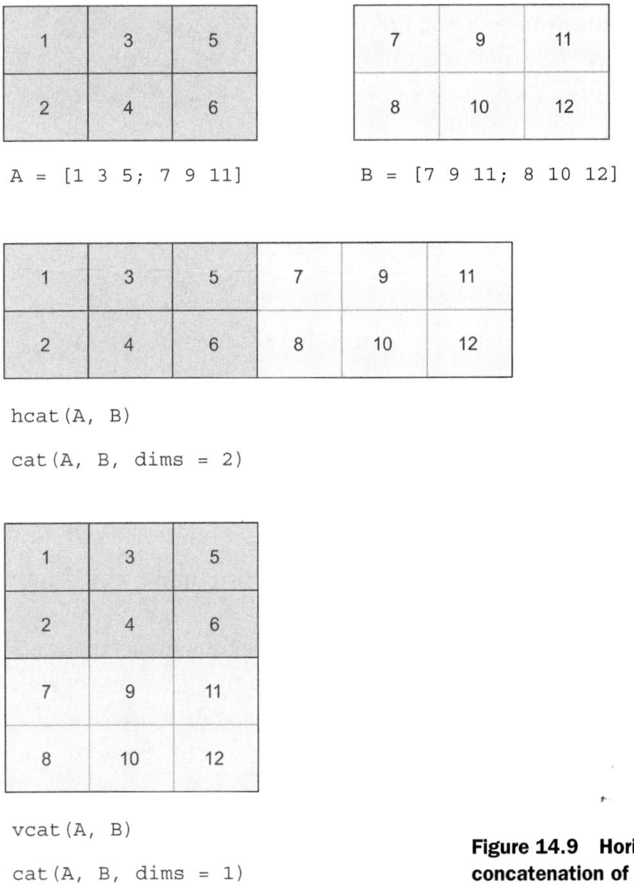

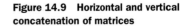

1 3 5
2 4 6
7 9 11
8 10 12
A = [1 3 5; 7 9 11]
B = [7 9 11; 8 10 12]
hcat(A, B)
cat(A, B, dims = 2)
vcat(A, B)
cat(A, B, dims = 1)

Figure 14.9 Horizontal and vertical concatenation of matrices

14.6 Creating matrices

When working with matrices, you often need special kinds of matrices. Creating matrices with only zeros or ones is so common there are special functions to do this:

```
julia> zeros(Int8, 2, 3)
2×3 Matrix{Int8}:
 0  0  0
 0  0  0

julia> ones(2, 3)
2×3 Matrix{Float64}:
 1.0  1.0  1.0
 1.0  1.0  1.0
```

Notice how you can optionally specify what type you want each element to be as the first argument. If you don't specify type, then it will default to `Float64`.

Creating a whole array of random numbers is also often practical. For instance in deep learning, large matrices with random values are frequently used. You will often use random values to create test data:

```
julia> rand(UInt8, 2, 2)
2×2 Matrix{UInt8}:
 0x8e  0x61
 0xcf  0x0d
```

Sometimes you just want to fill a whole matrix with a specific value:

```
julia> fill(12, 3, 3)
3×3 Matrix{Int64}:
 12  12  12
 12  12  12
 12  12  12
```

Vectors and matrices are huge topics, and if we had more time I would have covered the geometric interpretation of vectors and matrices. What are some possible uses? You could have represented the orientation of your rocket with a matrix and its position as a vector. You could have used matrices to rotate or move the rocket around in the coordinate system. For in-depth discussion on working with matrices, *Julia for Data Analysis* (Manning, 2022) by Bogumił Kamiński is an excellent resource.

Summary

- Arrays can be used to define column vectors, row vectors, and matrices.
- Matrices are two-dimensional arrays that can be constructed in many ways. It is most common to define it as a set of rows, but it is also possible to define matrices as a set of columns.

- Arrays have properties such as ndims, size, and length. These describe the number of dimensions, number of elements along each dimension, and total number of elements in the array.
- Arrays can be sliced by specifying ranges, which also generalize to matrices. You can give ranges for rows and columns to cut out a submatrix.
- Slices are copies of data. If you don't want slices to be copies, but directly reference data in the original array, then you can create a slice view with the @view macro.
- Matrices and vectors can be combined horizontally and vertically using hcat and vcat. For arrays of higher dimensions, you can use cat and specify the dimension to concatenate along as an argument.
- Matrices can quickly be created with functions such as rand, fill, ones, and zeros.

Part 4

Software engineering

Software engineering is about how we organize and structure larger programs, so they are easier to maintain, modify, and evolve. Chapter 15 covers functional programming and how it helps create more maintainable software and encourages new perspectives on how to think about code.

Chapter 16 focuses on the physical organization of software into modules, directories, and files, tying this in with dependency management. Large software is most often composed of many packages made by different teams. This part focuses on developing a solid system to handle versioning of software packages that depend on each other.

15
Functional programming in Julia

This chapter covers

- Why understanding functional programming is important in Julia
- The differences between functional and object-oriented program design
- Practical usage of higher-order functions
- Making your code more readable with function chaining
- Developing a password-keeping service

Julia is a multi-paradigm programming language, but a functional programming style is far more common in Julia than in other mainstream languages you may be familiar with, such as Python, Ruby, Java, or C++. Thus, it is natural to have an understanding of the principles of functional programming to become a good Julia developer.

Functional programming is not always the best approach to solving every problem. In this chapter, you will learn to build up a password-keeping service in both an object-oriented and a functional style, allowing you to explore the pros and cons of different programming styles (paradigms). Before building up a larger code example you will look at the core building blocks of functional programming, such as higher-order functions, closures, function chaining, and composition.

15.1 How does functional programming differ from object-oriented programming?

Let's take a high-level perspective on what functional programming is and why its covered in a Julia programming book. The first problem when discussing functional programming is that there is no single clear definition. In this chapter, I will use what I deem a pragmatic definition. Figure 15.1 shows how functional programming fits in with other programming paradigms.

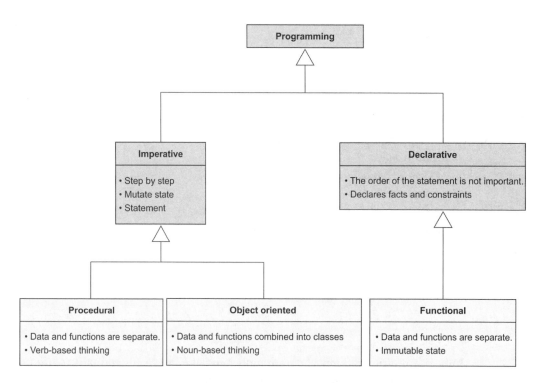

Figure 15.1   Diagram of different programming paradigms and how they are related

The most important thing I want to highlight in figure 15.1 is that *procedural* programming and *functional* programming are *not* the same thing. Writing code with a bunch of functions rather than using an object-oriented approach does not automatically make your code functional. That technique has been used for a long time in languages such as C, Fortran, and Pascal in an approach called procedural programming.

Instead, functional programming usually involves a variety of different practices and approaches:

- Handling functions as *first class objects*, meaning you can pass around functions and store them as if they were regular data
- Supporting *higher-order functions*, which are functions taking functions as arguments
- Using `map`, `filter`, and `reduce` instead of for loops when iterating over collections to perform different operations on them
- Preferring *closures* or *lambdas* instead of objects with methods to manage state

Functional programming offers many ways to combine functions in different ways and modularize your code at a function level.

15.2 How and why you should learn to think functionally

In functional programming, we try to avoid modifying (mutating) input data, which makes reasoning about the flow of data through your code easier. Functions take inputs and transform those inputs to produce outputs, which allows you to think about your programs as elaborate pipelines through which data flows.

The following listing illustrates this concept with the `camel_case` function from chapter 11, which is a nesting of multiple function calls. Each call produces input for the next function.

Listing 15.1 Converting snake case to camel case

```
"Turns hello_to_you into HelloToYou"
function camel_case(input::AbstractString)
    join(map(uppercasefirst, split(input, '_')))
end
```

We can use a data-flow diagram to visualize how the data flows between functions. The rounded boxes represent data transformations in a data-flow diagram, and the arrows are annotated with the type of data that flows along them. For instance string and character data flows into `split`, and then an array of strings flows out of `split` and into `map`.

Imperative programming styles, such as object-oriented programming, often make it very hard to perform such an analysis of data flow because functions or methods mutate their inputs. Instead of thinking about flows of data getting transformed, it is better to conceptualize the process as objects sending messages to each other to mutate their state.

15.3 Avoid deeply nested calls with function chaining

Before building up larger code examples demonstrating pros and cons of functional programming, I want you to get a better grasp of some of the fundamental building blocks you have at your disposal. The `camel_case` function in the previous section was implemented in quite a functional manner but isn't very easy to read because it is deeply nested. You don't end up with anything looking like the neat pipeline in figure 15.2.

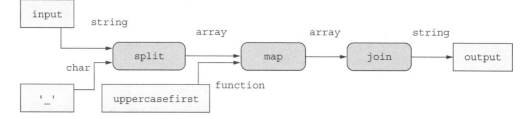

Figure 15.2   Data flow for the `camel_case` function

However, it is possible to build something like that figure using the Julia pipe operator `|>`. It allows you to pipe the output from one function into another function. The following is a complete example, which I'll break down afterward.

Listing 15.2   Camel case through function chaining

```
splitter(dlm) = str -> split(str, dlm)
mapper(fn) = xs -> map(fn, xs)

function camel_case(input::AbstractString)
    input |> splitter('_') |> mapper(uppercasefirst) |> join
end
```

In the REPL you can experiment with how the `splitter` and `mapper` functions work:

```
julia> f = splitter('_')
#13 (generic function with 1 method)

julia> words = f("hello_how_are_you")
4-element Vector{SubString{String}}:
 "hello"
 "how"
 "are"
 "you"

julia> g = mapper(uppercasefirst)
#15 (generic function with 1 method)

julia> g(words)
4-element Vector{String}:
 "Hello"
 "How"
 "Are"
 "You"
```

To understand listing 15.2 you need to understand the `->` and `|>` operators. The `->` operator is used to define what are called *anonymous functions* in Julia.

15.3.1 *Understanding anonymous functions and closures*

An anonymous function is a function without a name. You can create one-line anonymous functions with the -> operator. Without anonymous functions, you would need to write splitter and mapper, as shown in the following listing.

Listing 15.3 splitter and mapper without anonymous functions

```
"Create a function which splits on `dlm` character"
function splitter(dlm)
    function f(str)
        split(str, dlm)          The return is not needed; it
    end                          is just added to emphasize
    return f          ◁───┘      that f is returned.
end


"Create a function applying function `fn` on all its input"
function mapper(fn)
    function g(xs)
        map(fn, xs)      This return is also not needed,
    end                  but the last expression is
    return g      ◁───┘  returned anyway.
end
```

The example shows that the names of the functions being returned is not important. To the users of splitter and mapper it is not important that internally these functions got named f and g. Thus, anonymous functions are used whenever the name is not important. You can take one of the code examples from chapter 4 dealing with degrees and sine and make it neater, as in the following listing.

Listing 15.4 Simplifying code with anonymous functions

```
degsin(deg) = sin(deg2rad(deg))      Named function
map(degsin, 0:15:90)                 variant


map(deg->sin(deg2rad(deg)), 0:15:90)      ◁─── One-line variant


map(0:15:90) do deg
    rads = deg2rad(deg)      Multi-line
    sin(rads)                variant
end
```

If you cannot fit an anonymous function within a single line, then the -> operator is impractical. In these cases you can use the do-end form shown at the end of listing 15.4.

The f and g functions returned by splitter and mapper are called closures. A *closure* is a function that has captured some external state not supplied as an argument. The f function only accepts a string str as an argument. The delimiter dlm used to split the string str was captured from its enclosing scope. In this case the splitter function definition defines the scope f inside.

The g function only takes collection of data xs to work on. The function fn to apply to each element in xs was captured from its enclosing scope defined by the mapper function.

Closures don't need to be named. The splitter and mapper functions in listing 15.2 return anonymous functions. These anonymous functions are also closures, as they capture variables from their enclosing scope. In fact, it is a fairly common misunderstanding to believe that a closure is just a fancy term for an *anonymous function*. That is not a surprising misconception, given that anonymous functions are so frequently used to define closures.

15.3.2   *Using the pipe operator |>*

Julia pipeline syntax is used to chain together functions taking single arguments as inputs. That allows you to rewrite a call such as f(g(x)) to x |> g |> f.

That fact helps explain why you had to make the splitter and mapper functions. Normal split and map functions require multiple inputs and thus cannot be used with the pipe operator |>. The functions (closures) returned by splitter and mapper can be used in a pipeline:

```
julia> f = splitter('_');

julia> g = mapper(uppercasefirst);

julia> "hi_there_world" |> f
3-element Vector{SubString{String}}:
 "hi"
 "there"
 "world"

julia> "hi_there_world" |> f |> g
3-element Vector{String}:
 "Hi"
 "There"
 "World"

julia> "hi_there_world" |> f |> g |> join
"HiThereWorld"
```

The next important functional concept, *partial application*, is arrived at by simply asking the following questions: Why do you need to use the name splitter and mapper? Can't you just call them split and map as well?

15.3.3   *Conveniently produce new functions using partial application*

In computer science, *partial function application* refers to the process of fixing a number of arguments to a function, producing another function accepting fewer arguments.

This definition of partial application may sound complicated, but with a practical example you will see that it is a lot easier than it sounds.

If you import the `split` and `map` functions you can add new methods to them taking only single arguments, and thus you can define a slightly more elegant version of the `camel_case` function, as in the following listing.

Listing 15.5 Camel case with partial application

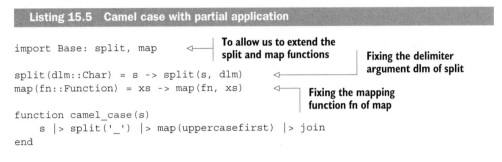

```
import Base: split, map          ◁────┐ To allow us to extend the
                                        split and map functions       Fixing the delimiter
                                                                      argument dlm of split
split(dlm::Char) = s -> split(s, dlm)   ◁─────────────────────┘
map(fn::Function) = xs -> map(fn, xs)   ◁──┐ Fixing the mapping
                                            function fn of map
function camel_case(s)
    s |> split('_') |> map(uppercasefirst) |> join
end
```

In essence you allow the user of the `split` function to *fix* the `dlm` argument. The new `split` function returned as the `dlm` value fixed. The same principle applies to `map`. This process of fixing specific arguments to a function is partial function application.

Since such capability is so practical many functions in the Julia standard library have been extended, with methods taking a subset of all required arguments, instead returning a function taking the rest of the arguments. Let me clarify with some built-in functions from the `Base` module (the built-in Julia module that is always loaded):

```
julia> images = ["bear.jpg", "truck.png", "car.jpg", "duck.png"];

julia> findfirst(img->img == "truck.png", images)
2

julia> findfirst(==("truck.png"), images)
2

julia> filter(img->endswith(img, ".png"), images)
2-element Vector{String}:
 "truck.png"
 "duck.png"

julia> filter(endswith(".png"), images)
2-element Vector{String}:
 "truck.png"
 "duck.png"
```

You can verify for yourself that when the `endswith` function is only given a single argument it calls a method returning a function:

```
julia> ispng = endswith(".png")

julia> ispng isa Function
true
```

```
julia> ispng("truck.png")
true

julia> ispng("car.jpg")
false
```

These are some good examples of mixing and matching functions in clever ways, which is a large part of what functional programmers do.

15.4   *Implementing Caesar and substitution ciphers*

I promised I would demonstrate how to build a password encryption service both in an object-oriented and a functional style. Before I do that, I need to explain how you can use ciphers to encrypt and decrypt passwords.

A *cipher* is an algorithm that takes as input what is called the *message* and, using a secret key, encrypts the message to produce what is called the *cipher text*. When you can use the same key to encrypt and decrypt it is called *symmetric* encryption (figure 15.3).

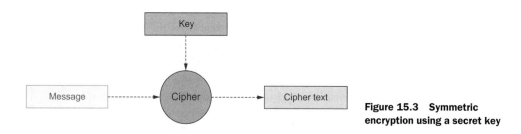

Figure 15.3   **Symmetric encryption using a secret key**

I will demonstrate implementing two different ciphers: the Caesar cipher and the substitution cipher (figure 15.4). By making two ciphers, I will show you how to configure a password-keeping service to use different ciphers. Making ciphers exchangeable requires making abstractions, which provides an opportunity to compare how abstractions are built using object-oriented principles and functional programming principles.

Each cipher algorithm is based on looking up a letter in the input message on the outer dial. Next, you will look at the corresponding letter at the inner dial to figure out what it should be translated to in the cipher text.

In the Caesar cipher, you can see that the letter A will translate to C, while B will be translated to D, and so on. Both the inner and outer dials of the Caesar cipher are alphabetical. The cipher *key* is how much you have rotated the inner dial (shifted two letters counterclockwise).

When Roman generals sent secret messages to each other, each general would have to know this secret key to know how much the inner dial had been rotated. Should the enemy learn this secret they could decrypt any message intercepted.

The substitution cipher is more complex in that the inner dial itself is the secret key. You don't rotate the dial but replace it entirely. For two parties to send secret messages to each other they need to have the same inner dial installed. We characterize the

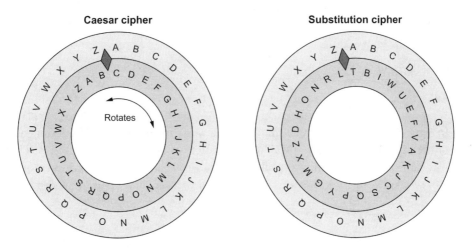

Figure 15.4 **The inner dial of a Caesar cipher can rotate. The inner dial of a substitution cipher is fixed, but the order of the alphabet will be random.**

substitution cipher as a mapping between two alphabets. The letters on the outer dial form one alphabet, which is mapped to the letters on the inner dial; this is known as the *substitution alphabet*.

I will start by demonstrating a straightforward implementation of both ciphers before showing an inflexible password-keeping service, which is hardwired to a single cipher. The next step involves showing how you can modify the ciphers and password-keeping service to allow the cipher used for encrypting and decrypting passwords to be swapped out. In the first approach, I will show how this goal can be accomplished using an object-oriented design, then I will demonstrate a functional approach.

15.4.1 *Implementing the Caesar cipher*

In listing 15.6, I demonstrate implementing the Caesar cipher. The number of letters rotated is passed in the `shift` argument, and `ch` is the character being encrypted or decrypted. For both `caesar_encrypt` and `caesar_decrypt`, you need to check if the input character `ch` is actually in the alphabet. This ensures special symbols and whitespace will not get encrypted or decrypted.

Listing 15.6 Caesar cipher encryption and decryption

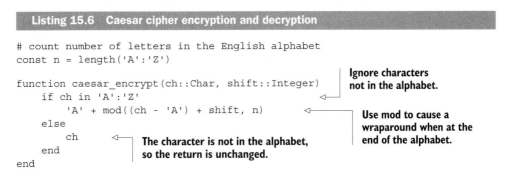

```
# count number of letters in the English alphabet
const n = length('A':'Z')

function caesar_encrypt(ch::Char, shift::Integer)
    if ch in 'A':'Z'
        'A' + mod((ch - 'A') + shift, n)
    else
        ch
    end
end
```

Ignore characters not in the alphabet.

Use mod to cause a wraparound when at the end of the alphabet.

The character is not in the alphabet, so the return is unchanged.

```
function caesar_decrypt(ch::Char, shift::Integer)
    if ch in 'A':'Z'
        'A' + mod((ch - 'A') - shift, n)
    else
        ch
    end
end
```

In figure 15.4 you will notice that we get a wrap-around effect. The letters at the end of the alphabet, such as Y and Z, map to letters at the beginning A and B. That is why you cannot just add a Shift to each letter, ch + shift. The mod function (modulo operator) makes your numbers work akin to what you see on a 12-hour analog clock:

```
julia> mod(1, 12)
1

julia> mod(9, 12)
9

julia> mod(13, 12)      <──┐
1
                           │  The input is larger
                           │  than 12, so it wraps
julia> mod(21, 12)      <──┤  around.
9                          │
                           │
julia> mod(17, 12)      <──┘
 5
```

In this example, I input ch - 'A' to mod, so that I can turn letters into values in the range 0 to 25. This makes it easier to calculate the wrap-around value. Afterward, I need to turn the numbers from 0 to 25 into a letter. Fortunately, Julia math operations between numbers and letters are set up to do that for you in a predictable manner, as illustrated in the next REPL session:

```
julia> 'A' + 1
'B': ASCII/Unicode U+0042

julia> 'A' + 4
'E': ASCII/Unicode U+0045                    You can separate
                                             statements with a
julia> ch = 'Z'; n = 26; shift = 2    <──┘   semicolon.
2
                                             Z wraps around
                                             to become B.
julia> 'A' + mod((ch - 'A') + shift, n)   <──┘
 'B': ASCII/Unicode U+0042
```

You may notice that I am using the same shift value as used in figure 15.4.

Now you know how to encrypt a single character, but how can you use that knowledge to encrypt and decrypt whole messages? You can use the map function to encrypt a message and then attempt to decrypt it afterward to make sure you get back what you put in:

```
julia> message = "THE QUICK BROWN FOX JUMPS OVER THE LAZY DOG";

julia> shift = 2;

julia> cipher_text = map(ch -> caesar_encrypt(ch, shift), message)
"VJG SWKEM DTQYP HQZ LWORU QXGT VJG NCBA FQI"

julia> map(cipher_text) do ch
           caesar_decrypt(ch, shift)
       end
"THE QUICK BROWN FOX JUMPS OVER THE LAZY DOG"
```

Notice I used the *do-end* form to call `decrypt`, so you can compare code readability. Sometimes I find the do-end form to be easier to read, even if only dealing with a single line of code.

15.4.2 Implementing substitution ciphers

To create a substitution cipher, I need to create a mapping between two alphabets. For this purpose I need to use the `shuffle` function found in the `Random` module.

Notice in the following code the use of the range `'A':'Z'` to quickly create a string containing all the letters in the alphabet. `collect` applied to this range would have given an array of letters, but in this case I want a string, so I use `join` instead.

`shuffle` will randomly rearrange the elements in an array. Remember that a range is a subtype of `AbstractArray`, which is why you can shuffle a range as if it were a regular array:

```
julia> using Random

julia> join('A':'Z')
"ABCDEFGHIJKLMNOPQRSTUVWXYZ"

julia> shuffle([1, 2, 3])
3-element Vector{Int64}:
 2
 3
 1

julia> shuffle(1:5)
5-element Vector{Int64}:
 1
 2
 5
 4
 3

julia> join(shuffle('A':'Z'))
"PKTAVEQDXGWJMBZOFSLICRUNYH"
```

These functions provide the tools needed to create a dictionary mapping between the two alphabets. When creating a dictionary you normally need key–value pairs, but in the following code, keys and values are created as separate arrays, so how can I make a dictionary out of this?

```
julia> alphabet = join('A':'F')        ◁──┤ Use range A–F to make
"ABCDEF"                                     examples shorter.

julia> substitute = join(shuffle('A':'F'))
"ACFBDE"
```

The zip function solves this problem. zip can take two arrays of elements and turn them into an iterable object, which when collected provides an array of pairs:

```
julia> collect(zip(alphabet, substitute))
6-element Vector{Tuple{Char, Char}}:
 ('A', 'A')
 ('B', 'C')
 ('C', 'F')
 ('D', 'B')
 ('E', 'D')
 ('F', 'E')
```

You can take the iterable object returned from the zip function and feed it to the Dict constructor. Because this iterable object returns value pairs on each iteration I will use the object returned from zip to create a dictionary:

```
julia> mapping = Dict(zip(alphabet, substitute))
Dict{Char, Char} with 6 entries:
  'C' => 'F'
  'D' => 'B'
  'A' => 'A'
  'E' => 'D'
  'F' => 'E'
  'B' => 'C'
```

This provides input data that can be used with an encryption function for the substitution cipher.

> Listing 15.7   Substitution cipher encryption based on dictionary lookup

```
function substitution_encrypt(ch::Char, mapping::Dict{Char, Char})
    get(mapping, char, char)
end
```

There is one glaring problem with this approach: decryption requires a reverse lookup. Looking at the mapping as equivalent to the encryption key is a bad solution. For symmetric encryption it is best to use the same key for both encryption and decryption. Thus, instead of doing lookup using a dictionary, I will instead search an array of pairs, as shown in the following listing.

Listing 15.8 Substitution cipher encryption based on an array lookup

```
using Random

alphabet = join('A':'Z')
substitute = join(shuffle('A':'Z'))
mapping = collect(zip(alphabet, substitute))

function substitution_encrypt(ch::Char, mapping::Vector)
    i = findfirst(row->first(row) == ch, mapping)
    if isnothing(i)
        ch
    else
        mapping[i][2]
    end
end

function substitution_decrypt(ch::Char, mapping::Vector)
    i = findfirst(row->last(row) == ch, mapping)
    if isnothing(i)
        ch
    else
        mapping[i][1]
    end
end
```

Find the index where first character is equal to ch.

If the character isn't in the mapping, nothing is returned.

Return the second character at mapping row i.

The solution is similar to the Caesar cipher solution in that you don't need to perform any encryption or decryption if the character ch is not in the alphabet. It is based on a linear search with the findfirst function to find the index of the tuple with the key you are interested in. If row is the tuple ('B', 'Q'), then first(row) is 'B', and last(row) is 'Q'. When doing encryption, first use first(row) as the lookup key then last(row) as the lookup key when doing decryption.

You might ask, *Isn't doing a linear search through an array a lot slower than doing a dictionary lookup?* No. For such a short array of simple values, a linear search would be faster. You would need at least 100 entries before there would be any noticeable difference in lookup performance.

15.5 *Creating a cipher-algorithm-agnostic service*

Imagine you have a service using a cipher and want to make it easier to swap out which cipher you are using. Here I will present a toy example to convey the concept of using a password-keeping service. It maintains a dictionary with logins as keys and encrypted passwords as values.

Listing 15.9 Password keeping service

```
mutable struct Vault
    passwords::Dict{String, String}
    shift::Int64
end
```

Vault is made mutable, since it must be possible to add passwords.

```
function Vault(shift::Integer)
    emptydict = Dict{String, String}()
    Vault(emptydict, shift)
end
```

Initialize with the empty passwords dictionary.

```
function addlogin!(vault::Vault,
                   login::AbstractString,
                   password::AbstractString)
    vault.passwords[login] = map(password) do ch
        encrypt(ch, vault.shift)
    end
end
```

Add an encrypted password to the password dictionary.

```
function getpassword(vault::Vault, login::AbstractString)
    map(ch -> decrypt(ch, vault.shift), vault.passwords[login])
end
```

Look up the password for the login name.

While the code works, there are numerous problems with this approach:

1   It is hardcoded to only support one encryption scheme: using a Caesar cipher. There should be a choice of any cipher.

2   The service assumes encryption, and decryption is done one character at a time. Encryption should be generalized to deal with whole strings because it is not necessarily implemented as character substitution.

15.6   *Building an encryption service using object-oriented programming*

In code listing 15.9 the cipher is hardcoded; you want to be able to swap the cipher with a different one. Let's look at how that can be achieved.

The solution is an abstract interface to the ciphers, so users of a password service do not need to know any particular details about each type of cipher. Listing 15.10 illustrates an object-oriented approach to this problem. First I define a Cipher as an abstract type, with a number of functions it has to support. I will add methods to each of these functions to add support for my particular cipher.

Listing 15.10   Defining an abstract cipher interface

```
abstract type Cipher end

function encrypt(cipher::Cipher, char::Char)
    error("Implement encrypt(::", typeof(cipher), ", char)")
end

function decrypt(cipher::Cipher, char::Char)
    error("Implement decrypt(::", typeof(cipher), ", char)")
end

function encrypt(cipher::Cipher, message::AbstractString)
    map(ch -> encrypt(cipher, ch), message)
end
```

```
function decrypt(cipher::Cipher, ciphertext::AbstractString)
    map(ch -> decrypt(cipher, ch), ciphertext)
end
```

The way this code has been set up, I have made implementing encrypt and decrypt for *message strings* and *cipher text strings* optional. The default implementation will use encrypt and decrypt of single characters. However, in your own code, if you have not implemented these you will get an error message if you try to perform encryption or decryption with your cipher.

You may notice that I have taken a slightly different approach in specifying interfaces here than I took in chapter 12. The normal recommended approach is defining functions and documenting which methods the user of your API is supposed to implement. Here I make an explicit error message explaining what you need to do. It is useful to know both practices. In this case, I felt it was more practical, as the same functions exist for dealing with strings as for dealing with individual characters. First, I will implement the Cipher interface for the Caesar cipher.

Listing 15.11 Caesar cipher implementing the Cipher interface

```
struct CaesarCipher <: Cipher
    shift::Int
end

const n = length('A':'Z')

function encrypt(cipher::CaesarCipher, ch::Char)
    if ch in 'A':'Z'
        'A' + mod((ch - 'A') + cipher.shift, n)
    else
        ch
    end
end

function decrypt(cipher::CaesarCipher, ch::Char)
    if ch in 'A':'Z'
        'A' + mod((ch - 'A') - cipher.shift, n)
    else
        ch
    end
end
```

This new Caesar cipher implementation is almost exactly like the previous implementation (listing 15.6), except in this example, I obtain the shift from the cipher object instead of getting it directly.

Listing 15.12 shows the object-oriented substitution cipher. It is similar to the original implementation (listing 15.8), except I am storing the mapping in the SubstitutionCipher object, and calling to encrypt and decrypt requires passing the cipher object rather than the mapping.

Listing 15.12   Substitution cipher implementing the Cipher interface

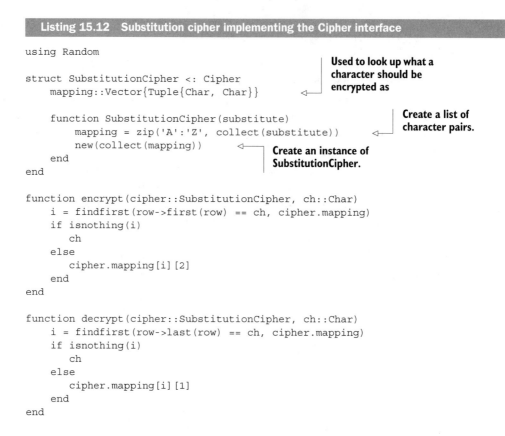

```
using Random

struct SubstitutionCipher <: Cipher          Used to look up what a
    mapping::Vector{Tuple{Char, Char}}        character should be
                                              encrypted as

    function SubstitutionCipher(substitute)            Create a list of
        mapping = zip('A':'Z', collect(substitute))    character pairs.
        new(collect(mapping))       Create an instance of
    end                             SubstitutionCipher.
end

function encrypt(cipher::SubstitutionCipher, ch::Char)
    i = findfirst(row->first(row) == ch, cipher.mapping)
    if isnothing(i)
        ch
    else
        cipher.mapping[i][2]
    end
end

function decrypt(cipher::SubstitutionCipher, ch::Char)
    i = findfirst(row->last(row) == ch, cipher.mapping)
    if isnothing(i)
        ch
    else
        cipher.mapping[i][1]
    end
end
```

You can now modify your password-keeping service to point to an abstract cipher rather than a concrete one (listing 15.13). That allows you to swap out the cipher used with any concrete cipher implementing the Cipher interface.

Listing 15.13   Cipher-algorithm-agnostic password-keeping service

```
mutable struct Vault
    passwords::Dict{String, String}
    cipher::Cipher
end

function Vault(cipher::Cipher)
    Vault(Dict{String, String}(), cipher)
end

function addlogin!(vault::Vault, login::AbstractString,
    password::AbstractString)
    vault.passwords[login] = encrypt(vault.cipher, password)
end

function getpassword(vault::Vault, login::AbstractString)
    decrypt(vault.cipher, vault.passwords[login])
end
```

I can now try the upgraded password-keeping service with different ciphers. I'll show an example with a Caesar cipher first. I start by creating a vault to store the passwords in. The vault is initialized with the cipher it will use to encrypt and decrypt passwords stored within it.

Next I call addlogin! to add passwords to the vault. Afterward I use getpassword to make sure I get the same passwords out that I put in:

```
julia> vault = Vault(CaesarCipher(23))
Vault(Dict{String,String}(), CaesarCipher(23))

julia> addlogin!(vault, "google", "BING")
"YFKD"

julia> addlogin!(vault, "amazon", "SECRET")
"PBZOBQ"

julia> getpassword(vault, "google")
"BING"

julia> getpassword(vault, "amazon")
"SECRET"
```

Next I'll show an example with the substitution cipher. In this case, I initialize the substitution cipher with a substitution alphabet. You can see from this that the letters ABC would get replaced by CQP:

```
julia> substitute = "CQPYXVFHRNZMWOITJSUBKLEGDA";
julia> cipher = SubstitutionCipher(substitute);
julia> vault = Vault(cipher);

julia> addlogin!(vault, "amazon", "SECRET")
"UXPSXB"

julia> addlogin!(vault, "apple", "JONAGOLD")
"NIOCFIMY"

julia> getpassword(vault, "amazon")
"SECRET"

julia> getpassword(vault, "apple")
"JONAGOLD"
```

15.7 *Building an encryption service using functional programming*

The point of showing how to accomplish the abstraction using an object-oriented approach first is that more programmers are already familiar with this approach. In this case *object oriented* means I am solving the problem by thinking in terms of type hierarchies and objects. I represented the cipher as an object and defined functions with methods that operated on these cipher objects.

With the functional approach, I will instead aim to solve the problem by thinking in terms of functions: higher-order functions and closures. The purpose is exposing you to two different mindsets on solving programming problems. To be a good Julia programmer you need to understand both.

15.7.1   *Defining a functional Caesar cipher*

I will define a Caesar cipher by using the partial application technique first shown in listing 15.5. This approach allows expansion of the original solution developed with the caesar_encrypt and caesar_decrypt functions (listing 15.6).

Notice in listing 15.14 how there are no cipher types in the code anymore. There is no data object representing the Caesar cipher. Instead I am adding new methods to the caesar_ encrypt and caesar_decrypt to allow partial application, so when only a shift argument is provided I will return a function taking a character rather than an character in the cipher text.

Listing 15.14   A Caesar cipher with functional flavor

```julia
const n = length('A':'Z')

# Original cipher functions
function caesar_encrypt(ch::Char, shift::Integer)
    if ch in 'A':'Z'
        'A' + mod((ch - 'A') + shift, n)
    else
        ch
    end
end

function caesar_decrypt(ch::Char, shift::Integer)
    caesar_encrypt(ch, -shift)          ◁──┐  Trick to avoid implementing
end                                         │  nearly identical code

# Implement a functional interface using partial application
function caesar_encrypt(shift::Integer)
    msg -> map(msg) do ch               ◁──┐
        caesar_encrypt(ch, shift)          │
    end                                    │
end                                        │  Return closure
                                           │  capturing shift
function caesar_decrypt(shift::Integer)    │
    msg -> map(msg) do ch               ◁──┘
        caesar_decrypt(ch, shift)
    end
end
```

Let's look at how these functions get used. I'll start by calling caesar_encrypt with a shift value of 1. It returns a function meant to be used for encryption. I'll then use that function to encrypt the text string "ABC". A similar pattern is used to create and use the decryption function:

```
julia> encrypt = caesar_encrypt(1)

julia> encrypt("ABC")
"BCD"

julia> decrypt = caesar_decrypt(1)

julia> decrypt("BCD")
"ABC"

julia> encrypt('A')
0-dimensional Array{Char, 0}:
'B'

julia> decrypt('B')
0-dimensional Array{Char, 0}:
'A'
```

> **This works because map can map across individual characters.**

A benefit of this solution is that it is easy to chain together results with the pipe operator | >:

```
julia> "HELLO" |> caesar_encrypt(2)
"JGNNQ"

julia> "HELLO" |> caesar_encrypt(2) |> caesar_decrypt(2)
"HELLO"
```

15.7.2 Defining a functional substitution cipher

To make the substitution cipher, I will expand on the substitution cipher code written in listing 15.8. I will employ the partial application technique again, adding two methods to the existing substitution_encrypt and substitution_decrypt (listing 15.15). They only take mapping as an argument but return cipher functions, which will encrypt or decrypt a message given to them.

Listing 15.15 A substitution cipher with functional flavor

```
function substitution_encrypt(mapping::Vector)
    msg -> map(msg) do ch
        substitution_encrypt(ch, mapping)
    end
end

function substitution_decrypt(mapping::Vector)
    msg -> map(msg) do ch
        substitution_decrypt(ch, mapping)
    end
end
```

I will use the substitution cipher in a similar fashion to the Caesar cipher. The main difference is that I use a mapping instead of a shift as the cipher key:

```
julia> alphabet = join('A':'Z');

julia> substitute = join(shuffle('A':'Z'));

julia> mapping = collect(zip(alphabet, substitute))

julia> "HELLO" |> substitution_encrypt(mapping)
"NEPPR"

julia> "HELLO" |> substitution_encrypt(mapping) |>
       substitution_decrypt(mapping)
"HELLO"
```

Now you know the pieces to make a password keeper based on functional design principles.

15.7.3 *Implementing a functional password-keeper service*

Now let's put it all together and create a password keeper that uses the encryption and decryption functions to allow logins and passwords to be stored and retrieved. There are many ways of doing this. In listing 15.16, I will deliberately go over the top to create a strong contrast with the object-oriented solution.

Listing 15.16   A password-keeper service with excessively functional style

```
function makevault(encrypt::Function, decrypt::Function)
    passwords = Dict{String, String}()

    function addlogin(login::AbstractString, password::AbstractString)
        passwords[login] = encrypt(password)
    end

    function getpassword(login::AbstractString)
        decrypt(passwords[login])
    end

    addlogin, getpassword
end
```

Let's look at an example of using this implementation to define a password keeper using a Caesar cipher. The Vault gets initialized with two function objects produced by calls to caesar_encrypt and caesar_decrypt, respectively:

```
julia> addlogin, getpasswd = makevault(
                              caesar_encrypt(2),
                              caesar_decrypt(2));

julia> addlogin("google", "SECRET")
"UGETGV"

julia> addlogin("amazon", "QWERTY")
"SYGTVA"
```

```
julia> getpasswd("google")
"SECRET"

julia> getpasswd("amazon")
"QWERTY"
```

With the substitution cipher there is a bit more setup to create the mapping vector. In all other aspects the password-keeper vault is set up the same way as the Caesar cipher:

```
julia> using Random

julia> alphabet = join('A':'Z')
"ABCDEFGHIJKLMNOPQRSTUVWXYZ"

julia> substitute = join(shuffle('A':'Z'))
"TQRBVPMHNFUESGZOLIDXCAWYJK"

julia> mapping = collect(zip(alphabet, substitute));

julia> addlogin, getpasswd = makevault(
                substitution_encrypt(mapping),
                substitution_decrypt(mapping));

julia> addlogin("google", "SECRET")
"DVRIVX"

julia> addlogin("amazon", "QWERTY")
"LWVIXJ"

julia> getpasswd("google")
"SECRET"

julia> getpasswd("amazon")
"QWERTY"
```

Now it is time to take a few steps back and reflect upon why exactly you would want to design the closures in the way shown in the examples. The objective is the same as that of the object-oriented case: presenting a generic interface to ciphers, so you can change which cipher is used without changing the implementation of the password-keeper implementation.

I did this by returning encryption and decryption functions, which don't expose any implementation details in their function signature. A *function signature* refers to what arguments a function takes, their order, and their type. The Caesar cipher and substitution cipher produce encryption and decryption functions with the same signatures. That is why they are interchangeable.

I attempted to make each presented solution as different as possible to make it clearer what the difference between functional and object-oriented programming is. Sometimes a caricature is helpful in getting a point across. Yet for real solutions you should always try to use good taste and find a sensible balance between an object-oriented and a functional approach.

In the case of making a password-keeper solution, the object-oriented approach was superior in my opinion, while converting snake case to camel case worked very well with a functional approach. Why the difference? Functional programming works very well when your problem can be reduced to some sort of data transformation. Instead, when you are dealing with something inherently stateful, such as a password-keeper service, an object-oriented approach is a more natural fit, as object-oriented programming is all about modifying state.

Summary

- Functional and procedural programming are often thought of as being interchangeable, but they are not the same. In functional programming, functions are first-class objects that can be passed around and manipulated with higher-order functions.
- Functionally oriented code is easier to analyze and debug, as it forms a clearer flow of data.
- Difficult-to-read function call nesting can be solved by using the function chaining operator |>.
- *Anonymous functions* are functions without names. They help simplify the creation of inline closures.
- Anonymous functions can be created with the -> operator or the *do-end* form.
- A *closure* is a function that captures state from its enclosing scope; it is a function with memory. Closures can be used to mimic objects with state, facilitate partial application, and manage resource acquisition and release (opening and closing a file).
- *Partial application* is a technique in which you return a function rather than a result when not all arguments have been provided to a function. This simplifies creating function arguments to higher-order functions, such as `map`, `filter`, and `reduce`.
- Elements in an array can be randomly shuffled around with the `shuffle` function from the `Random` built-in module. Many encryption algorithms need randomly shuffled input, and this is also a good way of creating input to test sorting functions on.
- Combine functional and object-oriented techniques for optimal results in Julia. Different problems require different approaches. Through practice you will develop a better intuition for when one approach is better than the other.

Organizing and modularizing your code

16

This chapter covers

- Introducing the concept of environments to managed dependencies
- Adding and removing package dependencies using environments
- Developing code in different environments and switching between them
- Creating a Julia package and adding dependencies to it
- Organizing code within a package
- Adding tests to packages
- Exploring the relationship between modules and packages

For large-scale software development you cannot dump code ad hoc into Julia source code files as has been shown in previous chapters. Instead, code must be modularized and organized. Organized code is easier to understand and navigate. In this chapter, you will learn how to take the geometry code you worked on earlier and organize it into a Julia package.

Packages are useful because they give you a way of bundling related code, distributing it, and version controlling it. Packages can depend on other packages in elaborate dependency trees. Real-world systems are built by combining numerous packages into one larger system. If you were working in a large organization on a wide-ranging project, then different teams would likely make different packages, which would then be combined to create the complete system.

In this chapter, I will teach you to organize code within a package, add and remove dependencies to other packages, and set up tests for your package. Remember to load modules with statements such as `using Statistics` and `using LinearAlgebra`. I will also explain how the *module* concept relates to the package concept.

16.1 *Setting up a work environment*

When developing software, you may want to use different versions of the same packages. While developing Julia code for your workplace, you may want to use the most stable and well-tested version of each package; this might not be as crucial for your hobby projects, and you may prefer instead to use the most recent versions with the latest cool features.

Julia environments let you switch between a *job* and a *hobby* environment setup with different package versions. I am using the word *job* instead of *work* to avoid confusing it with a working directory, which refers to the directory you are currently working in. In this section you will look at the following:

- Creating environments
- Adding and removing different package versions to and from an environment
- Activating and switching between different environments
- Understanding the relationship between a module and a package

Creating environments is just a matter of creating a directory to hold each environment. In this example, I will start Julia and go into shell mode by pressing ;, and then I will issue Unix shell commands to create directories. Using a graphical file manager, such as Finder or File Explorer, is a perfectly valid alternative approach:

```
shell> mkdir job hobby          ◁──┐  Make job and
                                    hobby directories.
shell> ls          ◁──┐  List current
hobby    job           directory contents.
```

Remember, in the Julia REPL you enter package mode by pressing]. In package mode you can execute commands to activate different environments and add packages to them. When you switch to an environment, the prompt will change to show which environment you are in. For instance, if you are in the `job` environment, the prompt will look like `(job) pkg>`. In this example, I will activate the `job` environment, so all following commands modify the `job` environment:

```
(@v1.7) pkg> activate job

(job) pkg>
```

I will add some package dependencies to this environment. For demonstration purposes it is not important which Julia packages I add, but I have chosen to demonstrate with the CairoMakie (https://makie.juliaplots.org) plotting package and the link ElectronDisplay (https://github.com/queryverse/ElectronDisplay.jl) package for showing plots in window. If you use Visual Studio Code you don't need the `ElectronDisplay` package, as it can already display any Julia plot.

> **NOTE** CairoMakie is part of a collection of related Julia plotting packages called `Makie`. All `Makie` packages give users the same types and functions, and the only difference is the type of graphics produced. `CairoMakie` offers the ability to create high-quality 2D vector plots, while `GLMakie` enables creating interactive 3D plots.

Let's assume you like to use the latest version of `CairoMakie` for your hobby projects, but your employer is a bit conservative. Instead, you must use the version 0.5.10 at work:

```
(job) pkg> add CairoMakie@0.5.10                           ◁─────┐   Add CairoMakie
    Updating registry at `~/.julia/registries/General.toml`      │   version 0.5.10 to
    Resolving package versions...                                 │   the job environment.
  [13f3f980] + CairoMakie v0.5.10
    Updating `~/dev/job/Manifest.toml`

(job) pkg> add ElectronDisplay                 ◁─────┐   Add the latest version
    Resolving package versions...                    │   of ElectronDisplay.
    Updating `~/dev/job/Project.toml`
  [d872a56f] + ElectronDisplay v1.0.1
    Updating `~/dev/job/Manifest.toml`

(job) pkg> status                              ◁─────┐   Check what
      Status `~/dev/job/Project.toml`                │   packages are added
  [13f3f980] CairoMakie v0.5.10                       │   to this environment.
  [d872a56f] ElectronDisplay v1.0.1
```

When you run the `add` package commands you will see a lot more info than I am showing you here. I edited out most of it because it would have filled several pages, but I have kept the most important bits of information.

When calling `add ElectronDisplay` you are informed that the ~/dev/job/Project.toml file is modified. What file is that? My job environment is in the ~/dev/job directory. If you don't have a Project.toml file in your currently active environment, then Julia will create it for you to store information about what packages you have added to your environment.

The `ElectronDisplay v1.0.1` line tells you what version of `ElectronDisplay` was installed. That was the latest version in 2022 when I wrote this book.

Notice how the add command for CairoMakie was slightly different. I tacked on a @0.5.10 to the package name to inform Julia's package manager that I wanted version 0.5.10 rather than whatever the current latest version of CairoMakie might be. When switching to the hobby environment I will use the latest version instead:

```
(work) pkg> activate hobby
  Activating new project at `~/dev/hobby`

(hobby) pkg> add CairoMakie ElectronDisplay
   Resolving package versions...
    Updating `~/dev/hobby/Project.toml`
  [13f3f980] + CairoMakie v0.7.5
  [d872a56f] + ElectronDisplay v1.0.1
    Updating `~/dev/hobby/Manifest.toml`

(hobby) pkg> status
      Status `~/dev/hobby/Project.toml`
  [13f3f980] CairoMakie v0.7.5
  [d872a56f] ElectronDisplay v1.0.1
```

In the hobby environment, I used the add command slightly different. I listed all packages I wanted to add, so I could do it all in one go. Afterward, Julia notifies me that the CairoMakie v0.7.5 package was installed.

You can always use the status command to get an overview of what packages have been installed in your currently active environment. The command reads info stored in the Project.toml. This information is used to locate the correct package in your local package depot at ~/.julia/packages:

```
shell> ls hobby
Manifest.toml    Project.toml

shell> cat hobby/Project.toml
[deps]
CairoMakie = "13f3f980-e62b-5c42-98c6-ff1f3baf88f0"
ElectronDisplay = "d872a56f-244b-5cc9-b574-2017b5b909a8"
```

The long strings of letters and numbers starting with 13f3f980 and d872a56f, respectively, are the universally unique identifier (UUID) of each package. Package names need not be unique. Several developers could be making a package named Cairo-Makie; thus, to be able to uniquely identify a specific package, they each need a unique UUID. Because there is currently no other package named CairoMakie, there is no package name conflict.

What if there was another CairoMakie package? In that case the package would need to be added with the following command:

```
(hobby) pkg> add CairoMakie=13f3f980-e62b-5c42-98c6-ff1f3baf88f0
```

The package system comes with its own help system, so you can write ? add to get a full overview of all the different ways of adding a package. To remove packages use the `rm` command. You can add a package and check how the Project.toml file changes as you remove it again. The following is an example of adding and removing the `Dates` package:

```
(hobby) pkg> add Dates
   Resolving package versions...
    Updating `~/dev/hobby/Project.toml`
  [ade2ca70] + Dates

(hobby) pkg> status
      Status `~/dev/hobby/Project.toml`
  [13f3f980] CairoMakie v0.7.5
  [d872a56f] ElectronDisplay v1.0.1
  [ade2ca70] Dates

(hobby) pkg> rm Dates
    Updating `~/dev/hobby/Project.toml`
  [ade2ca70] - Dates

(hobby) pkg> status
      Status `~/dev/hobby/Project.toml`
  [13f3f980] CairoMakie v0.7.5
  [d872a56f] ElectronDisplay v1.0.1
```

16.1.1 Using a package in the REPL

Adding a package to your active environment doesn't make the functions and types the package provides available in the Julia REPL or to the Julia project you are coding. Rather they become available after you run `using` or `import` statements. `Makie` has many different functions for plotting graphs. I will show how to use two functions: `lines` and `scatter`. Unless you use VS Code, you will need to load the `Electron-Display` package before anything becomes visible.

I will use `Makie` to plot a sine and cosine curve. To achieve that I will generate many *x, y* coordinates stored in `xs`, `ys1`, and `ys2`, respectively.

Listing 16.1   Plotting a sine and cosine curve with Makie

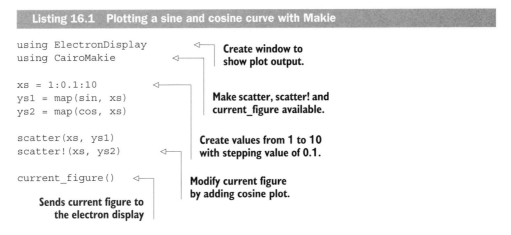

```
using ElectronDisplay          Create window to
using CairoMakie               show plot output.

xs = 1:0.1:10
ys1 = map(sin, xs)             Make scatter, scatter! and
ys2 = map(cos, xs)             current_figure available.

scatter(xs, ys1)               Create values from 1 to 10
scatter!(xs, ys2)              with stepping value of 0.1.

current_figure()               Modify current figure
                               by adding cosine plot.

        Sends current figure to
        the electron display
```

When Julia evaluates using CairoMakie it will look for a package named CairoMakie in its current environment. If your environment is hobby, then it will load the code for the v0.7.5 version of Makie. However, if you evaluated this code in the job environment the v0.5.10 version would be loaded instead. If you run the code in the Julia REPL you should get a figure with two dotted plots (figure 16.1).

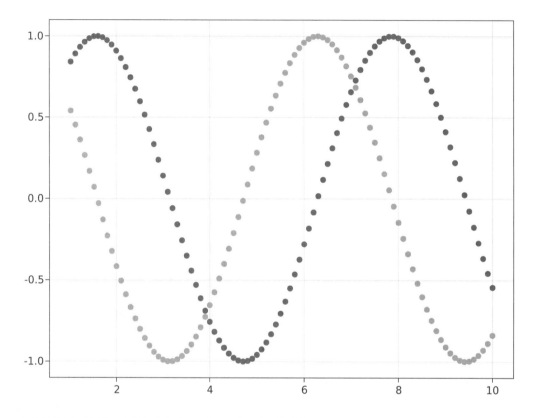

Figure 16.1 Makie scatter plot of the sine and cosine functions

These plots are called *scatter plots*. Every (x, y) coordinate produces a colored dot. If you want lines connecting each coordinate point you would use the lines and lines! functions instead, as follows.

Listing 16.2 Plotting sine and cosine with smooth lines

```
lines(xs,  ys1, linewidth=5)     Plot lines with
lines!(xs, ys2, linewidth=5)     thickness 5

current_figure()
```

Evaluating the code will give you the plot shown in figure 16.2. There are many named arguments that can modify the appearance of each plot. For example, the `linewidth=5` named argument makes the lines thicker.

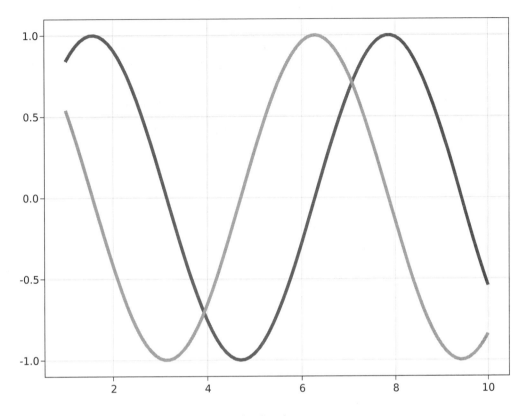

Figure 16.2 **Makie line plot of the sine and cosine functions**

You can visit the official Makie website (https://docs.makie.org/stable/) to learn more about plotting in Julia using Makie.

16.1.2 *How modules relate to packages*

My description of the package loading process was not entirely accurate. Packages define a module of the same name as the package. Hence, when you write `using Dates`, you are looking up the `Dates` package and loading the `Dates` module defined within it. The distinction will become much clearer once you define your own package and module.

You can think of a Julia package as a physical bundle of source code, resources, and metadata, such as version, name, and dependencies. These things matter to the package-loading machinery of Julia but are not language constructs. Just like there are the keywords `function` and `struct` for defining functions or composite types in Julia, there is also the `module` keyword for defining a module.

While functions allow you to group chunks of code, modules allow you to group related functions and types. Modules also create a *namespace*, just like a function. That means you can use variables with the same name in different functions, and they won't interfere with each other because each function forms a separate namespace. The volume functions in the following listing don't interfere with each other, since they are in two separate modules: `Cylinder` and `Cone`.

Listing 16.3   Functions with the same name in different modules

```
module Cylinder
    volume(r,h) = π*r^2*h
end

module Cone
    volume(r, h) = π*r^2*h/3
end
```

You could evaluate these modules in the REPL and call the different volume functions like this:

```
julia> Cylinder.volume(2.5, 3)
58.90486225480862

julia> Cone.volume(2.5, 3)
19.634954084936208
```

In this chapter you will, however, focus on defining a single module per package. That is the most pragmatic solution in Julia.

16.2   Creating your own package and module

On the following pages I will show you how to create your own package and module by taking the volume and trigonometric functions from chapter 2 and chapter 4 and organizing them into a module `ToyGeometry` stored in a package. You could build a package from scratch manually, but it is more convenient to use the Julia package manager to generate the scaffolding for you.

After generating the package and looking at its structure, I will show you how to add code to the package. You will then learn to expand your package with plotting functionality, so you can better grasp how to deal with package dependencies.

16.2.1   Generating a package

I start out in my ~/dev directory, where I have the hobby and job directories. You could, of course, organize this any way you want. I use shell mode to jump into the hobby directory, where I want to create my `ToyGeometry` package. The `generate` command is used in package mode to create a package:

```
shell> cd hobby/
~/dev/hobby

(hobby) pkg> generate ToyGeometry
  Generating  project ToyGeometry:
    ToyGeometry/Project.toml
    ToyGeometry/src/ToyGeometry.jl
```

A more sophisticated way of creating packages is using the PkgTemplate library, but generate is a good way of getting started, as it makes a minimalist package. If you look at the contents of the package, you will see it only contains two files: Project.toml and src/ToyGeometry.jl:

```
shell> tree ToyGeometry
ToyGeometry
├── Project.toml
└── src
    └── ToyGeometry.jl
```

You may be surprised to see the Project.toml file in there. Isn't that used to define environments? Exactly! And a Julia package is, in fact, its own environment. By being an environment, a Julia package can add other packages it depends on.

> **NOTE** Environments can be nested, but that has no practical implications. It is more useful to nest modules, but I will not cover module nesting in this book.

At the moment there are no dependencies, so the Project.toml file will only show data about the package, such as its names, the unique UUID identifying the package, the author of the package, and the current package version:

```
shell> cat ToyGeometry/Project.toml
name = "ToyGeometry"
uuid = "bbcec4ee-a196-4f18-8a9a-486bb424b745"
authors = ["Erik Engheim <erik.engheim@mac.com>"]
version = "0.1.0"
```

Let's add a dependent package to ToyGeometry to show how adding dependencies works. I will add two packages, Dates and Base64, which exist in the standard library bundled with Julia (no download from the internet is necessary). Since I don't want to add these dependencies to the hobby environment, but to the ToyGeometry environment, I first have to switch active environments:

```
(hobby) pkg> activate ToyGeometry/
  Activating project at `~/dev/hobby/ToyGeometry`

(ToyGeometry) pkg> add Dates Base64
  Resolving package versions...
    Updating `~/dev/hobby/ToyGeometry/Project.toml`
  [2a0f44e3] + Base64
  [ade2ca70] + Dates
```

```
    Updating `~/dev/hobby/ToyGeometry/Manifest.toml`
  [2a0f44e3] + Base64
  [ade2ca70] + Dates
  [de0858da] + Printf
  [4ec0a83e] + Unicode

(ToyGeometry) pkg> status
    Project ToyGeometry v0.1.0
     Status `~/dev/hobby/ToyGeometry/Project.toml`
  [2a0f44e3] Base64
  [ade2ca70] Dates
```

The Project.toml file in `ToyGeometry` will now be updated to show the dependencies of the package:

```
shell> cat ToyGeometry/Project.toml
name = "ToyGeometry"
uuid = "bbcec4ee-a196-4f18-8a9a-486bb424b745"
authors = ["Erik Engheim <erik.engheim@mac.com>"]
version = "0.1.0"

[deps]
Base64 = "2a0f44e3-6c83-55bd-87e4-b1978d98bd5f"
Dates = "ade2ca70-3891-5945-98fb-dc099432e06a"
```

I will have also gotten a new file called Manifest.toml, which stores information about the packages `Dates` and `Base64` depend on. For instance, `Dates` depends on the `Printf` package to format text strings of dates. Further, `Printf` depends on the `Unicode` package:

```
shell> cat ToyGeometry/Manifest.toml
julia_version = "1.7.2"
manifest_format = "2.0"

[[deps.Base64]]
uuid = "2a0f44e3-6c83-55bd-87e4-b1978d98bd5f"

[[deps.Dates]]
deps = ["Printf"]
uuid = "ade2ca70-3891-5945-98fb-dc099432e06a"

[[deps.Printf]]
deps = ["Unicode"]
uuid = "de0858da-6303-5e67-8744-51eddeeeb8d7"

[[deps.Unicode]]
uuid = "4ec0a83e-493e-50e2-b9ac-8f72acf5a8f5"
```

For packages not part of the Julia standard library, the entries will be more complex. The following is an entry from the Manifest.toml file in the `job` environment for the `Colors` package:

```
[[deps.Colors]]
deps = ["ColorTypes", "FixedPointNumbers", "Reexport"]
git-tree-sha1 = "417b0ed7b8b838aa6ca0a87aadf1bb9eb111ce40"
uuid = "5ae59095-9a9b-59fe-a467-6f913c188581"
version = "0.12.8"
```

You can see it doesn't just list the UUID but also the version of `Colors`. You don't need to know what the `git-tree-sha1` string means, except that it helps Julia locate the correct package in the local package depot to load.

16.2.2 Adding code to your package

At the moment, the package doesn't do anything, so let's add code by copying the volume and trigonometry code from chapters 2 and 4. I will start by creating two files, volume.jl and trig.jl, to hold this code:

```
shell> cd ToyGeometry/
~/dev/hobby/ToyGeometry

shell> touch src/volume.jl src/trig.jl

shell> tree .
.
├── Manifest.toml
├── Project.toml
└── src
    ├── ToyGeometry.jl
    ├── trig.jl
    └── volume.jl
```

Add the code shown in listing 16.4 to the src/volume.jl.

> **Listing 16.4 ToyGeometry/src/volume.jl**

```
"""
    sphere_volume(r)
Calculate the volume of a sphere with radius `r`
"""
function sphere_volume(r::Number)
    4π*r^3/3
end


"""
    cylinder_volume(r, h)
Calculate the volume of a cylinder with radius `r`
and height `h`.
"""
function cylinder_volume(r::Number, h::Number)
    π*r^2*h
end


"""
    cone_value(r, h)
Calculate the volume of a cone with radius `r`
```

```
and height `h`.
"""
function cone_value(r::Number, h::Number)
    π*r^2*h/3
end
```

Next I add the function from chapter 4 that used the Taylor series to compute sine; later I will add a cosine function. This code will go into the src/trig.jl file, as follows.

Listing 16.5   ToyGeometry/src/trig.jl

```
"""
    sine(x)
Calculate the sine of an angle `x` given in radians
"""
function sine(x::Number)
    n = 5
    total = 0
    for i in 0:n
        total += (-1)^i*x^(2i+1)/factorial(2i + 1)
    end
    total
end
```

The `ToyGeometry` package defines a module named `ToyGeometry`. I want all the functions I have written to be part of the `ToyGeometry` module. By running the `include` functions inside the `module` definition, all the function definitions get evaluated inside the `ToyGeometry` module and become part of it.

Listing 16.6   ToyGeometry/src/ToyGeometry.jl

```
module ToyGeometry

include("volume.jl")
include("trig.jl")

end # module
```

The `include` may not be obvious to you if you are thinking like a C/C++ developer, but it is really quite simple. Let's do a quick experiment to demonstrate.

Start by creating a file named arithmetic.jl, and write 3 + 4 inside it. `include` can be called anywhere, even inside a function definition:

```
julia> x = include("arithmetic.jl")
7

julia> function calc()
           include("arithmetic.jl")
       end

julia> calc()
7
```

You don't have to split up your code into multiple files and add them to the module with `include`. You could have defined the `ToyGeometry` module as follows.

Listing 16.7   ToyGeometry/src/ToyGeometry.jl

```
module ToyGeometry

sphere_volume(r)      = 4π*r^3/3
cylinder_volume(r, h) = π*r^2*h
cone_value(r, h)      = π*r^2*h/3

function sine(x)
    n = 5
    total = 0
    for i in 0:n
        total += (-1)^i*x^(2i+1)/factorial(2i + 1)
    end
    total
end

end # module
```

So why not define it this way? Putting all the code inside the module definition file ToyGeometry.jl does not scale well. As your package becomes larger it becomes impractical to have all your code in one file. That's why I split the code for a package up into multiple files and include those files inside the module definition.

16.3   *Modifying and developing a package*

If you are following along, you now have a correct package structure and definition; the next step is understanding the package development process. This is an iterative process in which you are testing the functionality of your package and adding new features over and over again.

While you develop your own package there are many Julia packages you may want to use to aid your development efforts but which should not be part of the dependencies of your package. The following are some packages I like to use to increase productivity:

- `OhMyREPL`—Provides syntax highlighting and history matching in the Julia REPL
- `Revise`—Monitors code changes to packages loaded into the REPL and updates the REPL with these changes

Returning to the example, I will now switch to the `hobby` environment, since I don't want these packages added as dependencies of `ToyGeometry`:

```
shell> pwd                          ◁──────┐  Just check where you
~/dev/hobby/ToyGeometry                    │  currently are.

(ToyGeometry) pkg> activate ..      ◁──────   The hobby environment
  Activating project at `~/dev/hobby`        is one directory up.
```

```
(hobby) pkg> add OhMyREPL Revise
   Resolving package versions...
    Updating `~/dev/hobby/Project.toml`
  [5fb14364] + OhMyREPL v0.5.12
  [295af30f] + Revise v3.3.3
    Updating `~/dev/hobby/Manifest.toml`
```

I can now load `OhMyREPL` and `Revise` into the REPL, but trying to load `ToyGeometry` will fail. Can you guess why?

```
julia> using ToyGeometry
ERROR: ArgumentError: Package ToyGeometry not found in current path:
- Run `import Pkg; Pkg.add("ToyGeometry")` to install the ToyGeometry package.
```

The error message in this case is not very helpful. Julia, for instance, never looks in the current filesystem path for packages. The actual issue is that I have not added Toy-Geometry to the `hobby` environment. The environment I am currently working in doesn't know about my custom package.

I could inform it about the package by using the `add` command in the package manager. However, the problem with using `add` is that it captures the latest package version and freezes it. Normally, that is a good thing because you don't want third-party packages added to your working environment to suddenly change. But when you actively develop a package your needs are different than when you are using a package. You want all your code changes to be available in your working environment without using an explicit `update` command to get latest changes. Thus instead of `add`, I will show how you can use the `dev` package command. The `dev` command needs the directory path of your package:

```
shell> pwd
~/dev/hobby

shell> ls
Manifest.toml    Project.toml    ToyGeometry

(hobby) pkg> dev ./ToyGeometry
   Resolving package versions...
    Updating `~/dev/hobby/Project.toml`
  [bbcec4ee] + ToyGeometry v0.1.0 `ToyGeometry`
    Updating `~/dev/hobby/Manifest.toml`
  [bbcec4ee] + ToyGeometry v0.1.0 `ToyGeometry`
```

Looking at the status of the `hobby` environment you can now see that `OhMyREPL`, `Revise`, and `ToyGeometry` have all been added:

```
(hobby) pkg> status
      Status `~/dev/hobby/Project.toml`
  [13f3f980] CairoMakie v0.7.5
  [d872a56f] ElectronDisplay v1.0.1
```

```
[5fb14364] OhMyREPL v0.5.12
[295af30f] Revise v3.3.3
[bbcec4ee] ToyGeometry v0.1.0 `ToyGeometry`
```

Now your current working environment knows where ToyGeometry can be found, so it knows what code to load when you write using ToyGeometry. Remember, there could be many packages with the name ToyGeometry, so your environment needs to be explicitly told which package should be loaded:

```
julia> using ToyGeometry
[ Info: Precompiling ToyGeometry [bbcec4ee-a196-4f18-8a9a-486bb424b745]

julia> ToyGeometry.sphere_volume(4)
268.082573106329

julia> ToyGeometry.sine(π/2)              Call your custom
0.999999943741051                         sine function.

julia> sin(π/2)         Julia's built-in sine function
1.0

julia> sine(π/2)                    Trying to call sine without
 ERROR: UndefVarError: sine not defined    specifying module name
```

It is awkward to write ToyGeometry.sine every time you want to call the custom sine function, but as the example shows, Julia doesn't currently know how to call it if you don't prefix it with the module name. Yet, as you have seen with other packages, such as CairoMakie, you don't need to prefix plot functions, such as scatter and lines, with the module name. How can you achieve the same?

The trick is to use the export statement to tell Julia which functions and types are to be exported (made public) from the module. While I'm at it, I'll add a cosine function and export that as well:

```
export sine, cosine          Make sine and
                             cosine public.
"""
    sine(x)
Calculate the sine of an angle `x` given in radians
"""
function sine(x::Number)
    n = 5
    total = 0
    for i in 0:n
        total += (-1)^i*x^(2i+1)/factorial(2i + 1)
    end
    total
end

function cosine(x::Number)
    n = 5
```

```
    mapreduce(+, 0:n) do i
        (-1)^i*x^(2i)/factorial(2i)
    end
end
```

You may notice that with `cosine` I am replacing the clunky for loop with a more elegant `mapreduce`, which was covered in chapter 4. `mapreduce` is a combination of the higher-order functions `map` and `reduce`.

You will notice it is now possible to write `sine` and `cosine` without any module name prefixing. The following simple test shows that the custom functions give similar output as the built-in functions:

```
julia> sine(π/2)
0.999999943741051

julia> sin(π/2)
1.0

julia> cosine(π)
-1.0018291040136216

julia> cos(π)
-1.0
```

How was Julia suddenly able to know `sine` and even `cosine` without any package reloading? This is thanks to the magic of `Revise`. Because I loaded `Revise` before `ToyGeometry` it will monitor changes to the module and incorporate them into the REPL automatically.

Should you always use `Revise`? Sometimes you make code changes you don't want reflected in the REPL immediately. Just use common sense. You can even use `Revise` for single files by calling `includet` instead of `include`.

When writing code you will naturally make mistakes. The REPL helps you quickly check your code to see if you are getting the right results. One of the best ways to quickly analyze a lot of data and spot problems is achieved by visualizing the data. So let's plot both the built-in `sin` and the custom `sine` to see if you get similar-looking plots. Evaluate the following code in your REPL.

Listing 16.8   Comparing built-in `sin` with custom `sine`

```
using ToyGeometry, CairoMakie, ElectronDisplay

xs = 0:0.1:2π
ys1 = map(sin, xs)
ys2 = map(sine, xs)

lines(xs,  ys1, linewidth=5)
lines!(xs, ys2, linewidth=5)

current_figure()
```

Ouch! They are not the same. At around 4.5 along the *x*-axis your custom `sine` function fails visibly.

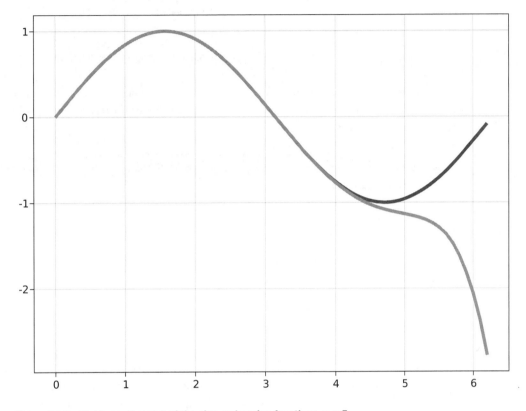

Figure 16.3 Makie scatter plot of the sine and cosine functions, *n* = 5

Fortunately, thanks to `Revise` you can modify the line that says n = 5. Try some different values for n to see how the plot changes. Setting n = 8 should solve your problem. There is no magical reason 8 works aside from the fact that higher values offer greater accuracy, meaning there is a tradeoff between performance and accuracy.

16.4 Tackling common misconceptions about modules

If you are coming from a different programming language there are likely many concepts relating to environments, packages, and modules you find confusing. For instance, in the Java world, a *module* is called a *package*, and a Julia *package* is closer to a *JAR file*.[1] Table 16.1 gives an overview of the differences in terminology used to described modules, packages, and environments in different programming languages.

---

[1] A Java Archive (JAR) is a package file format typically used to aggregate Java class files and associated metadata and resources (e.g., text and images) into one file for distribution.

Table 16.1   Differences in package and module terminology usage across popular programming languages

Julia	Java	C++	Python
Module	Package	Namespace	Module
Package	JAR	DLL	Package
Environment	Environment	Sandbox or container	Virtual environment

Another problem is that mainstream programming languages tend to put keywords such as `public` in front of functions that are meant to be exported or made public, as shown in the following listing.

Listing 16.9   Comparing Julia with a Java-style way of exporting functions

```
#### The Julia way ####
export sphere_volume

function sphere_volume(r::Number)
    4π*r^3/3
end

#### A Java-style way of exporting ####
# IMPORTANT: This doesn't work in Julia!
public function sphere_volume(r::Number)
    4π*r^3/3
end
```

While Julia's `include` function may seem similar to `#include` in C/C++, you have to take into account that `include` is a regular function call in Julia that returns a result. `#include` in C/C++ is not a function call at all but essentially a mechanism that pastes the content of the included files into the file with the include statements.

16.5   *Testing your package*

While you develop a package you can quickly test functions in the REPL. For long-term, large-scale development, that is not enough. You need to be able to quickly verify that a code you wrote weeks or months ago still works. In real-world software development you will make code changes in many different files. Keeping track of all functions affected by your code edits can be difficult; thus you need to have set up an extensive set of tests that can verify all previously written code still works.

Testing is a larger topic, so I will only cover the very basics in this book. You can read the following articles from my *Erik Explores* Substack to explore the topic further:

- "Organizing Tests in Julia" (https://erikexplores.substack.com/p/julia-test-organizing)
- "Julia Test Running: Best Practices" (https://erikexplores.substack.com/p/julia-testing-best-pratice)

Tests in Julia can be run from the package manager. It will try to execute a file named test/runtests.jl. In the example, I don't have this file or the test directory, so I will have to make both:

```
shell> pwd
~/dev

shell> cd hobby/ToyGeometry/
~/dev/hobby/ToyGeometry

shell> mkdir test

shell> touch test/runtests.jl test/trigtests.jl
```

Julia uses the concept of *nested test sets*, meaning a test set succeeds if all the test sets it contains succeed. The Julia convention is putting all test sets within one top-level test set. That is what I will demonstrate in the test/runtests.jl (listing 16.10); however, I will follow the same strategy by spreading tests across multiple files and including those files within the top-level test set.

Listing 16.10   ToyGeometry/test/runtests.jl

```
using ToyGeometry
using Test

@testset "All tests" begin

include("trigtests.jl")

end
```

Tests are run separately from your module, so you need to load the module you are testing with the using statement. Getting access to testing macros like @testset and @test requires importing the Test package. This package is not in your ToyGeometry environment. It does not make sense to add Test to this environment, since it will only be used while testing.

Julia offers a neat solution to this problem. You can treat the test directory as its own environment and only add Test to that environment:

```
shell> pwd                    ◁──────┐   Show what directory you
~/dev/hobby/ToyGeometry              │   are running package
                                     │   commands in.
(hobby) pkg> activate test
  Activating project at `~/dev/hobby/ToyGeometry/test`

(test) pkg> add Test
   Resolving package versions...
    Updating `~/dev/hobby/ToyGeometry/test/Project.toml`
  [8dfed614] + Test
    Updating `~/dev/hobby/ToyGeometry/test/Manifest.toml`
```

Before attempting to run the tests, you need to actually add them to your code. I will demonstrate this by adding tests to the test/trigtests.jl file, which contains tests related to trigonometric functions.

Each actual test is specified with the @test macro. Because floating-point numbers are difficult to make exactly the same, I will not compare function results using == but ≈, which you can write in the Julia REPL by writing \approx and pressing the Tab key.

Sometimes the default tolerance of ≈ is too strict and you need a looser definition of equality. In those cases use the isapprox function to compare values. It takes a named argument atol, which you can use to specify how great the difference between the two results you are comparing you consider acceptable, as follows.

Listing 16.11 ToyGeometry/test/trigtests.jl

```
@testset "cosine tests" begin
    @test cosine(π) ≈ -1.0
    @test cosine(0) ≈ 1.0

    for x in 0:0.1:2π
        @test isapprox(cos(x), cosine(x), atol=0.05)      ◁── Test if all cosine values
    end                                                         in range 0 to 2π with 0.1
end                                                             increments are roughly equal.

@testset "sine tests" begin
    @test sine(0)   ≈ 0.0
    @test sine(π/2) ≈ 1.0

    for x in 0:0.1:2π
        @test isapprox(sin(x), sine(x), atol=0.05)
    end
end
```

If you attempt to run this test while in the test environment it will, ironically, not work because test doesn't actually know about the ToyGeometry package. Hence you need to switch to the hobby or ToyGeometry environment to run the tests:

```
(test) pkg> test ToyGeometry
ERROR: The following package names could not be resolved:      ◁──── Cannot test
 * ToyGeometry (not found in project or manifest)                    from the test
                                                                     environment
(test) pkg> activate .
  Activating project at `~/dev/hobby/ToyGeometry`

(ToyGeometry) pkg> test ToyGeometry
    Testing ToyGeometry

Test Summary: | Pass  Fail  Total
All tests     | 108    22    130
  cosine tests |  43    22     65
  sine tests   |  65           65
ERROR: LoadError: Some tests did not pass:
   108 passed, 22 failed, 0 errored, 0 broken
```

Because of the for loops, I am able to perform a total of 130 tests in the preceding listing. The cosine test fails because I used n = 5, which does not make the results accurate enough. So I will set n = 9 instead for better accuracy. Please note that running tests causes a lot of output I've edited out.

Listing 16.12   Modifying a cosine function in trig.jl

```
function cosine(x::Number)
   n = 9   # modified
   mapreduce(+, 0:n) do i
       (-1)^i*x^(2i)/factorial(2i)
   end
end
```

When I run the tests again they should pass:

```
(ToyGeometry) pkg> test
     Testing ToyGeometry
Test Summary: | Pass  Total
All tests     |  130    130
     Testing ToyGeometry tests passed
```

The topic of testing and environments is much broader than I can cover here. What we have covered in this chapter provides you with a solid foundation from which to explore further. Here are some starting points:

- *pkgdocs.julialang.org*—The site for the Pkg module, which provides the functionality of the package manager.
- *docs.julialang.org*—The site for the official Julia documentation. You can look up detailed descriptions of modules, packages, and environments here, including testing.

Summary

- An environment is like a work area where you set up what packages you want to work with and use.
- Julia allows you to maintain different environments configured to use different packages and different versions of those packages.
- CairoMakie is a Julia package for plotting 2D vector graphics. It is part of a collection of plotting packages called Makie.
- scatter and lines are functions used in the Makie library to plot functions.
- ElectronDisplay is a package that provides a window for showing graphics, such as output from Makie. It is an alternative to plotting in the VS Code editor.
- You can switch between different environments using the activate package command. For instance, you might use this command when you want to modify the dependencies of another package you are developing.
- To make a module available in your code, add it with the add package command.

- Remove the package for modules no longer used in your program with the `remove` package command.
- Check what packages have been added to an environment using the `status` command. You can use this to check what dependencies your custom-made package has.
- In cases when many packages have the same name, specify the UUID of the package you are interested in when adding it to your work environment.
- Create a package with the `generate` package command.
- `Project.toml` shows direct dependencies of your environment, while `Manifest.toml` shows indirect dependencies.
- When adding a local package you are developing, use `dev` instead of `add`. That ensures the latest code changes are incorporated whenever you load a module from that package.
- Use the `Revise` package to monitor code changes to packages loaded after `Revise`.
- Use `test <package name>` to run tests for a package. For instance, `test ToyGeometry` will run tests for the `ToyGeometry` package.
- The `test` directory is its own environment that allows you to add the `Test` package as a dependency only to your test environment.

Part 5

Going in depth

You now have the foundation to go into more depth. In chapter 5, I/O could only be covered superficially because the Julia type system had not yet been covered. Chapter 17 expands on chapter 5 by focusing on the I/O type hierarchy.

In chapter 10, you saw how parametric types are used to represent various forms of nothing, and in chapter 6 how they help define strongly typed collections. In chapter 18, I will explain how parametric types aid in type correctness, performance, and memory usage.

Input and output

17

This chapter covers

- Understanding Julia's I/O system
- Using the most common functions for reading and writing to files
- Reading and writing to strings, sockets, and processes
- Adding code to the rocket example for loading rocket engines from CSV files

Real programs need to be able to read input from users and write out results. In this chapter, you will learn about the Julia I/O system (input and output system). It provides an abstraction for working with files, network communications, and interprocess communications as well as interacting with the console (keyboard and screen).

Julia is very popular in data science, where we work a lot with input data in the form of CSV files (comma separated values). That is why the main code example will center on parsing a CSV file containing data about rocket engines, as well as writing rocket engine data to a CSV file.

17.1   Introducing Julia's I/O system

Let's get a bird's-eye view of the I/O system in Julia. It is centered on the abstract type IO. It has concrete subtypes, such as IOStream, IOBuffer, Process, and TCPSocket. Each type allows you to read and write data from different I/O devices, such as files, text buffers, running processes (programs you started), or network connections.

From the type hierarchy in figure 17.1 you can see that functions such as print, show, read, readline, and write are available for all I/O types. Some functions, such as eof and position, are not available for all I/O types.

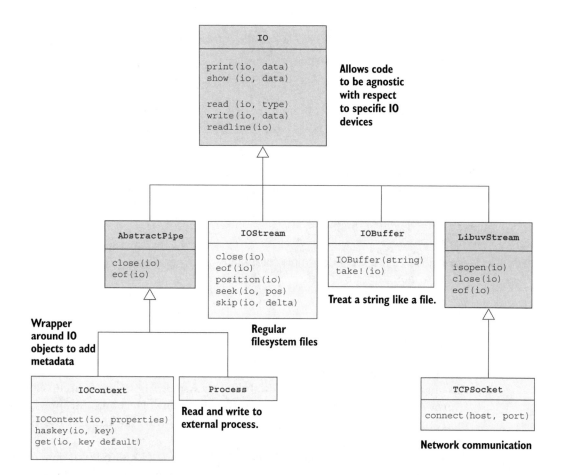

Figure 17.1   Type hierarchy of an I/O system showing what different subtypes are used for. Light gray boxes represent concrete types.

Different I/O objects are opened in different ways, but once created, you can use many of the same functions on all of them. I will demonstrate working with similar data from a file, string, and process. The data used will be from a CSV file called rocket-engines.csv with the following content:

```
name,company,mass,thrust,Isp
Curie,Rocket Lab,0.008,0.12,317
RS-25,Aerojet Rocketdyne,3.527,1860,366
Merlin 1D,SpaceX,0.47,845,282
Kestrel 2,SpaceX,0.052,31,317
RD-180,NPO Energomash,5.48,3830,311
Rutherford,Rocket Lab,0.035,25,311
```

I will open the file, read from it until I reach the end, and close it. In listing 17.1, I read one line at a time using the readline function and check whether I have reached the end of the file with eof. I split every line using the split function into multiple words by using commas as delimiters. Each read line is printed to the console. All these functions are in the Base module, which is always loaded.

> **Listing 17.1 Reading a CSV file line by line to demonstrate basic I/O functionality**

```
io = open("rocket-engines.csv")
while !eof(io)
    line = readline(io)
    words = split(line, ',')
    println(join(words, '\t'))
end
close(io)
```

You can process data from a text string in a very similar fashion. I'll demonstrate by creating a string with the first line in the rocket-engines.csv file and looking at how to process it with different I/O functions. I will use readuntil, which reads from an IO object, until hitting a particular character or string. I will use position to check how many characters into the IOStream I am, periodically using eof to check if I have reached the end of the I/O object:

```
julia> s = "name,company,mass,thrust,Isp";

julia> io = IOBuffer(s);

julia> readuntil(io, ',')
"name"

julia> position(io), eof(io)
(5, false)

julia> readuntil(io, ','), position(io), eof(io)
("company", 13, false)

julia> readuntil(io, ','), position(io), eof(io)
("mass", 18, false)
```

```
julia> readuntil(io, ','), position(io), eof(io)
("thrust", 25, false)

julia> readuntil(io, ','), position(io), eof(io)
("Isp", 28, true)
```

You can experiment with doing the same operations on an I/O object obtained by opening the rocket-engines.csv file. Remember to call `close(io)` when you are done; otherwise you will leak limited OS resources. Especially when writing to an I/O object, it is important to close it, or you may lose data.

17.2 *Reading data from a process*

Script languages such as Python, Ruby, and Perl gained popularity in part for being good *glue languages*. A glue language excels at connecting existing software components, often written in different languages.

You will briefly look at Julia's ability to work as a glue language. Let's pretend Julia lacks the ability to search through text files and you want to leverage the Unix grep tool[1] for that purpose. First you would jump into shell mode by pressing semicolon, just to demonstrate what your grep command will do: it finds lines with the text "Rocket Lab". By pressing backspace, you go back to Julia mode. Next you would open a connection to the grep process you launched (spawn). Notice the use of backticks to quote shell commands you want to run:

```
shell> grep "Rocket Lab" rocket-engines.csv
Curie,Rocket Lab,0.008,0.12,317
Rutherford,Rocket Lab,0.035,25,311

julia> io = open(`grep "Rocket Lab" rocket-engines.csv`);

julia> readuntil(io, ',')
"Curie"

julia> readuntil(io, ',')
"Rocket Lab"

julia> readuntil(io, ',')
"0.008"

julia> position(io)
ERROR: MethodError: no method matching position(::Base.Process)

julia> close(io)
```

Unlike many script languages, such as Perl and Ruby, the backticks in Julia do not cause a shell command to run right away. Instead they cause the creation of a command object of a type called `Cmd`. When you call open on a command object, the command actually

---

[1] grep is a standard command-line utility on Unix systems for finding lines in a file matching a given search criteria.

gets executed and spawns a process. The `io` object returned is of the `Process` type and represents a connection to the output of the running process. This way you can read from the process almost as if it were a file (figure 17.2).

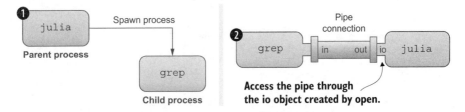

Figure 17.2   The `open` function spawns a child process. Both processes are connected through a pipe represented by the I/O object returned from the `open` function.

Why do you get an error message when calling the `position` function? Because there are no methods attached to `position` that work on `Process` objects. Only `IOStream` objects working on files have the notion of a position in the stream.

17.3   *Reading and writing to a socket*

A socket represents a network connection. I'll present a quick example demonstrating a network connection using the Unix `netcat` utility. Netcat is a simple tool for experimenting with TCP/IP-socket-based communication.[2] You can run netcat as either a client or a server.

> **NOTE**   `netcat` is already installed on Linux and macOS. Windows users can download the `nmap` utility as a substitute from `nmap.org/ncat`. Any time I write the `nc` command in the text, in Windows you should write `ncat` instead.

Follow these steps: Open two terminal windows. In the first window launch Julia, and in the second window launch `netcat` as a server listening for connections on port 1234. You can specify almost any port number you like as long as it is not already taken. After launching `netcat` write the line `"name,company,mass,thrust,Isp"` and press Enter:

```
shell> nc -l 1234
name,company,mass,thrust,Isp
```

In the Julia window use the `connect` function to connect to the local server running at port 1234. The `connect` function will return an I/O object of type `TCPSocket`:

---

[2] TCP/IP is the protocol used on the internet for communication.

```
julia> using Sockets

julia> sock = connect(1234)
TCPSocket(RawFD(23) open, 0 bytes waiting)

julia> readuntil(sock, ',')
"name"

julia> readuntil(sock, ','), isopen(sock)
("company", true)

julia> readline(sock)
"mass,thrust,Isp"
```

A socket is usually two-way, so you can write messages to the socket and see them pop up in the windows running netcat:

```
julia> println(sock, "hello netcat")

julia> close(sock)
```

Did you see the text string "hello netcat" pop up in the second window?

With these simple examples I have demonstrated that you can use the same functions, such as read, readuntil, readline, and println, for every type of I/O object, whether it represents a text string, file, or network connection.

17.4 *Parsing a CSV file*

Let's build up a more comprehensive code example. You will enhance your rocket code from the recurring example by adding the ability to load definitions of rocket engines from CSV files. To practice your Julia package making skills, make a Julia package called ToyRockets to contain your rocket code. I have already made this package and placed it on GitHub at github.com/ordovician/ToyRockets.jl, so you can follow along.

The ToyRockets package is created with the generate command in the Julia package manager. Next create a data directory to hold the rocket-engines.csv file. Add the following files to the src directory:

- *interfaces.jl*—Contains definitions of abstract types, such as Engine
- *custom-engine.jl*—The definition of a concrete engine type
- *io.jl*—A collection of functions for loading and saving rocket parts

Now run the necessary commands to make this happen, paying attention to the prompts. When the prompt says (@v1.7) pkg>, it means you must press] first to enter package mode. When the prompt says shell> it means you must press ; to enter shell mode:

```
(@v1.7) pkg> generate ToyRockets
    Generating  project ToyRockets:
    ToyRockets/Project.toml
    ToyRockets/src/ToyRockets.jl
```

```
shell> cd ToyRockets/
~/Development/ToyRockets

shell> mkdir data

shell> cd src
~/Development/ToyRockets/src

shell> touch interfaces.jl custom-engine.jl io.jl
```

If you followed the instructions correctly and put the rocket-engines.csv file in the data/ directory, then your `ToyRockets` package should look like this:

```
ToyRockets/
├── Project.toml
├── data
│   └── rocket-engines.csv
└── src
    ├── ToyRockets.jl
    ├── custom-engine.jl
    ├── interfaces.jl
    └── io.jl
```

Make sure you include all your source code files in the ToyRockets.jl file (listing 17.2), which defines your package module.

```
module ToyRockets

include("interfaces.jl")
include("custom-engine.jl")

include("io.jl")

end
```

Next you need to turn every row in rocket-engines.csv into a `CustomEngine` object, so first you need to define `Engine` types.

```
# interfaces.jl file
export Engine
abstract type Engine end

# custom-engine.jl file
export CustomEngine

struct CustomEngine <: Engine
    mass::Float64
    thrust::Float64
    Isp::Float64
end
```

In the next two sections you will load and save rocket engine data.

17.4.1 *Loading rocket engine data*

You will now take a look at the final code (listing 17.4) before I walk through all the details and explain how its different parts work. The code starts by reading all the rows in the CSV file, with each row representing a rocket engine. Loop over each row, parse it, and turn it into a `CustomEngine` object that gets added to a dictionary, `rocket_engines`, containing all the engines loaded from our input file.

> **Listing 17.4   An io.jl file containing code to load engine objects into a dictionary**

```
export load_engines

function load_engines(path::AbstractString)
    rocket_engines = Dict{String, Engine}()

    rows = readlines(path)
    for row in rows[2:end]
        cols = split(row, ',')

        if any(isempty, cols)
            continue
        end

        name, company = cols[1:2]
        mass, thrust, Isp = map(cols[3:end]) do col
            parse(Float64, col)
        end

        engine = CustomEngine(
                mass * 1000,          ⟵┘ From tons
                                            to kg
                Isp,
                thrust * 1000)        ⟵┐ kN to Newton
        rocket_engines[name] = engine
    end

    rocket_engines
end
```

`load_engines` take the path to the CSV file that contains rocket engine data and parses it to produce a dictionary of rocket engines. Here is an example of using it:

```
julia> using Revise, ToyRockets

julia> pwd()
"~/Development/ToyRockets"

julia> engines = load_engines("data/rocket-engines.csv")
Dict{String, Engine} with 6 entries:
    "RD-180"      => CustomEngine(5480.0, 311.0, 3.83e6)
    "Kestrel 2"   => CustomEngine(52.0, 317.0, 31000.0)
    "Curie"       => CustomEngine(8.0, 317.0, 120.0)
```

```
   "Merlin 1D"   => CustomEngine(470.0, 282.0, 845000.0)
   "RS-25"       => CustomEngine(3527.0, 366.0, 1.86e6)
   "Rutherford"  => CustomEngine(35.0, 311.0, 25000.0)

julia> engines["Curie"]
CustomEngine(8.0, 317.0, 120.0)
```

The `load_engines` function follows a pretty standard pattern I use when processing
data, which is neatly organized by lines such as CSV files (see chapter 5). You use
`readlines` here to get the rows in the file and `split` to get each of the columns of
every row (figure 17.3).

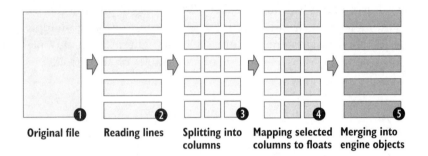

**Original file   Reading lines   Splitting into   Mapping selected   Merging into
                                        columns   columns to floats engine objects**

**Figure 17.3   The rocket engine's file is split into parts, transformed, and composed
into rocket engines in multiple steps.**

To better understand how the code works, copy and paste parts of the source code
lines into the REPL to see how the input data gets processed:

```
julia> path = "data/rocket-engines.csv"
"data/rocket-engines.csv"

julia> rows = readlines(path)
7-element Vector{String}:
   "name,company,mass,thrust,Isp"
   "Curie,Rocket Lab,0.008,0.12,317"
   "RS-25,Aerojet Rocketdyne,3.527,1860,366"
   "Merlin 1D,SpaceX,0.47,845,282"
   "Kestrel 2,SpaceX,0.052,31,317"
   "RD-180,NPO Energomash,5.48,3830,311"
   "Rutherford,Rocket Lab,0.035,25,311"
```

Next, pick an arbitrary row and split it into columns to verify the parsing works as
expected. Occasionally, there can be missing data, so be sure to check that every column contains data. You can achieve this with the higher-order function `any(isempty,
cols)`, which applies `isempty` to every column. If *any* of the columns are empty, it will
return `true`:

```
julia> row = rows[2]
"Curie,Rocket Lab,0.008,0.12,317"

julia> cols = split(row, ',')
5-element Vector{SubString{String}}:
    "Curie"
    "Rocket Lab"
    "0.008"
    "0.12"
    "317"

julia> any(isempty, cols)
false
```

Next, you will use a little Julia magic called *destructuring* to pull out the name of the engine and the company making it. With destructuring you place multiple variables on the left side of the assignment operator =. On the right side, you must place an iterable collection with at least as many elements as variables on the left side:

```
julia> name, company = cols[1:2]
2-element Vector{SubString{String}}:
    "Curie"
    "Rocket Lab"

julia> name
"Curie"

julia> company
"Rocket Lab"
```

cols[1:2] gives you a two-element array. Julia iterates over this array and assigns the elements in the array to name and then company. A tuple or dictionary would have worked just as well.

The next part is a bit more complex, as you take the three last elements, cols[3:end], and map them to floating-point values using the parse(Float64, col) function. This turns the textual representations of mass, thrust, and Isp into floating-point values, which you can feed to the CustomEngine constructor to make an engine object:

```
julia> mass, thrust, Isp = map(cols[3:end]) do col
           parse(Float64, col)
       end
3-element Vector{Float64}:
    0.008
    0.12
    317.0

julia> engine = CustomEngine(
                    mass * 1000,
                    Isp,
                    thrust * 1000)
CustomEngine(8.0, 317.0, 120.0)
```

The last step is storing this engine in a dictionary under the engine name.

17.4.2 *Saving rocket engine data*

At this point you can add code to your io.jl file to allow the saving of rocket engines to a file. By default a file is opened for reading. If you want to write to it you need to pass a "w" for the *write* argument to the open function. There are still a number of other new concepts in this code you will need to look at in greater detail.

> **Listing 17.5   An io.jl file with added `save_engines` code**

```
function save_engines(path::AbstractString, engines)
    open(path, "w") do io
        println(io, "name,company,mass,thrust,Isp")
        for (name, egn) in engines
            row = [name, "", egn.mass, egn.thrust, egn.Isp]
            join(io, row, ',')
            println(io)
        end
    end
end
```

Do you notice how you use the do-end form with your open function? That means it takes a function as the first argument. What is the point of that? Study the following implementation to see if you can make a guess.

> **Listing 17.6   Implementing `open(f, args…)`**

```
function open(f::Function, args...)
    io = open(args...)
    f(io)
    close(io)
end
```

The benefit of this solution is that you can pass the responsibility of closing your io object to Julia when you are done with it. You will also notice the use of the *splat* operator . . . . It is used to represent a variable number of parameters. Regardless of how many arguments you pass to open they will be collected into a tuple args. When calling open(args...) you expand this tuple into arguments again by using the splat operator.

What about the join taking an I/O argument as the first argument? Instead of returning the result of joining multiple elements with a separator, the join function will write the result to the supplied I/O object. Here is a demonstration of writing the result to standard out:

```
julia> join(stdout, [false, 3, "hi"], ':')
false:3:hi
```

You should now have a broad understanding of the I/O Julia system. Study the documentation of the functions and types covered here using the built-in help system to learn more.

Summary

- IOStream, IOBuffer, Process, and TCPSocket are I/O objects for reading and writing to files, text strings, running processes, or network connections.
- Use functions such as readuntil, readline, readlines, and read to read data from any I/O object.
- Use functions such as print and println to write data to an I/O object.
- split is a convenient function for turning strings into arrays of objects by splitting them up using a delimiter.
- Destructuring assigns multiple elements in a collection to multiple variables, providing a compact and elegant way of accessing elements.

18
Defining
parametric types

This chapter covers

- Working with and defining parametric methods and types
- Using parametric types to improve type safety and catch bugs
- Improving memory usage and performance by using parametric types

In chapter 10, I introduced parametric types to help explain how the union type works. We have also discussed parametric types in relation to collections such as arrays, dictionaries, and sets. With type parameters, you can restrict which elements can be used in your collections and thus get better type safety. However, all previous usage of parametric types have been as users of parametric types defined by others.

In this chapter, I will show you how to make your own parametric types and cover some common misconceptions and pitfalls when dealing with parametric types. But why would you want to make your own parametric types? Parametric types in Julia have two key benefits, which we will explore in detail in this chapter:

1 Enabling more type-safe code. Julia can catch errors early at runtime, such as trying to put a string into an array of numbers.

2 Improving performance when working with large datasets.

You will explore these topics through geometric code in 2D space (for simplicity). I will attempt to motivate you with a possible use in your rocket example project: to express the position of a rocket in space you need a `Point` type to represent a position in space and a `Vec2D` type to represent force, acceleration, and velocity in different directions.

18.1   *Defining parametric methods*

I'll start simply by presenting methods that take type parameters and exploring how type parameters can make your methods more type safe and reduce boilerplate. Before jumping in, let me refresh you on the concept of *type parameters*. Previously, I used an analogy with a function call `y = f(x)`, where the function `f` takes a value `x` and produces a new value `y` (figure 18.1). Likewise, you can think of the type expression `S = P{T}` as parametric type `P`, taking a type parameter `T` and returning a new concrete type `S`. Both `T` and `S` are concrete types, while `P` is just a template for making types.

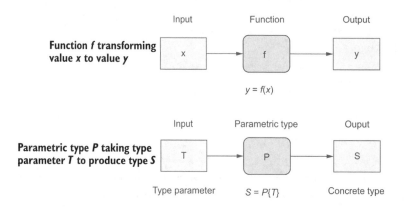

Figure 18.1   **Analogy between a function and a parameterized type. The former produces values, while the latter produces types.**

The `linearsearch` function defined in listing 18.1 does a *linear search* through the array `haystack`, looking for the element `needle`.

> **NOTE** Using a linear search means you are not doing anything clever. You just start at the first element and look at every element in succession. When you find the element you are looking for, you return the index of that element.

`linearsearch` is a parametric method because it takes a type parameter `T`. It is the `where T` clause that defines `T` as a type parameter.

Listing 18.1   `linearsearch` in collection `haystack` for element `needle`

```
function linearsearch(haystack::AbstractVector{T}, needle::T) where T
    for (i, x) in enumerate(haystack)
        if needle == x
            return i
        end
    end
    nothing
end
```

What advantages does using a type parameter provide in this case? Could you instead annotate `haystack` with the `AbstractVector` type and give `needle` the `Any` type annotation? No. That would not give the same strong type checking at runtime. You have defined `linearsearch` such that `needle` must have the same type as all the elements of `haystack`. Let me demonstrate in the REPL:

```
julia> linearsearch([4, 5, 8], 5)
2

julia> linearsearch([4, 5, 8], "five")
ERROR: MethodError: no method matching linearsearch(::Vector{Int64}, ::String)
```

The error message tells you there is no method taking a vector with `Int64` elements and a `String` search object. I have defined `linearsearch` such that whatever type `T` is, it must be the same for the `haystack` elements and the `needle` object.

Parametric types do not only improve type safety, but they also provide opportunities for reducing boilerplate code. Say you wanted to implement your own version of the Julia `typeof` function. A naive approach would be writing the code like the following.

Listing 18.2   Naive implementation of a `typeof`-style function

```
kindof(x::Int64)   = Int64
kindof(x::Float64) = Float64
kindof(x::String)  = String
```

You can try `kindof` in the REPL and see that it works for 64-bit integer values, floating-point values, and strings. However, that's it. Trying to add a method for every type in Julia is a fool's errand. As you may have guessed already, defining `kindof` as a parametric method solves the problem elegantly, as follows.

Listing 18.3   Implementing `kindof` using a type parameter

```
function kindof(x::T) where T
    return T
end
```

While names like `T`, `S`, `T1`, and `T2` are popular for denoting type parameters, you could use any name; the name is not essential. It is the `where` clause that turns the name into

```
julia> kindof(x::Int64) where Int64 = Int64
kindof (generic function with 1 method)

julia> kindof(3)
Int64

julia> kindof('C')
Char

julia> kindof(4.2)
Float64

julia> kindof(3 => 8)
Pair{Int64, Int64}
```

The fact that `Int64` is an actual type doesn't matter here. The `where` clause turns `Int64` into a type parameter and prevents it from being interpreted as a concrete type. Of course, you should avoid using known types as type parameter names, as this would massively confuse readers of your code.

18.2   *Defining parametric types*

Through the whole book we've used parametric types such as arrays, dictionaries, and tuples, but we have not defined such types ourselves. Let's look at how that can be done.

I will define the types `Point` and `Vec2D`. Figure 18.2 shows the relation between points and vectors in the coordinate space. Points are usually drawn like dots, while vectors are drawn like arrows. A vector represents a displacement along each axis in the coordinate system.

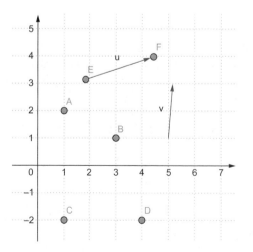

Figure 18.2   **The geometric relation between points and vectors**

Mathematically speaking, points and vectors are related through different operations. If you subtract the point E from point F, you get vector **u**. You could flip this around and add vector **u** to point E to get point F. I will discuss these details in greater depth later. First, I want to walk you through the details of a parametric type definition (listing 18.4). Don't define these in the REPL yet because you will modify the definitions.

Listing 18.4 Defining parametric types `Point` and `Vec2D`

```
"A point at coordinate (x, y)"
struct Point{T}
    x::T
    y::T
end

"A vector with displacement (Δx, Δy)"
struct Vec2D{T}
    Δx::T
    Δy::T
end

"Calculate magnitude of a vector (how long it is)"
norm(v::Vec2D) = sqrt(v.Δx^2 + v.Δy^2)
```

Use \Delta to get the Δ symbol. It is a symbol commonly used in mathematics to represent differences or displacements.

Point and Vec2D should not be thought of as types but templates for creating actual types. To create an actual type, you must provide a concrete type for the type parameter T. Without parametric types, you would have had to define numerous concrete types to deal with different numbers. Every method would have had to be defined for every type, leading to code bloat. For instance, with a parametric type, you could define norm once. Without it, you would need to define it for every concrete 2D vector type, as shown in the following listing.

Listing 18.5 Code bloat when you don't have parametric types

```
struct IntVec2D
    x::Int
    y::Int
end

struct FloatVec2D
    Δx::Float64
    Δy::Float64
end

norm(v::IntVec2D) = sqrt(v.Δx^2 + v.Δy^2)
norm(v::FloatVec2D) = sqrt(v.Δx^2 + v.Δy^2)
```

A Python, Ruby, or JavaScript developer, however, would object to this approach and say it is completely unnecessary to define multiple concrete types. If you want flexibility in the type for Δx and Δy just leave out the type annotation, as shown in the following listing.

Listing 18.6   Vec2 type without type annotations (any type)

```
struct Vec2D
    Δx
    Δy
end
```

Nothing prevents you from defining a 2D vector in this manner. So why not do it that way and avoid all the extra complexities introduced by parametric types? Dropping annotations is bad for numerous reasons:

1 You take away valuable type checking at runtime performed by the Julia JIT compiler.
2 You increase memory usage and reduce performance.

I'll cover each of these points in greater detail.

18.3   *Type safety benefits from parametric types*

I will compare 2D vectors with and without type annotations to show the type safety benefits of using parametric types. I'll start by creating two throwaway types, GVec2D and PVec2D, just for this comparison. I will not be building on these types further. Notice how it is perfectly valid to define a type definition on a single line—just separate individual statements with a semicolon. GVec2D is the weakly typed variant, and PVec2D is the strongly typed variant:

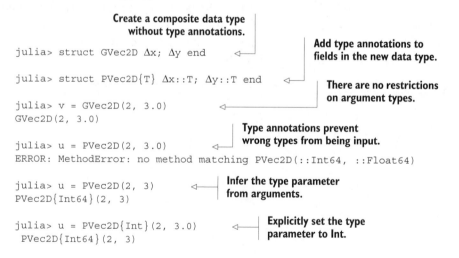

The GVec2D does not use type annotations, and thus when creating the q point I get no complaints from Julia about using two different numbers types for representing the *x* and *y* delta. If you were to try that with PVec2D, which has type annotations, the

Julia JIT compiler would complain because you are trying to use two different types of Δx and Δy. Because of this problem, Julia has no way of inferring what the type parameter T should be, and it must give up and throw an exception. That helps you catch cases in which you are not paying attention to the types of numbers you are passing around in your code.

This issue can be solved in two ways: Either make sure each argument is of the same type or use the curly braces {} to explicitly state what the type parameter is rather than asking Julia to infer it. Julia will then know the type of each field and perform an automatic conversion to that number type. Both are valid choices.

Type safety can be taken much further with parametric types. Do you remember the <: subtype operator? You have used this operator in a variety of cases, including testing whether one type is a subtype of another and indicating that a composite type is a subtype of an abstract type. You can also use this operator to impose constraints on the type parameter T. Currently, T can be any type, including nonnumerical types. That is not desirable, as coordinates are represented by numbers. The final Vec2D type, shown in the following listing, will constrain T to being a number.

Listing 18.7 Point and Vec2D defined so the type parameter must be a number type

```
import Base: +, -

struct Point{T<:Number}
    x::T
    y::T
end

struct Vec2D{T<:Number}
    Δx::T
    Δy::T
end

"Adding vector `v` to point `p` creates a new point"
function +(p::Point{T}, v::Vec2D{T}) where T
    Point(p.x + v.Δx, p.y + v.Δy)
end

"Subtracting two points gives a vector"
function -(p::Point{T}, q::Point{T}) where T
    Vec2D(p.x - q.x, p.y - q.y)
end
```

You can see there is no problem creating a PVec2D of characters because the type parameter T has not been constrained in any way. Vec2D, on the other hand, will not accept characters as arguments. Try experimenting with different values yourself to validate that the type constraints work:

```
julia> v = PVec2D('A', 'B')
PVec2D{Char}('A', 'B')
```

```
julia> u = Vec2D('A', 'B')
ERROR: MethodError: no method matching Vec2D(::Char, ::Char)

julia> u = Vec2D(8, 4)
Vec2D{Int64}(8, 4)
```

Thus far you have only used one type parameter in all expressions. But you know from using dictionaries, tuples, and pairs that there can be many type parameters. For the point subtraction operator in listing 18.7, I have required each point p and q to have the same number type, but this is not required. Listing 18.8 demonstrates the subtraction operator implemented with different number types for point p and q.

Listing 18.8   Substract defined so arguments p and q don't need to be the same type

```
function -(p::Point{T}, q::Point{S}) where {T, S}
    Vec2D(p.x - q.x, p.y - q.y)
end

function -(p::Point, q::Point)              ←——┤ Shorthand version without
    Vec2D(p.x - q.x, p.y - q.y)                │ explicit type parameters
end
```

Because in this example I am not using the type parameters T and S to constrain anything, I can omit them entirely. In Julia, writing Point is equivalent to writing Point{T} if T is unconstrained (figure 18.3 illustrates these type relationships). For instance, if you have a function sum that takes a vector as argument and you aren't concerned with the types of the elements, you could write sum(xs::Vector), which is identical to writing sum(xs::Vector{T}) where T.

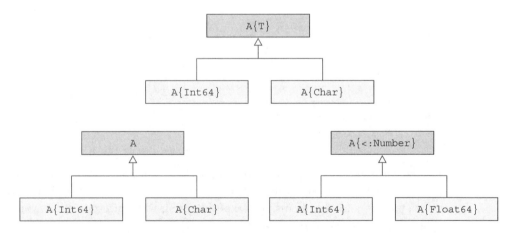

Figure 18.3   Subtype relations between parametric types. Functions taking parametric type A will, for instance, accept values of type A{Int64} and A{Char}.

In parametric methods, the key reason for using a named type parameter such as T is that you want to express that two or more arguments use the same type parameter. In other cases you don't want to enforce such a strict requirement. Instead you simply want the type parameters to be of a similar type. Say you want subtraction between points to only apply to integers (see the following listing).

> **Listing 18.9   Arguments p and q constrained to have integer-based type parameters**

```
function -(p::Point{<:Integer}, q::Point{<:Integer})
    Vec2D(p.x - q.x, p.y - q.y)
end
```

In this case, p could have UInt8 fields, while q could have Int16 fields. The example is, of course, contrived, as this particular restriction does not make sense. So why didn't I constrain p and q to Number? Wouldn't that be more realistic? It would not because there is no way to create Point objects that don't contain numbers. Remember that is a constraint on the type parameter to the Point type itself and its associated constructor.

18.4   Performance benefits from parametric types

Julia is a high-performance, dynamic language. Without parametric types, that would not be possible. Let's discuss how parametric types influence performance. A benefit of understanding this is that you can more easily anticipate performance problems in your code.

One of the key reasons dynamically typed languages are slow is because of something called *boxing*. Its name comes from the fact that most values have to be put in special containers that contain information about the value they contain, including its type and garbage collection details, which could be a mark or a reference count (see figure 18.4). The specifics of how the garbage collection occurs (i.e., how memory is freed) is not essential to this argument. The key point is that these generic containers have a bunch of bookkeeping data.

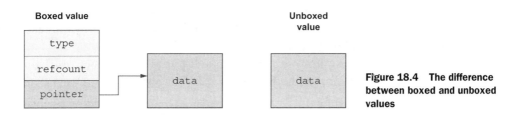

Figure 18.4   The difference between boxed and unboxed values

What is the point of this bookkeeping data? It is what allows you to handle arbitrary values at runtime. Imagine a simple function multiply for scaling a vector by a constant k (see the following listing).

Listing 18.10   Vec2D defined with abstract type fields to mimic regular dynamic languages

```
struct Vec2D          ⟵──┐  To support explanation
    Δx::Number             │  not for running
    Δy::Number             │  Need to be boxed
end
```

```
function multiply(u::Vec2D, k::Number)
    Vec2D(k * u.Δx, k * u.Δy)
end
```

This looks simple, right? But in a dynamic language, lots of code must run to perform this operation. In the following listing, I will walk you through a Julia pseudocode variant of what is going on.

Listing 18.11   Pseudocode of how `multiply` would work in a normal dynamic language

```
function multiply(u::Vec2D, k::Number)
    ux = getfield(u, :Δx)
    if !isa(ux, Float64)
        error("x must be a float")
    end

    uy = getfield(u, :Δy)
    if !isa(uy, Float64)
        error("y must be a float")
    end

    c = convert(Float64, k)
    Vec2D(floatmul(c, ux), floatmul(c, uy))
end
```

This code is not meant to be an accurate representation of what is going on. Think of it more as a form of pseudocode to help develop a rough intuition about how dynamic languages work under the hood.

In most dynamic languages, you don't know what fields a composite type has until runtime. That means you cannot generate code accessing fields directly, which is why you see the `getfield(u, :Δx)` line in listing 18.11. You must verify that each field is actually present and of the expected type.

Julia does not have this problem because it imposes a series of restrictions on its types that are not common in other dynamic languages:

- Fields are fixed by the type. Instances of a type cannot add or remove fields at runtime.
- You cannot store values that don't match the field types on a composite object.

These restrictions greatly simplify the job for the Julia JIT compiler when it tries to generate optimized machine code. For a refresher on Julia method calls see section 7.4.

The key takeaway is that when Julia generates code for a method, it knows *exactly* what the type of every input argument is. Since types cannot change in Julia, the JIT compiler will also know exactly what fields the arguments have and their types. This allows Julia to generate highly optimized machine code.

18.5 *Memory benefits of parametric types*

The benefits of parametric types don't stop at allowing the compiler to create more optimized code and include making it easier to have a more optimized layout of data in memory. If you define an array of type `Vector{Point{Int32}}` with *N* number of elements, then the Julia JIT can figure out exactly how many bytes are required to hold all those elements. That allows you to avoid memory fragmentation, which reduces the amount of available memory and performance of your applications. In short, parametric types give you better type safety, performance, and memory usage.

Summary

- Parametric types improve type safety at runtime.
- Julia determines whether a type is a type parameter in a function definition by looking at the `where` clause.
- Type parameters can be named anything, including actual type names, such as `Int8` and `Char`. However, to avoid confusing developers reading your code, try to use names such as `T`, `T1`, `T2`, and `S`.
- For composite types use `{T1, T2, T3}` to specify a type with three different type parameters.
- Use the subtype operator `T <: S` to constrain a parametric type `T` to being a subtype of another type `S`.
- Boxing is when values are stored with bookkeeping information to help determine the data type stored at runtime.
- Boxing kills the performance of dynamic languages. Parametric types combined with immutable types minimize the usage of boxing in Julia and thus allow the compiler to generate optimized machine code.
- Parametric types provide a more optimal memory layout for collections and individual objects, reducing memory usage and improving performance.

appendix A
Installing and configuring the Julia environment

This appendix covers downloading and installing Julia on Linux, macOS, and Windows. I will also cover how to configure your Julia environment to improve your efficiency.

The instructions in this appendix rely on understanding concepts such as the path for command utilities as well as knowing how to set it; these instructions will vary depending on operating system. For Unix-like systems such as macOS and Linux, you configure the search path by editing configuration files such as .zshrc, .profile, or .config/fish/config.fish. In these files, you can set environment variables such as PATH, EDITOR, and JULIA_EDITOR. If you are unfamiliar with the Unix command line, here are some resources from my Substack *Erik Explores*:

- "Unix Command Line Crash Course" (https://erikexplores.substack.com/ p/unix-crash-course)
- "Unix Commands, Pipes, and Processes" (https://erikexplores.substack.com/ p/unix-pipes)
- "Unix Shells and Terminals" (https://erikexplores.substack.com/p/unix-shells-and-terminals)

A.1 Downloading Julia

1 Navigate to the Julia downloads webpage (figure A.1): https://julialang.org/ downloads.
2 Select the correct Julia version for your operating system. I recommend installing Julia 1.7 or higher.

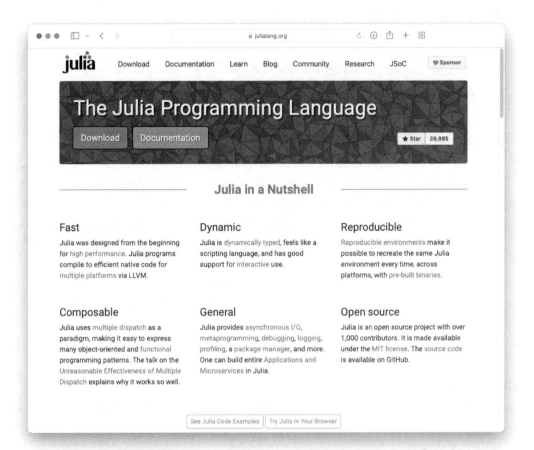

Figure A.1 The Julia homepage

A.2 Installing Julia

Read through the installation instructions for the operating system you use.

> **NOTE** Some shell commands are prefixed with sudo, which gives the command you are running superuser privileges. These privileges are needed to modify files or directories not owned by the logged-in user.

A.3 On Linux

There are many different Linux distributions, but in the instructions here, I am assuming there is a Downloads directory where you store downloaded files. Adjust command given based on where you store downloads on your Linux machine.

1 Unpack the .tar.gz file with a name similar to julia-1.7.3-linux-x86_64.tar.gz.
2 Move the unpacked directory to /opt. If /opt does not exist, create it. Create an /opt/bin directory as well, as it will be needed later:

```
$ sudo mkdir -p /opt/bin
$ cd $HOME/Downloads
$ sudo mv julia-1.7.3 /opt
```

Next, to run Julia from the terminal easily, make a symbolic link:

```
$ sudo rm /opt/bin/julia
$ sudo ln -s /opt/julia-1.7.3/bin/julia /opt/bin/julia
```
Remove any old link.

A.3.1   On macOS

1 Open your downloaded .dmg file named something like julia-1.7.3-mac64.dmg.
2 Drag and drop the Julia application bundle to your /Applications folder.

This completes the installation. It's that easy!

The next step is optional but convenient. Take the following steps if you would like to launch Julia by simply typing `julia` in the terminal rather than having to click the Julia application icon:

1 Open the `Terminal.app` console application.
2 Create a symbolic link from the installation location to a directory in your path, such as /usr/local/bin.

```
$ ln -s /Applications/Julia-1.7.app/Contents/Resources/julia/bin/julia
/usr/local/bin/julia
```

A.3.2   On Windows

Download the .exe file, which is a self-contained Julia installer. Double-click and follow the prompts to install Julia. The installation process is similar to installing most other Windows software.

A.4   Configuring Julia

Let's configure Julia to make it more convenient to use. Linux and macOS have very similar configurations, as they are both Unix-like operating systems.

A.4.1   On Linux and macOS

To make it easy to run Julia from the terminal, it is useful to configure your shell environment for Julia. If your shell is the Z shell (zsh), you need to edit the .zshrc file in your home directory. If you use Bourne Again SHell, `bash`, you need to edit the .profile file instead. Z shell is currently the standard on macOS.

Here is an example of configuring Julia for use with the bash shell on Linux, where Sublime Text (see https://www.sublimetext.com), `subl`, is used as the text editor for Julia code:

```
# ~/.zshrc file
export JULIA_EDITOR=subl
export PATH=/opt/bin:$PATH
```

You may use a custom shell. For instance, I use the fish shell, which is a modern, user-friendly shell for all Unix-like systems. In this case, you would edit the .config/fish/config.fish in your home directory. In the following code, I am configuring my Mac to use the VS Code editor, which is launched with the code command:

```
# ~/.config/fish/config.fish file
set -x JULIA_EDITOR code
set -x PATH /usr/local/bin $PATH
```

A.4.2 On Windows

On Windows, environment variables are configured through the GUI shown in figure A.2. The steps for opening this dialog depend on your windows version. For Windows 8 and newer, follow these steps:

1 In Search, search for and then select System (Control Panel).
2 Click the Advanced System Settings link.

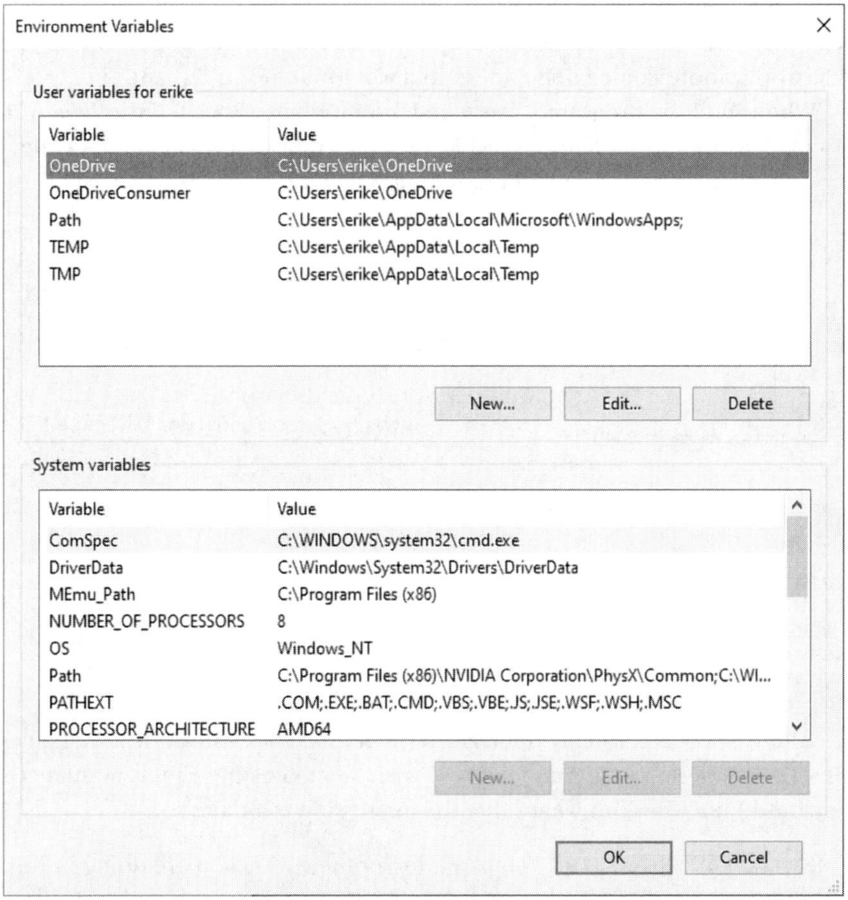

Figure A.2   Dialog for configuring the Windows binary search path

For Windows Vista and Windows 7, follow these steps:

1 From the desktop, right-click the Computer icon.
2 Choose Properties from the context menu.
3 Click the Advanced System Settings link.

You don't need to set the `JULIA_EDITOR` environment variable on Windows, as the operating system will open a dialog and ask you what editor to use when needed. Windows will then associate an application with .jl files.

Configuring the shell environment is likely less needed on Windows than on Linux/macOS because command-line interfaces are not as frequently used by Windows developers. Developers interested in the command line on Windows may prefer to use the Window Subsystem for Linux (WSL; https://docs.microsoft.com/en-us/windows/wsl/about). If you use WSL, then follow the Linux installation and configuration steps instead.

A.5 *Running Julia*

Now that Julia is installed and configured, you can try running it. Either click on the Julia application icon or open a terminal window, type `julia`, and then press Enter.

When the Julia program is launched, it enters what is called the *Julia REPL* (read–evaluate–print–loop). The Julia REPL is a program that accepts Julia code, evaluates it, and then prints the result of evaluating that code:

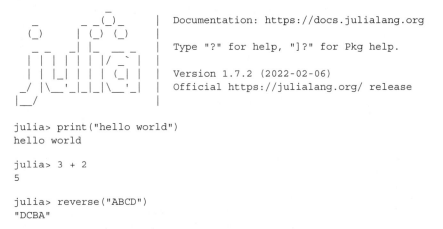

```
$ julia

               _
   _       _ _(_)_     |  Documentation: https://docs.julialang.org
  (_)     | (_) (_)    |
   _ _   _| |_  __ _    |  Type "?" for help, "]?" for Pkg help.
  | | | | | | |/ _` |  |
  | | |_| | | | (_| |  |  Version 1.7.2 (2022-02-06)
 _/ |\__'_|_|_|\__'_|  |  Official https://julialang.org/ release
|__/                   |

julia> print("hello world")
hello world

julia> 3 + 2
5

julia> reverse("ABCD")
"DCBA"
```

Each line of code is usually referred to as an *expression*. (Many other languages distinguish between statements and expressions.) After pressing Enter, evaluate the expression, and Julia will show what value the expression evaluates to.

> **HOW DO YOU EXIT JULIA?** You can interrupt anything you are doing in Julia by holding down the Ctrl key and pressing C. We write this as Ctrl-C. To exit Julia, hold down Ctrl-D or type `exit()`.

Ctrl-C is commonly used to stop execution of Julia code that has gotten stuck. For instance, you may want to stop execution if you are executing an infinite loop.

A.6 Julia REPL Modes

The Julia REPL can be in different modes indicated by the prompt currently showing. A green prompt with the name `julia>` means you are in the standard Julia mode. Here are the other modes you will see in code examples:

- `help?>`—Look up help about a function or type. Enter help mode by pressing ?.
- `pkg>`—Package mode is intended for installing and removing packages. Enter package mode by pressing].
- `shell>`—Shell mode allows you to issue Unix shell commands, such as `ls`, `cp`, and `cat`. Enter shell mode by pressing ;.

You can exit a mode by going to the start of the line and pressing backspace. That will take you back to Julia mode.

While reading this book, look at the prompt to determine which mode we are in. If you don't put the REPL in the correct mode, the commands you issue will not work. The following is an example of being in help mode. The prompt will be yellow:

```
help?> 4 / 2
  /(x, y)

  Right division operator: multiplication of x by the inverse of y on the right.
  Gives floating-point results for integer arguments.
```

REPL modes are covered in greater detail in chapters 5, 16, and 17.

A.7 Installing third-party packages

There are several third-party packages that, while not necessary, can improve your workflow. Packages are covered in greater detail in chapter 16.

Enter package mode to install packages. We will install the packages `OhMyREPL`, `Revise`, and `Debugger` here:

```
(@v1.7) pkg> add OhMyREPL, Revise, Debugger
  Resolving package versions...
```

Load the package into the Julia environment with the `using` keyword. Multiple packages can be loaded by separating them with a comma.

```
julia> using OhMyREPL, Revise, Debugger
```

The `OhMyREPL` package provides syntax highlighting and a better search history in the REPL. `Debugger` allows you to step through code with the `@enter` macro. For instance, the following code will step into the execution of the `titlecase` function. Step by pressing N, and exit by pressing Ctrl-D:

```
julia> @enter titlecase("hello")
```

The most interesting and useful package is Revise, which allows you to monitor code changes. Normally, you load the code of a single file into the Julia REPL with the `include` function. If you use the `includet` function from the Revise package instead, the code in the file will be monitored. Say you create a file named hello.jl with the following code:

```
greet() = "hello world"
```

You could load this file in the Julia REPL using Revise:

```
julia> includet("hello.jl")

julia> greet()
"hello world"
```

You could modify the source code file to say `"hello Mars"`, and this change would be picked up without needing to explicitly load the file again:

```
julia> greet()
"hello Mars"
```

appendix B
Numerics

This appendix covers some common issues and questions about numbers in programming. These topics are not entirely unique to Julia; for instance, I will discuss what happens if the result of an integer arithmetic operation results in a higher or lower number than can be represented by the integer type. I will also discuss why floating-point numbers, unlike integers, are inaccurate.

B.1 *Different number types and their bit lengths*

A number is not just a number. There are different *types* of numbers, such as integers, real numbers, irrational numbers, and so on. For example, *integers* are whole numbers, such as 2, 7, 43, 820, –52, 0, 6, and –4, while *real numbers* contain numbers that have a decimal point, such as 3.45, 0.042, 1331.0, 78.6.

However, the way a mathematician and the way a programmer tend to look at numbers is fundamentally different. On a computer, we care about things such as the bit length of a number and whether the number is signed or unsigned.[1] If you have used programming languages such as Java, C#, C, or C++, then you may be very familiar with this already.

If your programming background is in another dynamic language, such as Python, Ruby, JavaScript, or Lua, these concepts may be unfamiliar to you. While Julia is also a dynamic language, numbers play a more central role. In, for example, Python and JavaScript, you don't have to pay much attention to different number types. In Julia, this is more important, as numbers have been carefully designed to make Julia suitable for high-performance computing.

I'll provide you with the basics. When filling out a form, you are probably familiar with restrictions on the number of digits you can enter. Computers are the

---

[1] Signed numbers can be negative, while unsigned numbers can only be positive.

same. If you store your numbers as four digits, then the largest number you could use in any calculation is 9999. The key difference is that for a modern digital computer, all numbers are stored in memory as binary numbers, not decimal numbers. Thus the number types you select from are not 4-digit numbers, 8-digit numbers, and so on. Rather, the number types you pick from are, for example, 8-bit, 16-bit, or 64-bit numbers. How does this affect you in practice?

Numbers are written with ones and zeros. An 8-bit number is a number with 8 binary digits. The largest number you can represent with 8 bits, written in binary form, is `0b11111111`. The `0b` prefix on this number is intended to clarify it is not a decimal number. Translated to decimal notation, this would be 255. Thus, if you try to store 256 as an 8-bit number, it will fail. (Note that I have shortened the error messages for clarity.)

```
julia> UInt8(256)
ERROR: InexactError: trunc(UInt8, 256)

julia> UInt8(255)
0xff

julia> Int(ans)
255
```

But why should you restrict the size of the numbers you work with? Why not simply use the largest possible number every time? Because you don't have infinite amounts of memory on your computer. If you only use a few numbers, it doesn't matter if they are large. However, if you process millions of numbers, then the bit length starts to matter. Secondly, it frequently takes a longer time to perform calculations on large numbers compared to small numbers. Julia defaults to 64-bit numbers because they are very practical to work with. A signed 64-bit integer has a maximum value of 9,223,372,036,854,775,807. You are unlikely to work with larger numbers than that.

But how do you know the largest and smallest value a number type can hold? Fortunately, Julia gives you the functions `typemax` and `typemin`, which let you find that out for yourself. However, for now, you will just have to take at face value how these functions work. You give them the name of a Julia number type, such as `Int8`, `Int16`, or `UInt8`, and these functions give you back the lowest and highest number value you can represent with that number type. For instance, an 8-bit signed integer, `Int8`, cannot represent values larger than 127:

```
julia> typemax(Int8)
127

julia> typemin(Int8)
-128

julia> typemax(Int16)
32767
```

```
julia> typemax(Int64)
9223372036854775807

julia> typemin(Int32)
-2147483648
```

typemin(Int8) returns the value -128 because a signed 8-bit integer cannot represent number values smaller than -128.

While all these number types can seem complicated, you rarely need to think about them in practice. Sticking with the default types, such as Int64, is the best choice in most cases. You only need to consider other integer number sizes if you process many numbers and get into performance or memory problems. Or you may need a bigger number because you are working with very large values. In that case, you could consider Int128 or even BigInt.

> **DIFFERENCES BETWEEN 64-BIT AND 32-BIT JULIA INSTALLATION** If you downloaded and installed a 32-bit version of Julia, then the default integer type will be Int32 rather than Int64. Code examples in this book will assume you run 64-bit Julia.

Did you try to find the maximum value of a BigInt but could not get it to work? Read on to find out why.

To learn what type is used to represent a particular number literal, you can use the typeof function. Just give it a number, and it will return the number type used to represent that number. Actually, it can be used for any type. If this doesn't make a lot of sense, don't worry, as typeof will be covered more extensively later:

```
julia> typeof(797298432432432432)
Int64

julia> typeof(797298432432432432709090)
Int128

julia> typeof(797298432432432432709090697343)
Int128

julia> typeof(797298432432432432709090697343430912321321)
BigInt
```

BigInt is a very special number type, as it does not have a predefined number of digits. Instead, it simply keeps growing to fit all digits, so your computer memory is its only real limit; that's why there is no well-defined maximum value for a BigInt.

Why not use BigInt all the time? Then you wouldn't have to think about what bit size you need. The obvious answer is that it would make for bad performance. Thus, you should try to limit the use of BigInt to sections of your code that benefit from it and which are not performance critical.

B.2   *Overflow and signed and unsigned numbers*

Let's put together everything we have learned about number formats and bit lengths in chapter 2 to cover some important topics. The first is the concept of *overflow*. Think about mechanical counters, like the one shown in figure B.1. It has four digits, so what happens when you get to 9999? It wraps around, and you get to 0000 again.

Figure B.1   A mechanical counter. It increments each time you click the metal button.

Numbers work exactly the same way on computers. Because each number type can hold a maximum value, you can end up performing arithmetic operations that give results larger than the values that can be held in your variables. Here are some examples of this in practice:

```
julia> UInt8(255) + UInt8(1)
0x00

julia> UInt8(255) + UInt8(2)
0x01

julia> 0xff + 0x01
0x00

julia> 0xff + 0x05
0x04
```

Because an UInt8 can only hold values up to 255, you get a wraparound when you add more—or to use more accurate language, you get an overflow. In this case, it is easier to understand the concept by working with hexadecimal numbers. An 8-bit number can hold a max of two hexadecimal digits, and the last digit value in a hexadecimal is F. For 16-bit numbers, you need much higher values to get overflow:

```
julia> UInt16(65535) + UInt16(1)
0x0000
```

```
julia> UInt16(65535) + UInt16(3)
0x0002
```

The way overflow works differs for signed and unsigned numbers. Look at the following behavior of signed and unsigned numbers, and see if you can make sense of it:

```
julia> UInt8(127) + UInt8(1)
0x80

julia> Int(ans)
128

julia> Int8(127) + Int8(1)
-128

julia> Int8(127) + Int8(2)
-127

julia> Int8(127) + Int8(127)
-2
```

This output looks odd, right? You are adding positive numbers and ending up with negative ones. How on Earth is that possible? This has to do with the fact that computer memory can only store numbers. There is no negative sign stored anywhere. Instead, you will use the wraparound behavior to simulate negative numbers. Returning to the mechanical counter example in figure B.1, storing four-digit decimal numbers; *4 + 9998* would end up as 2. Imagine clicking four times on the mechanical counter starting at 9998. The counter would wrap around and end up as 2.

   That means an alternative way of thinking about the number 9998 is to imagine it as the number –2. *4 + (–2) = 2.* This way, 9999 becomes –1, 9995 becomes –5, and so on. By following this logic, 1 could be interpreted as –9999. However, one should not go that far; otherwise, it isn't possible to represent positive numbers with four digits.

   The scheme used on modern computers is to divide each number range roughly in half, so half the values are used to represent negative numbers and the other half are used to represent positive numbers. An unsigned 8-bit integer can represent numbers from 0 to 255; however a signed 8-bit integer represents values from –128 to 127, which you already saw earlier:

```
julia> typemin(Int8)
-128

julia> typemax(Int8)
127

julia> typemin(Int16)
-32768

julia> typemax(Int16)
32767
```

Thus, what is stored in memory is actually no different. The only difference is how to interpret what is stored there when doing different calculations. When using unsigned numbers, it is assumed all the numbers are positive. When using signed numbers, it is assumed half of the values are negative. In fact, Julia can show you how the exact same bits in memory can be interpreted differently using the `reinterpret` function:

```julia
julia> reinterpret(Int8, UInt8(253))
-3

julia> reinterpret(UInt8, Int8(-1))
0xff

julia> Int(ans)
255
```

Reinterpret the unsigned 8-bit number 253 as a signed 8-bit number. 253 interpreted as signed is -3.

Reintepret the bits in memory for the signed number -1 as an unsigned number. Unsigned -1 is the same as 255 for 8-bit numbers.

B.3   *Floating-point numbers*

Integer numbers cannot represent numbers with decimal points, such as 4.25, 80.3, or 0.233; there are different ways of representing such numbers. Historically, *fixed-point numbers* have been used, but on modern computers we tend to use what are called *floating-point numbers*. Fixed-point numbers are used for such things as currency calculation. The number of decimals after the decimal point is fixed in this type of number representation: you always have two decimals.

Computers cannot store signs or decimal points in memory. Computer memory only stores numbers, and it only stores them in binary format. This is not all that different from, say, an abacus. There is no way to explicitly store negative numbers or represent a decimal point on an abacus; however, one can establish conventions.

You could simply decide, for example, that the two last digits of the numbers you work with are supposed to be after the decimal point. That means that if you wish to input 1, you actually need to input 100. Likewise 23 becomes 2300. In a similar fashion one can *simulate* fixed-point numbers using only integers. You could take integer numbers such as 4250 and 850 and *pretend* there is a decimal point before the two last digits. Thus you could interpret those numbers as 42.50 and 8.50. This works fine in calculations:

```julia
julia> 4250 + 850
5100

julia> 42.50 + 8.50
51.0
```

For calculations with money, this is the appropriate choice; as such calculations typically involve rounding to the nearest two decimals. But for scientific calculations with lots of digits after the decimal point, this is simply too impractical. That is why we have floating-point numbers, which are based on the idea that you can represent any number in this fashion (figure B.2).

$$12.34 = 1234 \times 10^{-2}$$

$$1.234 = 1234 \times 10^{-3}$$

$$0.1234 = 1234 \times 10^{-4}$$

Figure B.2   Representing any decimal number using integers multiplied by a number with base 10 and a positive or negative exponent

Consider the first line: The number 1234 is referred to as the *significand*. The second part indicates the *base* of the number. In this case the *base* is 10, and the *exponent* is –2. Internally, a floating-point number stores the significand and exponent separately. This arrangement is what allows the decimal point to *float*. Floating-point number types can represent much larger numbers than integers but with the downside that they are not entirely accurate. Why? That is too large of a topic to get into in this beginner's book, but I can offer some hints about it. Consider a number such as ⅔. With decimal numbers we write this as 0.6666666666666666. The digits just keep on going. With decimal numbers, the digits behind the decimal point represent fractions in which the denominator is a multiple of 10. Thus we approximate as shown in figure B.3.

$$\frac{2}{3} \approx \frac{6}{10} + \frac{6}{100} + \frac{6}{1000} + \cdots$$

Figure B.3   Approximation of a fraction with decimal numbers

This can never be entirely accurate. In the examples I use in this book, this will generally not be a problem, but it is something worth being aware of if you start working seriously with floating-point numbers. But don't assume every floating-point number has to be inaccurate. Many numbers can be expressed accurately, such as 0.5 or 42.0. For computers, floating-point numbers are obviously not represented as fractions using base 10, but fractions using base 2.

index